6-30-22

THE GREAT ABNORMALS

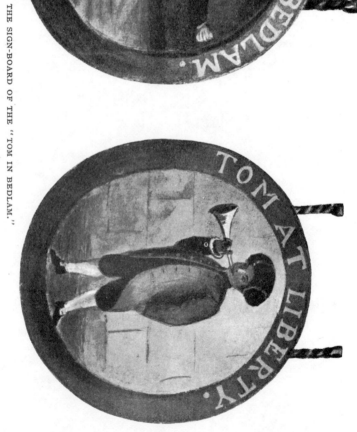

THE SIGN-BOARD OF THE "TOM IN BEDLAM."

(*Drawn by Mr. James Arrow, after a photograph.*
By courtesy of Mr. Fisher Unwin.)

THE GREAT ABNORMALS

BY

THEO. B. HYSLOP, M.D., F.R.S.E.

*Gaskell Scholar in Psychological Medicine; formerly President, Psychological
Section Royal Society of Medicine: Society for the Study of Inebriety
and the Chelsea Clinical Society; late Senior Physician, Bethlehem
Royal Hospital, and Lecturer on Mental Diseases at St. Mary's
Hospital; Demonstrator in Experimental Psychology,
Guy's Hospital, and Senior Physician to King
Edward's Schools, London and Witley*

LONDON

PHILIP ALLAN & CO.

QUALITY COURT

1925

Republished by Gryphon Books, Ann Arbor, Michigan, 1971

Library of Congress Catalog Card Number 79-162514

PREFACE

In the foreword to Dr. L. A. Weatherly's *Plea for the Insane* the present writer said : " The public is naturally and rightly anxious to guard the liberty of the subject and at the same time to ensure its own safety. In other words, it wishes to prevent the reception and detention, under the Lunacy Administration, of persons who might possibly be better dealt with either at their homes or elsewhere ; it seeks to protect the unfortunate invalids who are compelled by circumstances and the nature of their maladies to surrender for the time being their legal and social responsibilities ; and it desires to make adequate provision for the ventilation of any grievances of patients so unfortunately placed. The medical faculty has for long attempted to enforce upon the notice of the public the need for the better protection of the interests of both the invalids and itself by methods short of actual certification of insanity, but so far without avail."

The contents of the present volume are meant as a further plea for the greater spirit of tolerance with regard to the aspirations and activities of those who do not conform to our own self-opinionated standards of mentality ; for the individuals whose ' abnormalities ' about to be described have been among ' the great ones of the earth.' We are at present so shackled by traditions pertaining to religion, law, science, and work, that an artificial code of restriction and prohibition has become imposed upon our individualities to such an extent that, in order to remain free, we must perforce not only refrain from self-expression, but adopt, advisedly, an artificial attitude of hypocrisy which, instead of leading to light, is manifestly sham and subversive. The time does indeed seem opportune to state in definite terms the sociological impasse at which we have arrived, and if by so doing the writer helps in any degree to lighten the perplexity and burden of those who have to do with the mentally afflicted, his efforts will not have been made in vain.

In collating the following pages reference has been made to well-known works such as *The Story of Bethlehem Hospital*, by E. G. O'Donoghue : *Historic Oddities and Strange Events*, by S. Baring Gould : *Civilization in England*, by H. T. Buckle : *Extraordinary Popular Delusions*, by Chas. Mackay : *Foibles and Fallacies of Science*, by D. W. Hering : *Mad Majesties*, by Angelo S. Rappoport : *Royalty in all Ages*, by T. F. Thisleton-Dyer : *The Blot upon the Brain*, by W. W. Ireland : *The Insanity of Genius*, by G. F. Nisbet : *The Man of Genius*, by Caesar Lombroso : *Devils*, by Chas. J. Wall : and to many other works.

To the critic, the writer confesses that this volume is not meant to be either historical or literary, and in the collation of ' cases ' he has chosen them merely as illustrations of the main contention that the segregation of many of those who are alleged to be mentally unstable though harmless has been productive of suffering to the individuals concerned : whereas the importance of segregation of the mentally perverted who are harmful to the community has been under-rated. This means that the whole question requires a readjustment of values, and it is only by a frank admission of actualities that justice can be done.

CONTENTS

INTRODUCTION

THE frontispiece—'Mad Tom in Bedlam' and 'Tom at Liberty'—might well serve as a text to this book.[1]

Poor 'Tom in Bedlam' was treated as an 'irresponsible' and sometimes dangerous person, whereas 'Tom at Liberty' was free to blow his own trumpet and fill his pocket in proportion to the mental capacity and credulity of the people. That such imitators still exist in large numbers is only too readily evidenced when we note the present-day vagaries in art, music, science, literature, and religion. Inasmuch, however, as these have been dealt with in a previous volume,[2] the following pages will be devoted to the consideration of some of the more serious mental and moral aspects of human beings as recorded in history.

In reviewing the activities of dwellers 'within' and 'without' the precincts of Bedlam, no attempt is made to form a diagnosis as to their sanity or insanity; the

[1] E. G. O'Donoghue, *The Story of Bethlehem Hospital*, p. 140, says, "So familiar and fantastic a figure on the road as Tom o' Bedlam naturally found its way into the sign-boards of wayside inns. There still exists an example of such a sign in the village of Redbourne, Herts. On one side of a copper plate you may see 'Tom o' Bedlam'; he is in a barred cell with fetters round his legs. On the reverse side is 'Tom at Liberty'; he is attired in a gorgeous red coat, blue knee breeches, and white stockings. With a turban on his head this gay impostor struts along the road blowing his horn—with an oration and a collection at intervals."

[2] *The Borderland: Some Problems of Insanity*, by Theo. B. Hyslop.

making of a diagnosis being well within the capacity of every thinking person. Before the reader proceeds to peruse the data offered for his consideration, it is advisable to realise that ' perversion of mind ' does not necessarily imply ' irresponsibility in conduct,' or *vice versa*. That certified inmates of asylums for the insane may possess, and generally do possess, comparatively sound control over their conduct, no person with experience can deny : *i.e.* many do not lose their control to so great an extent as to render them a source of danger either to themselves or to others.

When visiting the ' Chamber of Horrors ' at Madam Tussaud's the thought may have arisen that therein were recorded the chief criminals. The record, however, is inadequate in its scope, for history tells us that the greatest of criminals have been free to exercise their inhumanity, *i.e.* many persons suffering from insanity have been saved from death by finding sanctuary in asylums, while ' irresponsibles ' have flourished in the midst of a welter of human blood. The question may well be asked by each one of us, Am I my brother's keeper, or is he so down on his luck, so mentally enfeebled, so irresponsible, that he must be handed over to the care of others ?

One of the conclusions to be derived from the data recorded in the following pages is that in the drama of history the spirit of toleration has played a leading part. That intolerance has been an active factor throughout the ages has been exemplified on every platform of human endeavour, in spite of the fact that only under the influences of tolerance can each individual unit work, live, and expand his being. Whether ' tolerance ' is in all respects compatible with the theories of Darwin, Malthus, and Spencer is another matter. At this stage of our evolution the trend of humanity must be for tradition to give way to knowledge, and for knowledge to give way to moderation and a more complete toleration. To live and let live, to know and let know, to have and let have, to do and let do, are all excellent guides, although the real charter for the evolution of humanity is to be and let be.

When estimating the scope or depth of the human mind, one can but wonder what influences are at work to prevent some communities from attaining to greater heights. Power and wealth are of but little value to evolution so long as they do not lead to higher planes of thought and existence. Science has but paved the way towards rationalism. It has considered the evolutions, the mutations, the energies, the gravitations, and the relativities, of the cosmos; biology has dealt with life as regards structure, reaction, etc.; psychology has observed, classified, and endeavoured to explain the various processes of mind; whilst religion has gathered together the resultant philosophic conclusions thereon and has sought, with the aid of inspired traditions, to formulate conceptions as to our existence as a subservient and fractional part of a greater whole. Religion stands, therefore, on the highest platform of human thought and endeavour. It is, however, only by a right interpretation of its data that it can realise itself as having bridged the ages since truth was first revealed in all its strength and virility.

We note how humanity is gradually scaling the ladder of an emergent evolution to a self-realisation, *i.e.* a realisation of self as but an integral part of a greater whole. Egomania implies belief in self as being ' the one and only,' whereas self-realisation means evolution. Chesterton's claim, that the man who believes in himself ends either in Hell or Hanwell, applies to those who struggle on the level of a divergent evolution. On this lower level are to be found the philosophy of Nietzsche, with its Napoleonic lust of power, Omar Khayyam's dream of 'Paradise enow,' and Oscar Wilde's egoism of self-indulgence.

Roberts [1] endorses the view of Chesterton, and suggests that there is so ominous an increase of insanity and suicide in Europe and America as justly to raise the question whether the white race is not under sentence of death. He says it is the story of Peer Gynt writ large. Peer Gynt set out to live his philosophy of egoism ; and the lunatics in the Cairo madhouse hailed him their king and natural leader, and crowned him the Great Monarch of Himself. This extravaganza applies, however, to self-realisation *per se*, that is to say, to a megalomania brought about merely by many accidental factors of causation such as hashisch, psychopathia-sexualis, and a misinterpretation of vital truths. In egomania, man enthrones himself as his own god, as all-sufficient, and as forming no part of an all-pervading medium. He does not uplift himself to the higher platform of subservience to a greater whole.

Between the Alpha and the Omega of human inspiration there is a seething cauldron of those who are struggling for air to breathe, light to see, and freedom to exist, on a higher plane where there is no need of armaments, dogmata, or prohibitions. Meredith had his being on the platform of sight and sense, Swinburne on that of unbelief and revolt, William Morris of beauty and socialism.

[1] Dr. R. Roberts, " The Doctrines of God," *Hibbert Journal*, October, 1924.

Browning, Tennyson, and Francis Thompson had glimpses of spiritual insight. Browning wrote :

> " Then take and use Thy work,
> Amend what plans may lurk,
> What strain o' the stuff,
> What warpings past the aim.
> Our times are in Thy hand,
> Perfect the cup as planned,
> Let age approve of youth,
> And death complete the same."

Religion is not infrequently assigned as a cause of insanity. A philosophy of the infinite is, however, far from being a source of aberration of thought amounting to actual insanity. A true and philosophical religion raises the mind above incidental emotionalism and gives stability. Christianity is the truest form of philosophy.

The typical cases of religious insanity [1] directly developable from sectarian or even undenominational religious enthusiasm, from religious meditations, exercises, devotions, or superstitions, are by no means so common as they are supposed to be by the uninitiated observer. Many mental cases bear a strongly marked religious, or, at least, moral aspect, but these are not necessarily caused by religious over-excitement or enthusiasm. The form of their appearance may be shaped by the prevailing ideas and creed of the patient, but the reason for their existence lies deeper. As the late Sir Thomas Clouston used to say, ' Far more depends upon the brain one takes to church than anything one sees or hears therein.' Schools and churches are as gardens for the cultivation of the moral being. Religion, instead of being a source of mental disturbance, is really the greatest asset to stability

---

[1] Theo. B. Hyslop, British Medical Association, Leicester, on *Occupation and Environment as Causative Factors of Insanity.*

of mind and body. Faith inspires courage to overcome life's cares and perplexities.

Huxley and Tyndall were loyal to a faith which transcended actual verification; whilst Lodge and Julian Huxley have advanced speculative thought to the extent and meaning of existence. Scientific methods have tended to displace conventional ideas derived from tradition. Concepts as to the essence or nature of a supreme being have varied according to the imagination of the various exponents. Theologians have ever tended to rise to a more philosophic platform of thought until they are now within reach of a conviction that credulity, agnosticism, and rationalism are not in reality incompatible. Rationalism but leads to personal humility with regard to the evidences of omniscience, omnipotence, and omnipresence: agnosticism is but a humble admission that there are matters which cannot be known to the human intellect; whereas credulity is a part of ' being ' which requires no proof.

Clement Webb distinguishes between the two expressions : the personality of God and the personality *in* God. It may well be urged that the topmost rung of existence can only be attained by those who are imbued with faith, hope, and charity. One thing is certain, *viz.* : there is always plenty of room at the top of the ladder of human thought, feeling, and endeavour; and it rests with each individual either to remain on one particular rung, or to mount to where he can breathe more freely, see more clearly, and realise that above and beneath there is a cosmos of which he knows but little.

In historical literature little attention has been paid to discovering the principles which govern the character and destiny of humanity. Most writers have confined their

attention to the consideration of one or other of the
various aspects of thought or action. Plato was struck
with the extreme difficulty of finding a standard in the
human mind whereby we may test the truth or falsehood
of spectral phenomena and dreams. Among an ignorant
people, there is a direct tendency to ascribe all serious
dangers to supernatural intervention. A strong religious
sentiment being thus aroused, it constantly happens that
not only is the danger submitted to, but it is actually
worshipped. " In the world at large, every advanced
thinker, enthusiastic reformer and popular teacher is almost certain to be classed with the insane. The ' friends '
of the Master said, ' He is beside Himself,' St. Paul was
declared ' mad ' by the highest tribunal." [1]

The Thracians weep and wail when a babe is born, and
deliberate on all the sorrows and hardships which the
child will in all probability be called upon to suffer ;
while, on the other hand, they rejoice and hold high fes-
tival when they bury their dead. The Mexicans hold
much the same idea, but they welcome the newly-born
infant with these words—" My child, thou art born to
endure, therefore endure, and suffer, and be silent."
Swift must have been imbued with something of the same
conviction, for Sir Walter Scott relates of him that he
invariably kept his birthday as a day of mourning, when
he would read over and over again the passage in the
Bible where Job grieves over the day when in his father's
house ' a son is born.'

In India most of the natives, especially the Brahmins,
have a great reverence for the mad, and consult them in
any trouble or adversity. Amongst many semi-barbarous
people also, the madman is both dreaded and worshipped,

[1] *The Great Society : A Psychological Analysis*, by Graham Walles.

and he is often made their ruler.　The Ottomans hold the mad in the same reverence as they do their dervishes, and they believe that the ' All Powerful ' has for them an extra tenderness.　They even call them divine ones, sons of God, and the priests feel honoured to receive them in their homes.　Amongst the dervishes themselves the strangest customs prevail.　Each monastery has a prayer and dance of its own, if their convulsive movements can be called by the name of dance.　Some bend their bodies backwards and forwards, some from side to side, and as they proceed with their prayer the movements become more and more rapid until they attain almost to frenzy. This ' dance ' they term praising the unity of God.

The Moors say of the insane, that Allah has retained their reason in the Land of the Blessed though their bodies remain for a while on earth, but that their words should be treasured as precious inspirations, because reason returns to them in their speech.　In some districts, the mad are often made saints of, and permitted to follow their own impulses.　One of these strange saints strangled every person who approached the Mosque.

The Kuffais are known far and wide for their extraordinarily exaggerated piety.　They allow themselves little sleep, and then only with their feet in cold water; they fast for weeks at a time.　They commence the chant of Allah by coming forward with the left foot, and, holding each other by the arm, they make a circular movement with the other.　As they advance, the chant becomes louder, the dance movement becomes quicker, until with glazing eyes, tired out and perspiring, they fall into ' sacred ' convulsions.　In this condition of religious hysteria they endure the ordeal of hot iron, and, when the fire has subsided, they cut and mutilate their flesh with knives.

The Patagonians appoint women as doctors and magicians, and these women do all their prophesying during convulsive attacks. If men are raised to the priesthood they are compelled to wear women's dress, and they must also give proof of the possession of the special qualifications essential for the post. In China the followers of Tao have complete faith in demoniacal possession, and strive to discover the future from the words of the insane, thinking that, being ' possessed,' the spirit will speak through them. To us of the twentieth century, the thought of being possessed by a devil is almost inconceivable, and the idea of being under anyone's will except our own is ridiculed. There are, however, still a few people —the ' die-hards ' to tradition—for whom the devil is a real and terrible force to be reckoned with.

The inauguration of bells had for its purpose the exorcism of the evil spirits with which the air was thought to abound, the office of baptising and blessing the bells being held to make them thus powerful. This fact is vouched for by the inscription on several of our ancient bells, which begins—" By my lively voice, I drive away all harm." The custom of " ringing the hallowed bell in great tempests and lightnings," was resorted to when our Church of St. Paul was blazing. The passing bell, which is now called the funeral bell, was rung at the death of all Christian persons, and in the sixteenth century it was tolled day and night for the dying. A bell was also rung (and still is) during the passage of the body into the church and to the grave, following out the same thought of keeping evil spirits away from the dead person. In this, as in many other customs, there still lurks a trace of the superstitions of the past, the past which is not so extinct as many people imagine.

On a ruined wall which was once the Church of St. Pancras near the monastery of St. Augustine at Canterbury, marks are still supposed to have been imprinted by the devil when he was driven out of the chapel by the Mass read by St. Augustine. In his rage he tried hard to destroy the chapel, and his violent efforts caused his hoofs to leave their indelible marks upon the wall. In Central Africa, when a drought occurs, many of the natives believe it to be caused by the swallowing of every particle of moisture by the Devil.

The events usually recorded in history can be of service as records, but it is by their interpretation that greatest benefit can be gained ; hence it is that much has been done during recent years towards discovering the principles or motives which govern the character and destiny of races. Nowadays, the foundations for belief, as set by Kepler, Newton, and many others, have become scientific, and to their efforts have been added those of innumerable scientists with regard to biology and psychology, until we have arrived, not at the parting of the ways between science and religion, but at a junction of the two whereby they become reconciled and interdependent, *i.e.* theological and metaphysical hypotheses have tended to displace tradition and dogmata respectively.

As Buckle [1] says, metaphysics will never be raised to a science by the ordinary method of observing individual minds. Its study can only be successfully prosecuted by the deductive application of laws which must be discovered historically, and which must be evolved by an

[1] *Civilization in England.*

examination of the whole of those vast phenomena which the long course of human affairs presents to our view. Plato could not find a standard in the human mind whereby to test the truth or falsehood of spectral phenomena and dreams. Needless to say, we are still without conclusive tests as to the limits of interpretation of such phenomena. In fact, we can only form provisional diagnoses as to their being manifestations either of progress or of decay.

The revolt against the advances in civilization during the Christian era has been steadily maturing for many generations. Subversive movements have arisen in consequence of the growth of a mental and moral chaos through the warring of factions. Russia has based its programme on an economic policy of acquisition with the idea that subversion of life and moral attainment is a practical necessity. Lenin was undoubtedly affected mentally, and he has but served as a text for the Russian ' Toms o' Bedlam ' who now act as his imitators. Viewed in the light of history, other despots have perverted the moral instincts of the Russian people, and there has been a throw-back to barbarism owing to the initiative of a disordered mind. As stated by the Duke of Northumberland (*National Review*, cit.) there have been other movements which closely resemble the modern Bolshevist movement, *viz.*, that of the Albigenses in the twelfth century, the subversive Bohemian sects in the fifteenth, the Anabaptists in the sixteenth, and in the French Revolution. Revolt against the growth of the tree of humanity is due nowadays also to the undergrowth of ' mental weeds.' This undergrowth has been fostered, and even encouraged, by subversive make-shifts, sociological fallacies, biological incongruities, and economic delusions, until the world finds itself threatened with a cataclysm, which, instead of being local, may become general. To search abroad for the ' hidden hand ' is futile, for the hidden hand belongs to each individual unit ; and it is to each individual unit that appeal should be made. Crowd-psychology cannot with justification seek protection against arbitrary compulsion and intoleration so long as the masses themselves do not practise what they desire to uphold. In order to retain freedom each unit has to cultivate tolerance towards his fellow-beings, otherwise subversion is bound to occur, and the victims become relegated to the ranks of the unfit, the unsound, or the irresponsible. That the attainments of mind, feeling, and conduct, and all that pertains to civilization are being strangled by mental, moral, and industrial perverts is evidenced to-day in those mass-movements which recognise no moral or spiritual obligations, no legal restrictions, and no standards of conduct.

In the history of the rise of civilization, ignorance has been followed by fear and superstition, superstition by revelation, revelation by religion, religion by law, law by prohibition, and prohibition by loss of freedom, until humanity manifests itself as an aftermath of mockery, paradox, and irresponsibility, together with a hypocritical counterfeit of reverence, truth, and self-control.

The Sudras (labourers) of India used to stand in a relationship to the Vaisyas (capitalists) very different from that of capital to labour in Europe. Buckle [1] records some minute and curious legal provisions. " If one of the Sudras presumed to occupy the same seat as one of the Vaisyas he was banished with a mark on his

[1] *History of Civilization*, vol. i. pp. 58-9.

hinder parts, or branded with a gash on his buttock. If
he spoke of them with contempt, his mouth was to be
burned ; if he actually insulted them, his tongue was to
be slit ; if he molested a Brahmin, he was to be put to
death ; if he sat on the same carpet with a Brahmin, he
was to be maimed for life ; if he listened to the reading of
sacred books, burning oil was to be poured into his ears ;
if, however, he committed them to memory, he was to
be killed ; if he were guilty of a crime, the punishment
for it was far greater than that inflicted on his superiors ;
but if he himself were murdered, the penalty was the
same as for killing a dog, a cat, or a crow." One may
well ask, of what avail are the present-day outstretched
hands of free education and philanthropy to chained
slaves who are allowed neither to think nor act for themselves ?

In Western civilisation, release from a somewhat ana-
logous condition of thraldom has but been followed by
individual surrender to a form of slavery in which the
units in every department of thought and labour are
shackled together as slaves to an organisation which
represses any individual effort to attain to freedom either
mentally, morally, or economically. That each unit
should so surrender his freedom of thought and conduct
to impositions which serve to arrest ascent from a level
which is tuned to the lowest level of efficiency, is a matter
which suggests questions as to loss of the sense of indi-
viduality. But the various unions of modes of thought
and industry have yet to realise that their shackles are
subversive and imposed from below. We learn from the
History of Peru (Prescott, vol. i. p. 159) that the people
were so shackled that they could follow no craft, could
engage in no profession, labour, or amusement, but such

as was specially provided by law. In their case, however, the shackles were not self-imposed through lack of imagination, understanding, or initiative. That the ordinary individual should possess an imagination like that of Dante, Shakespeare, or Newton is not essential to ascent from conditions of inhuman slavery. The real trouble is to be found in an atavistic trend to barbarism similar to that of some of the Hindus of Malabar, who from feelings of reverential fear refuse to destroy wild beasts and noxious reptiles ; the mischief these animals inflict being the cause of the impunity they enjoy.

The natural powers of the human brain may be transmitted by inheritance, as advocated by Gall, Comte, Prichard, and others, *i.e.* there may be a progress of mental capacity for reason, feeling, volition ; but the direct transmission of knowledge of data can, so far as we know, occur only vicariously and by means of circumstances afforded by environment. That reasoning powers, memory, aesthetic sense, and control may be transmitted is probable, and such transmission appears to be just as evident as is the transmission of life and mind. That such qualities can be transmitted is proved by the history of mankind, and although his existence has been imperilled by waves of fanaticism and subversion he has maintained himself throughout the ages ; whereas knowledge, wealth, and modes of activity have varied considerably. This means that certain qualities are stable, whilst others have been not only unstable but also ever-changing.

The Royal Commission on Lunacy and Mental Disorders, which is now sitting, has to consider such problems as must inevitably arise in connection with the safeguarding of the interests of the individual and of the community. That such an enquiry should be held is indeed necessitated by the existence of many curious anomalies with regard to individuals and communities. Firstly a definition is required as to what is meant by ' abnormality of mind.' ' Normal ' means conforming to natural order or law. ' Natural order ' refers to the ways we do think and act ; ' natural law ' refers to nature's trend of thought and action. The ways we do think and act are not co-extensive with the ways we ought to think and act ; for, were they co-extensive, but few human beings would be normal. When we realise that no human individual is at all times stable in his perceptions, cognitions, reasonings, judgments, memory, feelings, or conduct, we must confess that we possess minds somewhat akin to many of those who are relegated to institutions for mental instability. The question of certifying an individual solely on account of his beliefs should not arise in a civilised community where tolerance of other people's vagaries prevail. Unfortunately, however, the conventional prohibition of a natural expression of our inner beliefs has been followed by an intolerance by those who either do not give vent to their fully formed convictions, or who possess ideas of so nebulous a character as to render them incapable of expression.

It is also yet to be recognised that so-called mental disorder, *per se*, is not co-extensive with the sense of responsibility, and that the wildest imaginings portrayed through the history of civilisation have not necessarily been incompatible with the highest attainments in the realms of thought and conduct. When, however, faulty reasonings have encroached upon the domain of personal responsibility in thought or behaviour, and have become subversive and a source of danger to the individual or to the community, then, and then only, should it be considered necessary to relegate the individual from the majority of the unsound to a minority of the unsafe.

Questions of responsibility have been made to include questions of insanity. This absurdity has been due to defective knowledge and to a consequent faulty reasoning whereby the normally unsound have been acquitted on the grounds of irresponsibility, whilst the abnormally irresponsible have been convicted on the grounds of sanity. The present rulings of our Courts demonstrate these paradoxical relationships, and it is still the legal prerogative to deprive a man of his liberty, or even his life, by reasoning based on the faulty assumption that insanity implies irresponsibility, or irresponsibility insanity. That our asylums are replete with instances of faulty reasoning, comparable to those in vogue in the outside world, I do not dispute ; but that these faulty reasonings are attended in all instances by a corresponding want of sense of responsibility I deny, and many of such persons should, in my opinion, be freed from some of the restraints now imposed upon them. That many of the patients in asylums do conduct themselves in an orderly and even useful manner no person can gainsay. For such conditions, home life and family surroundings would be beneficial and conducive to happiness were the home influences more suited to their needs, and were there more tolerance displayed towards them by the community. One of the saddest of asylum experiences is the knowledge that it is to the interest of some patients that they should not be subjected to the influences prevailing in some forms of home life. Poverty through drink and extravagance, vanity and discomfort, nagging and discord, constitute some of the bars to release from control, just as they may have been the real factors of causation of loss of freedom.

The ' Right of Asylum ' has a twofold significance, and England, if it is to be thorough in its administration, should enquire still further into its abuses.   The ' Right of Asylum ' should not be denied to those who are qualified to exist as independent and unharmful units of the community ; but, where they are subversive in their social, biological, or economic trend, then no such right should be granted.   It is also open to all to consider the question as to who, of our selves, can also claim the ' Right of Asylum ' by reason of subversive tendencies which are of evil import morally or economically either to ourselves or to the community.

Were a census to be taken of those who are disordered mentally, without losing their sense of personal, moral, and economic responsibility, and those who are apparently sound mentally yet unsound in their sense of responsibility, we would realise how misguided we have been in our comprehension of the real issues in some of the complex problems now before us.   When once the reader has grasped the fact that there is a fundamental and real difference between ' insanity ' so-called and ' irresponsibility,' he will begin to realise that hitherto the diagnosis, classification, and treatment of the insane have been illogical, because they have been based upon false data followed by faulty reasoning.   The outcome of this illogical procedure is now evidenced by a confusion which permeates and influences medico-legal practice. When Church and Science, Law and Medicine, Capital and Labour, have come into line with each other on a higher platform, then, perhaps, we may witness the birth of a greater spirit of rationality and tolerance.

Insanity may be regarded as a degree of defect or perversion of the faculties of perception, judgment, morality,
or of conduct, whereby the individual falls out of harmony
with his environment to such an extent as to render it
advisable or necessary that either he or the community
should be afforded protection. Irresponsibility may be
regarded as a condition of defect or perversion of the
power of control due to (*a*) congenital or acquired causes
(*e.g.* abnormal states without insanity, as in dreams,
somnambulism, minor epilepsy, etc.) ; (*b*) morbid impulsion
or uncontrollable action ; or (*c*) insanity with halluci-
natory or delusional states arising through disease, and
by reason of which either he or the public should be safe-
guarded from the effects of the perverted activities.

To realise the fundamental distinction between these
two conditions is imperative if we are to unravel the
medico-legal confusion which exists to-day. That this
confusion has long prevailed is exemplified, on the one
hand, by the ' responsibles ' who through illness of mind,
conscience, or body, are now under lock and key, gazing
sadly out of barred windows, and praying for a home to
which they might with safety return ; and, on the other,
by the ' irresponsibles ' who are not only free but also a
source of danger either to themselves or to others, and
who should, by reason of their lack of sense of responsibility, be segregated.

The former class has attained to great proportions in
asylums, and the main cause has been intolerance ;
whereas the proportionately small number of the latter
has been due to a misguided tolerance of subversive pol-
lutors of the community. Needless to say, the following
pages are collated as a plea both for many of the insane
who have been deprived of their liberty, and for the out-

side public, which is also in need of care and protection. That some who are beneficent are segregated, whilst others who are harmful are free, is a fact for which the public itself is in great part to blame.

All the world is indeed a stage, on which the farces, comedies, and tragedies of life are enacted for the education, cultivation, and entertainment of the occupants of box, stall, pit, or gallery ; whilst outside there is to be found a long queue of those who are waiting their turn for admission, and who are being entertained by minstrel, clown, or acrobat. The Toms o' Bedlam, who derive financial benefits from queues ' without,' are to be seen at the portal of every church, law court, art gallery, concert hall, public library, press bureau, and refreshment saloon.

The reader who does not wish to witness the play of humanity as gleaned from history may now turn aside and refuse to learn anything from the doings of the ' madding crowd.' For him the following pages can be but of little interest or purport. Should, however, he feel it to be his duty to ascertain for himself his own and others' place on the scale of humanity, then let him diagnose the meanings of events and arrive at his own conclusions.

CHAPTER I

TYRANTS AND DESPOTS

SAUL (*c.* 1075 B.C.), the first King of Israel, was subject to fits of depression from his early youth, and there is little doubt that Samuel, who elected him King, had hallucinations which appeared chiefly as a craving for power, and possibly the reasons why he selected Saul were his good looks and handsome bearing, knowing that his lack of energy would still leave the power in his own hands. Saul was one of the many beings who fancy themselves to be objects of persecution, and spend their lives in persecuting people from whom they dread some injury. He suffered from attacks of what he termed the ' evil spirit,' and during his fits of dire depression, he could be consoled only by music. David often soothed him by playing to him ; yet Saul became jealous instead of grateful, and twice essayed to kill him. He even gave instructions to have him executed, but weakened and wept copiously. His suspicion and jealousy were extended to his son Jonathan, whom also he essayed to have killed. Suspecting nearly one hundred priests of treason, he had them and their wives and children put to death. In the house of the witch of Endor, he imagined he could hear the voice of Samuel. He finally put an end to his miserable existence by casting himself on his own spear.

Saul, to his own astonishment probably even more than to that of the assembled crowd, became suddenly imbued with the prophetic spirit just before his coronation. Some time afterwards the spirit of evil genius took possession of him, and urged him to try to pierce David with a lance. In the first Book of Samuel, we read of " Saul as a prophet running naked through the fields," [1] and in 1 Kings, xviii. we see the prophets of the groves of Baal crying out like madmen, eating filth and refuse, and cutting their flesh.

There is a pretty legend told of Nimrod that, when in the fields, happening to look up he beheld in the heavens a figure which resembled that of a crown. The mighty hunter summoned to his side the most skilful craftsman in gold who resided in the vicinity, and asked if he could fashion a head-piece like that intended for Nimrod by Heaven, whence the pattern had expressly come. The artist answered confidently in the affirmative, sketched the model, and in a short time produced a radiant crown which the King wore ; at which his subjects could seldom look without peril of being blinded by its dazzling glory.

Nebuchadnezzar (B.C. 602-556), the great ruler and conqueror of many nations, suffered from a more than ordinary swollen head, and fancied himself to be some Heaven-sent being of Divine origin.

Theopus (c. B.C. 550), the Greek poet, wrote idealistic moral maxims—several eulogising a happy death—and he left all his property to a prostitute.

Socrates (B.C. 469-399) believed that poets create, by means of an inborn instinct, beautiful verses in the same way as a diviner makes predictions in a trance, without consciousness of the thoughts they string together. We are told by his biographers that he firmly believed that a

---

[1] See also 1 Samuel, xix. 24.

familiar spirit was always by his side, and, according to his own writings, he constantly heard the ' spirit voice.' This great philosopher wore the same robes in winter as in summer, and he was in the habit of removing his sandals to walk barefoot on the ice. He would sometimes pause in his walk and commence to dance and leap ; and he enjoyed venting his sarcasm on all with whom he came in contact. He also frequently relapsed into fits of profound meditation varied by sudden outbursts of wild ecstasy.

Democritus (born B.C. 470-460), the Greek philosopher, blinded himself, because he was not able to see a woman without craving to possess her.

Dionysius, the Tyrant of Syracuse (B.C. 430-367), combined the qualities of a distinguished general with those of a poet, and it is a strange fact that a prize that he won for a poem gladdened him more than all the victorious laurels he had gained in battle. Intense cruelty was his predominant instinct. It was he who evolved and brought into use the remarkable ' ear cave ' for his prisoners. This was a device by which he could sit far off and yet hear all that his captives said of him, and then he would wreak an awful vengeance. He upbraided his son for his debauched conduct, but was himself the most licentious and profane of kings. Knowing full well that he had made himself hated by his people and his so-called friends, and even by his own family, he lived always in suspicion and alarm. But not until he turned on Plato and made him a slave did the nation rise up against him and send him to exile to Locris, where he continued his unspeakable cruelties for ten years. His return to the throne was of short duration, for he was again exiled ; this time to Corinth, where he became a schoolmaster, whether as a means of continuing a petty tyranny over

his pupils, or as a deed of humility, is open to conjecture.
But certain it is that the formerly proud, aggressive king,
degenerated and scarcely ever sober, was always ragged
and unclean. He had no property, and lived on what he
could scrape together by teaching or by shaving and
haircutting. As to the latter he was singularly proficient.
Sometimes he stood outside drinking houses amusing
the crowd with ribald jokes, or sometimes he solicited
alms for the altar as though he were a monk. Unlike
these holy men, however, Dionysius bared his arms,
tucked up his robe, played vigorously on the tambourine,
or danced till he was breathless. And yet, even when
practically in the gutter, he had an ambition to establish
a public academy. His death was occasioned through
excessive joy on hearing that a play which he had written
had won a prize.

Aristippus (died B.C. 399), beneath an outward mask
of extreme asceticism, gave himself up completely to a
debauched life.

Among the few great military commanders the world
has ever known, Alexander the Great (B.C. 356-323) holds
a high place. Born of a father with an ungovernable
temper, and a depraved mother, Alexander was, in spite
of his wonderful victories, a man of thoroughly debauched
character. He was troubled throughout his life by a
contraction of the muscles on one side of the neck, which
made his head appear lop-sided, and he died at the early
age of thirty-three.

Ptolemy II. married the wife of his brother Philometer,
and on the wedding day he killed their baby son in its
mother's arms. After awhile he put his wife aside, and
married her daughter by his brother. He murdered two
of his own children by this wife, sending the limbs of one

as a little present to its mother. He was finally turned
out of his palace, and spent some years in exile. In
spite, however, of his dire atrocities, he returned to power
and continued his reign of terror. Ptolemy II was a
clever scholar, a brilliant author and an apt linguist.

Sallustius (B.C. 86-34), the Roman historian whose
writings on virtue are almost celestial in their purity and
beauty, lived a life of utter licentiousness.

Augustus, Emperor of Rome (63 B.C.–A.D. 14), the son
of Julius Cæsar's sister Atia, was very delicate as a child,
prone to fears, terrified of darkness and thunder, and
subject to epileptic fits. Suetonius tells that he was a
cruel and treacherous debauchee, and Seneca writes that
it was only through utter fatigue of cruelty that his reign
became less brutal and even benevolent towards its close.
But, on the other hand, it cannot be denied that Augustus
was well endowed with brains and the capacity to use
them. His brain power, however, was not handed on
to his children. His daughter Julia led a thoroughly
depraved life, whilst his son Drusus had hallucinations
and was inhumanly cruel.

Julia (39 B.C.–A.D. 14), daughter to the Emperor Augustus, was first princess of the Cæsars, and inherited all that
was evil in her father's nature, without the power of
restraint which kept the head of Augustus well balanced
even in the midst of his self-indulgent and dissipated
life. To say that Julia was not a moral woman would be
an entirely inadequate way of explaining her ; she had not
even the innate sense of decency which many animals
possess. There was no path of vice that she did not
tread. She went, in brazen wantonness, from one atrocious orgy to another, until Augustus, horror-stricken
at the shameless behaviour of his own daughter, even

contemplated putting her to death. Finally, however, he placed her in strict confinement for five years, and never consented to see her again. He also made a clause in his will forbidding that Julia's ashes should be placed beside his in the Imperial mausoleum. Of Julia's three children, two of her sons died almost in infancy, the third, Agrippa Posthumous, was feeble in body and mind.

Tiberius (A.D.14–37), who became the third husband of the notorious Julia, was by nature cruel and vicious, like all the Claudian-Julian family, and it is hardly to be expected that such a union could develop any good traits. Indeed it was greatly owing to the disgust he felt on fully realising the true character of the woman to whom he was married, that he went into self-banishment at Rhodes for seven years. During that time, Tiberius spent his life in secret cruelties and vicious pleasures, whilst planning evil deeds for the future. And when, in his fifty-fifth year, he ascended the throne his reign became a succession of despotic and unexampled cruelties, whilst his personal life was passed in excesses so shameless and corrupt as to defy description. His hatred of mankind seems to have increased with his years, and he committed murders without remorse or ceremony. Tiberius could look on and smile whilst those whom he had sent to terrible torture were flung into the sea, where sailors had orders to dash to pieces any who might still have any life in them. He believed that death put an end to existence, and he had no faith in an after-world.

He found intense joy in tormenting men, animals, and even insects and birds, and he rejoiced in their shrieks of agony. Yet his intellect was of a high order, and in his early youth he had high ambitions. But depression of spirits seized him, and in a craving for solitude he went

to Rhodes, where, Suetonius tells us, he behaved like a
guilty man and was filled with humble contrition. He
also imagined himself to be an object of persecution, and,
fearing that danger menaced him on every side, found
refuge in the uninhabited parts of the mountains for over
two years. Then he returned to Rome, but only to live
in obscurity in a quiet garden on the Aquiline Hill. In
this misanthropical condition, Tiberius came to the throne
on the death of Augustus. It is therefore not to be wondered at that the iron-willed Accius Sejanus for many
years ruled the Emperor and his Empire. Tiberius
went to Capri, where no one was allowed to land. When
Sejanus left him to attend to affairs of State in Rome,
his enemies poisoned the mind of the Emperor against
his favourite, and Tiberius, believing that Sejanus had
treasonable intentions, ordered not only his assassination
but also the assassination of many others of his counsellors
who, he imagined, were also implicated. Indeed the
River Tiber could scarcely contain all the corpses, so
numerous were the victims of the panic-stricken Emperor.
He even mistrusted his brother Drusus and his mother
Livia. At the latter's death he annulled her will, and
executed all her friends to whom she had bequeathed
legacies. Suetonius says that as many as twenty people
were put to death daily, and frequently twice that number,
including women and children. Yet it was fear, fully as
much as the lust for blood, which prompted his cruelty.
Later in life his fear took a new phase. He became
obsessed with the idea that he might die of poverty and
hunger. His lavishness changed to avarice. He frequently refused to pay his servants, and seized the
property of his nobles. Seeking forgetfulness from his
tormented mind, Tiberius entered on a life of lust and

obscenity, and scenes of hideous cruelty and debauchery became the order of the day. In his seventy-fifth year he died in a fit of apoplexy during one of these horrible revels.

Claudius (10 B.C.–A.D. 54), son of Drusus and grandson of Augustus and Livia, was physically weak, and, giving up all ambition, spent his days in drink and play. He was twice made consul, but incurred the derision of the Court by his poltroonery. He divorced his first two wives and then married Messalina, a woman of infamous character. Claudius was sixty when his nephew Caligula was assassinated. Being petrified with fear, he hid behind a portière, where the soldiers found him trembling with alarm. He was so weak-minded that his wife, Messalina, made no secret of having a lover. Claudius was also a glutton and a drunkard. His absent-mindedness was so great that having at last consented to give orders for Messalina's execution, he was surprised not to see her at his table the next day, and actually sent for her. Similarly, he frequently invited people to dinner whom he had sent to assassination the day before. He was a coward, and affrighted at the least noise. After fourteen years, he died by poison given by his niece Agrippina, whom he had married after the death of Messalina.

Claudius was tall and well built, but moved unsteadily, and his knees appeared to be lacking in strength. He had a hard, hoarse laugh, and leered hideously, and foamed at the mouth when in a rage. His head shook from side to side, and his speech was stuttering. Under able tutorship he had become a good scholar, especially in Greek, and was even the author of a long historical work. His character was a strange combination of dull stupidity and shrewd cunning. Whatever better faculties may have lain latent within him he drowned in drunkenness. At fifty he became Emperor—then the cruelty which had been slumbering broke forth in full measure. Claudius delighted in looking on at tortures and executions and in watching the faces of his victims.

Messalina, wife of Claudius, instead of seeking to uphold her power by her fidelity, gave herself up to a life of excesses which could not have been surpassed by even the most vicious man of that corrupt period. She passed shamelessly from one paramour to another, and even had the effrontery to go through the marriage ceremony with one of her lovers.

Caligula (A.D. 12–41), the youngest son of Germanicus and Agrippina, also had hallucinations. Caligula soon proved that he too had a mania for persecution. He actually delighted in the sight of blood, watching with delight the agonies of the wounded and dying. Thus, when all the criminals whom he had condemned to death had been killed, he gave orders to seize some of the spectators in the arena—had their tongues torn out, and they were then thrown to the wild dogs and torn to pieces. Peaceable citizens he would suddenly imprison in low caves, so that they could only crawl, or have them cut in halves. Even his brother and father-in-law he had assassinated. One of his amusements consisted in showing his wife Cæsonia in a nude state to his friends. Now and again he ordered the public granaries to be closed, so that he might be entertained by the sight of starving people. He suffered greatly from insomnia, and was disturbed by terrible dreams and nightmares. According to Suetonius, his extravagance was almost incredible; he even swallowed pearls dissolved in vinegar, and when short of money stole and robbed from his people. At

last the sword of Cassius Chærea rid the world from his
tyrannical cruelty.

Nero (A.D. 37–68), son of Agrippina by her first marriage
with Dimitrius, inherited the characteristic traits of Germanicus, Julia, and Agrippina. The latter had always
participated in the orgies of her imperial brother Caligula,
and, with the connivance of her lover, the freed-man
Pallas, had succeeded in marrying the weak Emperor
Claudius in his dotage, and forced him to adopt her son
Nero as his successor. Claudius, it is chronicled, replied
to congratulations at the birth of his son in these words :
" From Agrippina and me only a monster and a scourge
of humanity can come forth." And he spoke truly, for
although Nero's reign opened with good promise, his cruel
instincts soon manifested themselves. He poisoned his
brother Britannicus, put to death his mother and his wife
Poppæa, and massacred all who stood in his way. He
was utterly deficient in the instincts of humanity. Nero,
like Caligula, was killed during a revolution, and died a
most humiliating death. Like all the Cæsars, Nero's
vanity was developed at the expense of altruistic feelings ;
his sexual instincts were perverted, and his destructive
instincts led to refinements of cruelty, debauchery, patri-
cide, and sanguinary gloatings.

Agrippina became a wife at the age of thirteen, and nine
years afterwards gave birth to a son—Nero. Sister to
Caligula, she attended all his orgies, and his name figures
on the long list of her paramours. Niece to Claudius, she
obtained influence over him by pandering to the sensual
desires of his weak mind, and gratified her ambition by
becoming his wife and empress of the world. She mercilessly condemned to death all those whom she considered
might become her rivals, and even ordered the head of

one to be sent to her that she might put her fingers into its mouth and recognise the owner by a peculiarity in the formation of the teeth. Agrippina was cruel and avaricious, she sold places for wealth and power, and ordered rich people to be killed so that she might seize their possessions.

It has been said of Nero's grandfather, Domitius, that it was no wonder he had a beard the colour of brass, when he had a mouth of iron and a heart of lead. And yet, in spite of his parentage, so impressive were the teachings of Nero's tutors Seneca and Burrhus, that he commenced his reign with wisdom and benevolence. But four years of absolute power brought to the surface all the savagery and sensuality of his predecessors. His cruelty remains a by-word even to this day. Amongst the enormous number of his victims, nine of his own family were put to death by his orders. His passion for music seems strangely incongruous, and it is historical that after setting fire to Rome he went on playing whilst the magnificent city was burning.

Commodus (A.D. 161–192) seems to have been extremely bored by the lessons to which in his boyhood " he was forced to listen like a young lion yawning and showing his formidable teeth." His one desire appears to have been to do in all things exactly the opposite to his tutor's teachings. All his thoughts and tendencies were cruel and perverse. Accompanying his father in the wars beyond the Danube probably encouraged the boy's lust for blood. At nineteen he became emperor, but was utterly incapable of ruling the vast Roman Empire, and even putting his name to a document was too much trouble for him. The favourites who ministered to his pleasures governed the nation in a vile and corrupt

manner. He himself kept three hundred concubines and
as many boys. His harem was shared by his favourites.
And so little was he open to a sense of shame that, by his
special wish, his most infamous actions were engrossed in
the public records. He had the cravings of a savage beast
for slaying, and he often put to death the companions of
his debaucheries. He gloried in his vigorous strength, and
fought over seven hundred times in the gladiatorial games.
We are told that one of his pet amusements was to bleed
men with a surgeon's lancet. For thirteen years Rome
endured his tyranny, until he met his death at the hands
of a band of conspirators.

Heliogabalus (A.D. 204–222), the reputed son of Cara-
calla, mounted the throne at the age of fourteen. He did
not possess one single quality which could have entitled
him to rule over a great nation, but merely used its wealth
and power to gratify to the full his sensuality and love of
self-indulgence. His life was spent in inexpressible infamy,
and he looked upon one and all of his subjects, however
high their rank, with utter indifference and contempt.
Quite aware of the fate which awaited him, of the violent
death which sooner or later ended the orgies of the dissolute emperors of Rome, he yielded to the passions which
bore him to the tomb. Lampridius tells us that he had
prepared silver ropes with which to strangle himself, golden
swords to stab himself, and solutions of poisons flavoured
with spices, and he had a high tower erected, the inside
of which was adorned with pictures, gold and gems, from
which he might precipitate himself, vaunting that even his
death should be costly.

Constantine (A.D. 288–337), the Christian Emperor of
Rome, forbade the habit of putting out eyes, asserting
that the human face was a throne of celestial perfection,

and therefore should never be maimed; but this same Constantine murdered his own son in cold blood.

The Emperor Constantine is stated to have had a dream, on the night of the death of his son Constantine, that he saw him falling into hell, and, in an excess of terror, he hastily sent messengers to Rome and Jerusalem to implore the prayers of the faithful. He also summoned the monks from the monasteries around to assemble in his palace. The day was Holy Thursday, and at the moment of the elevation of the Host, Romanus divested himself of all his upper garments, and stood in the midst of the assembly with nothing on but his shirt. With a loud voice he read his general confession, at the conclusion of which he knelt before each monk in turn and received absolution. And, according to Suetonius, Romanus was entirely sure that the ceremony received divine sanction.

Childeric II, King of France (died A.D. 673), was known as the ' Phantom King,' because he went so little among his people that he was scarcely ever seen. He spent most of his time trimming his beard and curling his hair. Charles the Bald, King of France, justified to himself and others all the atrocious deeds he committed by asserting that he was possessed of a devil. Ferrand (A.D. 862), Count of Flanders, was an extremely keen chess player, and when playing with his wife he constantly defeated her. This caused the Countess to conceive such a fierce hatred for him that when he was taken prisoner at the battle of Bouvines, she rejoiced, and, although she might easily have procured his release, she did not take any steps towards it, but allowed him to remain in prison for a long time. And yet it is chronicled that she was a dutiful and loving wife until the chess-playing commenced.

Cunegunde (A.D. 972) was himself assured, when building

the Cathedral of Bamberg, that he had raised the devil, and assigned to his satanic majesty all the heaviest and more laborious portions of the work.

Edward the Confessor (died 1066) is credited with having possessed visionary powers.   On one occasion, when on a visit to the royal treasury with his chamberlain, he beheld the devil in all his hideousness dancing with saturnine glee on the casks wherein the Danegelt tax was kept.   The king deduced the fact that this tax must be evil and unjust or it would not cause the devil so much joy, so he immediately ceased to collect it.

King Boleslas II of Poland (1058–1101) whilst on one of his hunting expeditions could not be found ; but, many days later, he was discovered in the market-place dressed as a porter and carrying heavy loads.   His ministers and gentlemen of the Court took him severely to task for such unseemly conduct, and entreated him to return to the throne ; but Boleslas replied : " Upon my honour, gentlemen, the load which I quitted is by far heavier than the one you see me carry here.   The weightiest is but a straw compared with the world under which I laboured.   I have slept more in four nights than I have during all my reign. I begin to live and to be a king myself.   Elect whom you choose—for me, who am so well, it were madness to return to the Court."

William Rufus (1060–1100) was so firmly convinced of the divine right and protection for kings that, when his sailors were afraid of putting to sea in a storm, he cried out : " I have never heard of a king who was shipwrecked ! Weigh anchor, and you will see that the winds will be with us ! "

Frederick II (1194–1250) took enormous delight in every conceivable form of petty malice, and at times he did not even hesitate to chastise his friends with blows. He asserted that " vengeance is the pleasure of the gods," and that his most ardent desire was to cause more harm to his enemies than he had ever endured at their hands. He included among his enemies all his friends and courtiers, at any moment that their words or actions varied even slightly from his own opinion or frame of mind. Thus one unfortunate courtier who had a weakness for pomade had his clothes saturated with oil by the Emperor's order.

Louis IX of France (1215–1270) was continually oppressed with fits of wild restlessness, and at such times only Jacques Coetier, one of the royal physicians, was able to exercise any control over him. He succeeded in diverting the King's attention by arranging for the performance of country dances outside his window.

Edward I of England (1239–1307) combined in his nature a love of merry pranks with a temper of unusual violence. He would often be " seized with fierce rage," and it is reported that in these tempestuous outbreaks he more than once threw coronets on the fire. One day, in a mischievous mood, he made a wager with Matilda of Waltham, the Queen's laundress, that she could not ride with them to the hunt, and be in for the stag's death. The King was so astonished when she accepted the challenge, and she rode so successfully that Edward gleefully paid his fine of forty shillings.

Edward I believed so implicitly in the divine right of kings that he felt convinced that a royal corpse would be immune from the corruption which overtakes the bodies of ordinary mortals, and in support of his belief he left instructions in his will that his tomb should be opened at least every two years, and his body wrapped in a new cere-cloth.

Margaret, second wife of Edward I, carried her passion for hunting to such excess that, when enthusiastically following the hounds, she was seized with the first pangs of child-birth and barely able to seek a neighbouring house before her first-born saw the light.

Mohammed Toghlak, Sultan of India (1325), until his accession was known as Juna, the son of Gheias-u-din-Toghlak. He had been originally only a foot-soldier, then governor of Debalpur. Juna led a revolt against the reigning sultan, who took refuge in flight. Gheias-u-din-Toghlak was then asked to rule over the kingdom, and on being told that, if he refused, his son Juna would certainly seize the throne, he consented to become sultan. On Juna discovering the hiding place of the late sultan, Khusru Khan, he conducted him before his father and had him put to death, in the same way as Khusru himself had done to his predecessor.

During his absence on a Bengal expedition, Gheias-u-din-Toghlak left his son as Viceroy in Delhi, and on his return was crushed to death by the falling of the pavilion which had been erected in honour of his reception. It is said by Batuta that Juna had ordered the pavilion to be built up in such a way that it would collapse as soon as the elephants walked over a certain part. Historians differ as to whether the sultan was picked up dead or merely stunned. If the latter, he was certainly despatched with all haste by Juna's orders. Juna thus became sultan, and henceforth was known as Mohammed Shah Toghlak. He was then about thirty years old. His two great proclivities were oddly incongruous : he loved to make presents and to shed blood. The new sultan was fearless yet humble, and extremely punctilious in his attention to his own devotions, as well as those of his people. In one day, he ordered nine citizens to be put to death because they had been neglectful in the performance of prayer. There is no doubt that Toghlak was a man of many accomplishments and great eloquence, also a poet of no mean ability. He was the possessor of a marvellously retentive memory, and a student of many sciences.

Toghlak discouraged licentiousness in any form and was temperate in his own habits. Nevertheless the lust for power, and the intoxication thereof, completely perverted his judgment, and he was continually planning unwise and reckless schemes to satisfy his own vanity and ambition, without a thought of the sufferings he caused his subjects or of their disastrous effects upon the nation. Ferishta writes that this sultan, " who established hospitals for the sick and almshouses for widows and orphans on the most liberal scale," was entirely pitiless, and gloried in ordering wholesale executions. " Every day," says Ibu Batuta, " they brought to the hall of audience hundreds of people in chains, their arms attached to their necks and their feet tied. Some were killed, others tortured or beaten." The elephants belonging to Toghlak were trained to throw men up in the air and catch them again on their trunks, to cut their bodies with knives which were fixed to their trunks, or to trample upon them. Beha-u-din, a cousin who refused to pay homage to the new sultan and who sheltered with a Hindu rajah, was eventually given up to Toghlak, who ordered him to be flayed alive and his flesh to be sent to his family.

In crushing revolts against his power and authority Toghlak was utterly without pity. When he moved the capital of India from Delhi to Diogiri, he ordered that " after three days no one should be found in the city of

Delhi." He also ordered a careful search to be made for those who might remain in hiding. His slaves found in the streets two men, one paralytic and the other blind. They brought them before the sovereign, who ordered the paralytic to be thrown from a catapult, and the blind man to be dragged from Delhi to Doulatabad, a forty days' march. He fell to pieces during the journey, and only one leg was dragged into Doulatabad. Ferishta records that Toghlak " was afflicted with violent toothache and lost one of his teeth, which he ordered to be buried with much ceremony at Bhir, and caused a magnificent tomb to be reared over it, which still remains a monument to his vanity and folly."

If any person denied an accusation which the Sultan through rumour or malice chose to make against him, he was tortured or put to death ; his own brother was publicly decapitated. When giving orders for execution Toghlak usually concluded with the words : " God have pity upon him, or them." The tyrant had none. Sixty-two adherents of the Governor of Oude, who revolted against him, he had torn to pieces, or tossed by elephants, and portions of the victims were thrown to the leader of the revolt.

When hunting in Beiram, for no reason whatsoever, he commenced a general massacre and hung some thousands of heads on the city walls ; this he repeated in Canouj. Fearful, not of revolt but of assassination, Toghlak's spies were everywhere. To maintain his enormous army, and enable him to indulge in his favourite whim of giving costly presents to strangers, the people were oppressed with taxes so heavy that many left the towns and lived like wild men in the woods. Revolt after revolt Toghlak crushed, and he punished his enemies with the utmost barbarity. When advised to abdicate, he only persisted more mercilessly in scourging the rebels ; but an excessive meal of a favourite dish caused the despot's death after a reign of twenty-seven years.

Frederick III, Emperor of Germany (died 1330), frequently slept soundly in the Council Chamber whilst most urgent State affairs were discussed. When the Turks invaded his domains and destroyed the villages and harvests, he strolled in his garden, picked caterpillars off his roses and slugs from the cabbage leaves. We are told that he was so lazy and lethargic that even turning the handle of a door was too much for him—he would kick it until someone came to open it, or occasionally he would become irritated and burst it in. One day he injured his foot doing this, and, owing to the possibility of mortification setting in, the surgeon amputated it. " Ah me ! " said Frederick, " a healthy boot is better than a sick Emperor."

Charles VI of France (1368–1422) spent his entire time thinking out some fresh plan of pleasure, and often he would adopt a new and original disguise. On one occasion he and his boon companions dressed themselves as satyrs, wearing linen costumes to which they fixed tow with pitch. And thus garbed, they joined a gay wedding party at the Hotel St. Pol, and executed wild dances. Whilst these dances were in progress, the Duke of Orleans madly suggested setting fire to the masqueraders' dresses, which naturally flared up instantly, and but for the presence of mind of the Duchess of Berri, who covered the king with her dress, he would assuredly have been burned to death, as were three of the other dancers, the fourth only saving himself by jumping into a water-butt.

Henry V, King of England (1387–1422), when Prince of

Wales, was extremely wild and dissipated.   His thought-
less extravagance made him continually short of money.
He mingled only with low companions, and became
involved in vulgar brawls.   A popular (though not historical) story relates that one of these brought him to
the inside of a London prison.   When his servant was
arrested and brought before Judge Gascoigne, Prince
Henry tried to set him free with his own hands, and
struck the judge when he frustrated his purpose.   Gascoigne severely reprimanded the young Prince and sentenced him to prison.   Scapegrace as he was, Henry took
the reproof with such good grace that his father, Henry
IV, said he was proud of having a son who would thus
submit himself to the laws, and that he had a judge who
could so fearlessly enforce them.   On another occasion,
John Hornesley, Mayor of Coventry, committed Henry
to gaol, " for that he, with some of his friends, did raise
a riot."

The whole line of the Austrian house of Spain from
Philip the Fair (1285–1314), who married Joanna (Joana
la Loca), was marked by weakness and cruelty.   Perhaps
it was partly owing to the greater brilliancy and charm
of her brother John and her sister Isabella that Joanna,
the third daughter of Ferdinand of Aragon (Ferdinand
the Catholic) and Isabella of Castile, spent rather a
neglected childhood, which may have increased her
natural melancholy.   In 1496 she married the Arch-
duke Philip of Austria, for whom she evinced intense love.
When parted from him her grief was terrible, and she was
utterly indifferent to all her surroundings.   Joanna was
entirely without will power, although occasionally giving
proof of sound judgment.   At times she would persist in
some obstinate caprice, as, when travelling through

France, on returning from Flanders to her native land, she refused to pay homage to the French king, and not even her husband's persuasions could alter her decision. Her behaviour was so inexplicable that her mother, Isabella, made the Cortes of Toledo agree that her husband Ferdinand should retain the regency of Castile until his grandson should become of age—"if, after her own death, Joanna should be absent or unable or unwilling to rule." This measure had become necessary in consequence of the early deaths of the Queen's two elder children, John and Isabella, which made Joanna the heir-presumptive to the Castilian crown. When Philip returned to Flanders, leaving his wife in Spain, she fell into complete apathy, varied at times by furious fits of rage, and when, in 1503, he summoned her to join him in Brussels, she wanted to start off at once, although it was mid-winter and France in the throes of war. She even rushed from the castle insufficiently clad. Her attendants followed and begged her to return. But even when the outer gates of the castle were closed upon her she stood at the barrier, furious and indignant, refusing even to re-enter the castle to complete her toilet. The next day she commenced her journey to Flanders, where she found her husband under the influence of a golden-haired lady of the Court. Joanna's conduct caused a complete, though temporary, separation between Philip and herself; he could not endure her alternating fits of mad love and furious jealousy, being himself a lover of an easy-going, pleasurable life, with a distinctive aversion for worry or serious occupation of any kind.

In 1506, after the death of her mother, Joanna and Philip returned to Spain, where the people had prepared a splendid welcome for her. But she refused to attend the gorgeous ceremonials, or to lessen the mourning she was wearing.   In spite of so much contrariness, Joanna is said to have been most punctilious in inspecting the credentials of the deputies and in making sure that all were duly authenticated.   During the same year, with unexpected and tragic suddenness, Philip died after only five days' illness.   Joanna stayed day and night beside him, giving orders and attending personally to his needs ; but neither during his short illness, nor on its fatal termination, did she ever shed a tear.   She sat in a darkened room, with her eyes fixed on the floor, immovable as a marble statue, except when at rare intervals she broke into feeble paroxysms of discontent and petulancy.   The new " Queen of Spain " was " equally regardless," says Martyr, " of herself, her future subjects, or her afflicted father.   Her one slight solace was music, of which she was extremely fond."

For some time Joanna would not permit the burial of Philip, the body being laid in the church of Miraflores, where she attended dressed as a nun.   She ordered the coffin to be opened, kissed the hands and feet of her dead husband, and spoke to him in terms of endearment. After doing this for several weeks, Joanna gave orders to convey the corpse to the royal sepulchre at Granada. When they rested, the body was laid in a church or monastery, where Joanna had the funeral rites again performed just as though Philip had only just died.   She was constantly fearful lest some person should profane the place ; she certainly had no love for her own sex.   It has been suggested that, in delaying the burial of Philip's remains, Joanna was acting on the suggestion of a foolish Carthusian monk, who had told her that a certain Prince had once returned to life after being dead for fourteen years.

When, in 1507, Ferdinand met his daughter Joanna at Tortoles, he found her in a lamentable state ; her face was haggard, her figure emaciated, and her clothing torn and shabby. He had her taken to Tordesillas, where she persisted in living an isolated life, often imagining herself, or her attendants, to be possessed by evil spirits. Often she fancied she could see a black cat rend the soul of her father, her husband, or her own, and at those times her rage and terror were very acute. In her ordinary life, she lived as the beasts lived, her personal habits even descending to the unclean.

This woman was the mother of two German Emperors, and the founder of a mighty dynasty of emperors and kings of Austria and Spain. Her son, Charles V, was an epileptic, and was harassed constantly by funereal and morose yearnings, and eventually sought seclusion in the monastery of St. Juste. Philip III and Philip IV of Spain were indolent, debauched, and weak in body and mind. Charles II also suffered from hallucinations.

Amongst the unaccountable freaks of Don Sebastian (1480) one of the most extraordinary was the removal of the body of John II, which had lain in Batalha Abbey for the best part of a century. He ordered the corpse to be taken from its resting place, and being in a state of complete preservation, he had it stood upright, dressed in royal robes, and even placed in the withered hand the sword which the long-dead King John had once owned. Then Sebastian commanded the Duke of Aveiro to do homage to the body and kiss its hand, whilst he cried out, " Behold the best officer of our kingly service." The King then proceeded on his round of sepulchral visitations.

Don Sebastian's vagaries and restlessness were the absolute despair of all around him. The royal quarters had

continually to be shifted from one end of the little kingdom
to another in obedience to the King's command. Repose
was to him unbearable, and midnight often found him
pacing the sandy shores of the Tagus and in the forest of
Cintra.

Francis I of France (1494–1547) had a mind for nothing
but his own entertainment, and " framed a court of which
licentiousness was the custom, and from which justice,
temperance, and every Christian as well as chivalric virtue
were banished."

Henry VIII of England was over fond of the punch
bowl, and frequently became intoxicated. He also preferred low company to his Court surroundings. The
marriage adventures of the eighth Henry will of course
never cease to be the source of wonder. His favourite
sport was the chase, and indeed hunting was such a passion
with him that when the death gun sounded, announc-
ing the execution of his once " entire beloved Anne
Boleyn," he gleefully exclaimed—" Ha, Ha ! the deed
is done, uncouple the hounds, and away."

Charles V (born 1500), though strong of mind in many
ways, yielded to the superstitions of his time and believed
firmly in talismans and amulets. He always kept ' infallible ' styptics for stopping blood, English crampings,
a blue stone magnificently carved, to cure gout, bezoar
stones for driving away plague, and other charms and
mascots. Charles insisted on having his funeral rites
celebrated before him, but did not attend the service in
a shroud, nor did he lie down in his coffin. In all other
points, however, the ceremony was fully complete. He
ate enormously, and drank still more. His repulsive
excesses brought on diseases which hastened his end.
Often at dinner he would stick a knife into the joint, or

tear off with his fingers a piece from any special part he fancied.

Charles was possessed of great vigour and strength, also of extraordinary intellectual power. His personal character was strangely contradictory; he was deeply religious, but capable of acts of meanness and unscrupulousness. His articulation was hampered by his teeth, which failed to meet properly, and therefore interfered with thorough mastication. He was also subject to epilepsy, attacks of depression, and violent headaches. The latter caused him to cut off his long hair. When he was only thirty, he was also much troubled with gout.

In spite of all these drawbacks, however, he was one of the greatest and most powerful monarchs who ever reigned in Europe. That, at the age of fifty-six, he voluntarily abdicated, and spent the remainder of his life in seclusion, is conclusive proof that he felt that his health unfitted him for continuance of his office. He never ceased to entreat that the burning of heretics should be continued, and he regretted bitterly that he had not sent Luther to the stake.

Ferdinand of Austria (1503–1564) was of an amazingly apathetic disposition. One day he is reported to have remarked in the Imperial palace at Vienna, " I once very readily paid a visit to one of the theatres in the suburbs, but I cannot make out whether they wanted me or not." The Emperor seems to have fancied that he was there to put his signature to a document of some sort, and he was puzzled as to whether he had been asked to do so or not.

Don Pedro I of Portugal, when desperate with sorrow at the loss of his wife, would—after tossing sleeplessly for hours—order a troop of soldiers to form a hedge from his palace, and he would rise from his bed and dance between the soldiers who held lighted torches. It was Pedro's way of " giving bodily expression to the vehemence of his grief."

Philip II (1527–1598) took his losses at chess so much to heart that his extreme vexation was always manifest to the entire Court, but most of all to any clever but injudicious player who had won. When that untactful man returned to his home, Philip would inform him that he could expect no further favours.

CHAPTER II

TYRANTS AND DESPOTS (*Continued*)

IVAN IV, ' the Terrible ' (1530–1584), was a striking and awful figure in Russian history. He combined in his character all the opposites—enlightenment and superstition, intelligence and cruelty, culture and savagery. His great grandfather Vassily Vassilevitch, a weak-minded Prince, capable of the meanest cruelties, had his eyes put out by Dimitri Shemyaka. Vassily's son, and Ivan the Terrible's grandfather, Ivan III, from his youth upwards showed signs of brutality. He filled the prisons ; the knout and other torments became the order of the day. He replaced judgment with torture. The son of Ivan III, Vassily Ivanovitch, was a man of changing moods, varying many cruel actions by occasional sudden fits of generosity. His second wife, mother of Ivan IV, suffered from partial paralysis, and Ivan III himself died from the results of a wound which deprived him of speech and brought on paralysis.

From his infancy, little Ivan lived in the midst of atrocities—murders and tortures—and from being merely a spectator, he soon became the principal actor in the sanguinary deeds enacted. As a child, although on all public occasions he was treated with Oriental submission, he was neglected in private life and treated with insolence by the boyarins. Probably even then he was chuckling with delight at the thought that in a few years he would be able to revenge himself on his tormentors. As a little child, Ivan showed signs of excessive barbarity, and found savage joy in torturing animals, which he would throw from a window in order to enjoy their agony. When riding through the streets of Moscow, he loved to trample men, women, and children under his horse's hoofs, and he laughed aloud at the fright and suffering he caused. The crowd of courtiers, anxious to win favour, flattered and applauded all his actions.

At the age of thirteen, he ordered the arrest and execution of the Regent, Andrew Shouysky, dispensing even with the farce of a court-martial. Shouysky was seized, thrown to the dogs, and torn to pieces. In 1547 Ivan was crowned ' Tsar ' with great pomp and ceremonial. Once on the throne, he gave absolute rein to his hereditary sanguinary desires and to his unbridled fury. Though unable to concentrate his mind on any subject for long, he had acquired a vast amount of learning, and was possessed of a very lively imagination. He was also at times convinced that he possessed a dual personality, and inclined to take fiction for reality. Fired by reading of the greatness and magnificence of Babylonian, Assyrian, Roman, and Byzantine emperors, he fancied himself to be one of them, hence his adoption of the title of ' Tsar ' (Cæsar).

He married Anastasia Romanovna in 1547, but did not break away from the disorderly life he had been living. He took no interest in the affairs of State, though always asserting that he was Autocrat and Ruler of Russia, and that he could do anything he wished. Ivan never permitted his subjects to bring to him complaints of any sort, and once, when a deputation of peasants came to the village of Osteov, at the first words they uttered the Tsar shook with rage. He ordered the unfortunate peasants to be seized, stripped of their clothing, soaked in boiling brandy, and their hair and beards burned.

When the city of Moscow was reduced to ashes by the great fire and more than 1700 people were burned to death, a rumour became current that the fire had been brought about by evil magical machinations of wicked people who served Satan. Ivan believed the rumour, and found victims even amongst his own relatives, the Glinskys, who had made themselves unpopular with the nation. Ivan's grandmother, Anna Glinskaya, was accused of witchcraft, her son was torn to pieces, and all their friends were assassinated.

The new Tsar was a coward and terrified at the phantom of a possible revolution. He allowed himself to fall under the influence of Sylvester, who, supported by Alexis Adashev, ruled for Ivan for thirteen years. In spite of all his pretended intrepidity and independence, Ivan was constantly in the power of his favourites. " But his mind was too superficial," writes Kovalevski, " too narrow-minded and not far-seeing, so that he never perceived that he was acting under the influence of others, but, vain and proud by nature as he was, he readily imagined the ideas of others to be his own."

There were times, however, when the Tsar was seized with a desire to throw off the yoke of his advisers ; but, doubting the strength of his position, he awaited the moment when he would be able to give full vent to his revenge and hatred. When the Tsaritsa Anastasia died in 1560, rumours were circulated that Sylvester and Adashev had caused her death. They demanded a fair trial, but their request was refused and both were exiled.

Ivan then drew to his side other friends who shared his love of debauchery and praised his sanguinary atrocities. In all his actions he allowed himself to be completely ruled by the urgings of his impulses and passions; in his mind an autocracy stood above all else on earth, and in crime he was most assuredly an artist. His wild imagination created fictitious crimes, so that he put to torture and death scores of innocent people. These tortures and elaborate executions were a source of utter delight to him, he enjoyed them even more than theatrical performances. He devastated entire districts, sparing neither women nor children. Love and pity were unknown to him—if he sent gifts or money to churches or monasteries, it was in order to still some superstitious fear.

A week had barely passed after the death of his wife, for whose loss he professed intense grief, before he married Maria of Circassia. But still he did not cease from his drunkenness and vice; indescribable and terrible scenes were the order of the day. The older boyarins, though disgusted at the orgies in which they were compelled to participate, had to submit. Prince Ryepnin did indeed attempt to protest, but he was assassinated in Church during prayers. All the friends of the once favourite Sylvester were put to death or exiled, as were hosts of other families. Indeed, tyranny and the shedding of blood grew to a terrific pitch. It was evident that the Tsar's fiendish cruelty invariably became more appalling after his fits of imaginary piety. Even in his wars he evinced excessive savagery.

Ivan took refuge in a coward's ruse to give his tortures and executions a semblance of justice. In 1564 he set rise to a rumour that the Tsar had resolved to abdicate and leave Russia. He summoned to Moscow the sons and families of the boyarins, and laid down his sceptre and crown. All the valuables were carried away from the Kremlin and packed in sledges ere the Tsar and his boyarins started on their journey. None dared to disobey, although Ivan pretended to have given up the government. The Tsarita, his children, and favourites accompanied him to Alexandrovskaya Sloboda. But the comedy was of short duration. After a few months, Ivan sent a message by Constantino Polivanov in which he accused the boyarins of treachery and the clergy of aiding and abetting the traitors. He likewise sent another message inciting the merchants and common folk against the nobles.

His cunning plan was successful, as he had felt sure it would be, in bringing a deputation begging him to resume government and so come to the rescue of his unhappy people. He graciously consented to do this on condition that the clergy would swear never to shield traitors, but allow him to kill or exile them, and to confiscate their property. He ordered the people to erect a new palace for him on the Neglinna, and to surround it with high walls. He took every possible precaution to ensure his own safety, and no one was permitted to leave the castle without his consent. The guards of the royal household became notorious for their bloody and scandalous deeds.

Ivan, whose personal appearance had undergone a frightful change owing to the debauched and perverted life he lived, knew no bounds to his cravings and bloodthirstiness. The followers of all his old enemies suffered torture and death. Then all of a sudden, a new idea possessed him—he turned his palace into a monastery, with himself as Abbot, and spent hours in fervent prayer, he himself playing the part of chaplain.   In the midst of these prayers he would give some cruel order, which his actor-monks rushed forth to execute, and put some wretched victim to death with long knives which they carried beneath their cowls.   Women and even very young girls were violated and, in a fit of Sadism, murdered, whilst their husbands were poisoned or killed by violence.   More than once the Tsar commanded that a woman whom he and his suite had dishonoured should be hanged over her husband's threshold.   Anyone of whom Ivan had, or fancied he had, the least suspicion was assassinated, tortured, or impaled.   Opritshinky were dashing round the town killing ten to twenty people daily, and nobody dared to remove the corpses which lay about.   A list of the disgusting torments invented by the Tsar's evilly fertile brain would be too long and revolting to chronicle.   And yet, in the midst of his horrible crimes, he convened an assembly to consider urgent political matters.   Prince Vladimir Andrevitch, whom he suspected as being a possible menace to his throne, was invited to the Tsar's castle, where both he and his mother were murdered.

When the Tsar's second wife died, he asserted that she also had been poisoned, and made that an excuse for fresh assassinations.   All the boyarins of whom he had the least doubt were put to death, and he got rid of independent priests.   Then his murderous instincts started on a still vaster scale.   Entire towns and districts were depopulated, the people being put to torture and death and the towns burned.   Men, women, and children were cut to pieces, and the Tsar's savage hordes carried off everything they could.

At Novgorod, abbots and monks were murdered, the richest and most influential inhabitants were arrested and brought with their wives and children before the Tsar. They were stripped naked and put to horrible tortures. Ivan himself had invented a machine by which his victims could be roasted alive. They were then bound to sledges, dragged through the town, and cast into the river; Ivan's hangmen and servants then rowed about in boats, murdering any poor victims who rose to the surface.

On his return to Moscow he ordered three hundred people to be executed, and prepared on a grand scale for the wholesale assassination. But as the day neared, either through cowardice, or perhaps malice, he chose one hundred and eighty and spared their lives. The rest were subjected to indescribable and frightful tortures, Ivan himself inventing a fresh horror for each—because he hated monotony! Some were cut to pieces, others cast into boiling water, and so on. He not only superintended, but took personal part in all the massacres. He then went to the houses of some of the accused men and violated their wives and daughters. When the Russian armies were being overthrown by foreign enemies, and the country was in the throes of famine, Ivan sat in his palace hiding from his enemies, leading the same drunken, debauched life. In a paroxysm of fury he killed his own son and heir apparent, Ivan.

He was at that time slightly over fifty, but looked like a very old man. He was suffering from a terrible malady, which caused his limbs to rot and his flesh to fall off in pieces. For days he remained speechless, and yet even when death was near and his daughter-in-law came to visit him, she had to rush away to escape his obscene embraces. Astrologers had predicted the day of his death, and the Tsar in agonies of terror, awaited the dread event.

It has been said of Ivan that he was always most rigidly

pious and reverent when he was idiotically drunk, or planning some super-fiendish crime. He gave way, in his more sober moments, to fits of ungovernable fury. When only in his teens he had one of his attendants killed by dogs on the public highway, and in his self-styled frolicsome moods he would let loose wild bears in the streets. Then, whilst the affrighted citizens were being tormented and killed, ' the Terrible ' calmly knelt down and said his prayers the while he watched the terrible scene. And when he rose from his knees, he flung a few coins to the wounded as compensation. Ivan would compel parents to murder their children, and children one another, and whenever there was a survivor, " the amiable monarch, if not too weary," would slay him himself, and laugh uproariously at this conclusion to such a huge joke. He is reported to have sent to the city of Moscow ordering " a measure of fleas for a medicine." The citizens replied that they could obtain the fleas, but it was not possible to measure them on account of their hopping art. Upon receipt of their answer, Ivan set a mulct of 7000 roubles upon the city.

At the time of the birth of Ivan, the Russian people had suffered the intensest cruelty from the Tartars, who had laid their country waste. Misery, bloodshed, and despotism were the order of the day, even among the families themselves. Children were actually the slaves of their father, who could sell them again and again. Wives were under the same despotic rule. The peasant in his hut of wood was as despotic a tyrant as the great ruler himself. Prisoners of war were made slaves. Only a great concentrated power could save the nation, and so the people of Russia looked to the young Tsar as their ' little father,' their saviour.

Rendered fatherless at three years old, little Ivan had grown up under the regency of his mother Helena, who for four years led a life of cruelty and licentiousness until her death was brought about by poison. The boy, thus reared, fell into the power of self-seeking conspirators, who committed one atrocity after another. All his boyish love of brutality was fostered and encouraged. And yet, through his inconceivably atrocious brutalities and all the horrors he committed, the people endured his oppression and cried, " If the Tsar leaves us, we shall perish. Who will be our defence in war with the stranger ? How can the sheep do without the shepherd ? " Ivan's caprices and insensate cruelties followed each other in unrestrained frightfulness. For twenty-six years he indulged remorselessly in his worst passions of lust, cruelty, and murder. He personally committed murders only for the sake of killing. On one occasion he cut off the ear of a nobleman who was making obeisance to him, saying to him, " You are worthy of our grace." And it is noteworthy, as testifying to the servitude of all ranks of the nation, that the unfortunate nobleman repressed every sign of pain and " thanked the Tsar for his gracious pleasantry ! "

Ivan ran a knife through Theodore, who had been master of his house for nineteen years, after dressing the old man in his royal robes and crown, and placing him on the throne with a sceptre in his hand. The Tsar bowed low before him, saying, " I wish you health, great Tsar of the Russians. But, as I have the power to raise you to the rank of Tsar, I have also the power to throw you down again ! " In the midst of his feasts Ivan would frequently put down his knife and fork to order the execution of prisoners. His ministers would return triumphantly singing ' Goida, goida,' after murdering a hundred or more men, and con-

tinue the feast. Ivan killed numberless prisoners to test
a poison which he ordered his doctor to prepare, which
could be so graduated as to do its deadly work in from
half-an-hour to several hours.

In 1569, on hearing that the people of Kostromo had
formed a procession to meet his cousin Vladimir, whom
he had sent to command the army in Nijni Novgorod,
Ivan was so furious that he ordered the execution of all
the leaders of the reception, and invited Vladimir to come
to him at Alexandrova. He then ordered a poison bowl
to be handed to his cousin, his cousin's wife, and their
four children. Their ladies in waiting and servants
were stripped before the people's eyes and shot, whilst
Vladimir's aged mother was drowned.

At Novgorod, every day five hundred to one thousand
people of all classes were brought before Ivan ; men,
women, and children were put to death by inconceivable
forms of torture, houses were gutted, horses and cattle
killed. It is roughly estimated that twenty-seven thousand people were butchered. The climax to Ivan's terrible cruelty was reached when, in a fit of passion, he
struck his own son a fatal blow with an iron-headed staff.
But in spite of all his atrocities, Ivan IV showed conclusively at times that he was capable of planning and
carrying out a steady policy, and that he possessed an
intellect which, if not brilliant, was by no means de-
spicable, and it is a truth, if an extraordinary one, that
the people bewailed his death when in 1584 he passed
away.

Eric XIV of Sweden (1533-1577) was extremely handsome and courageous. His mother, Princess Catherine of
Sachsen-Lunenberg, had been a dangerous hypochondriac,
and after her death, his father, Gustavus, suppressed and

neglected Eric, but pampered and favoured his two sons by his second wife. This treatment warped the boy's naturally amiable disposition, and he ascended the throne full of jealousy, distrust, and suspicion. Eric's coronation was on a scale of great magnificence. He early turned his thoughts to marriage, and negotiated with Queen Elizabeth of England, who wrote him a letter, in 1561, confessing that she esteemed and admired him, but could not bestow her royal hand upon him until she had made his personal acquaintance. He therefore resolved to go to England, never doubting that Elizabeth would favour his suit.

But in spite of his eagerness for the success of his wooing, Eric was spending his life amid impure pleasures and excesses of every description, and was continually surrounded by women of the worst type. During the delay caused by inclement weather which rendered the immediate journey to England impossible, the King displayed much energy, intelligence, and far-seeingness in the ruling of his kingdom. He ordered the abolition of many superstitious ceremonies, made much progress in the condition of schools, encouraged the scholars, artists, and musicians, and welcomed the wandering Huguenots. When Elizabeth rejected him, he sought the hand of Mary, Queen of Scots, but she also did not favour his offer.

Astrology was one of his favourite studies, and he fancied he read in the stars that his brother John, whom he had imprisoned, would become king during his lifetime, and that he himself would take his place in prison. Several times he dashed off to Gripsholm, fully determined to kill his brother, but could not bring himself to do the deed. Then he knelt before his prisoner, and in great humility craved his forgiveness for all the suffering he was forced to inflict upon him, imploring him to be merciful when he should be in his place in prison.   Refused by the royal ladies, he obtained permission to marry a Swedish lady, and chose his favourite mistress, Catherine Mansdotter, to whom he was blindly faithful.   This attachment made him intensely jealous of a corporal to whom Catherine had been formerly engaged.   He had him arrested and tortured to confess to a deed of which he was innocent, and then thrown, with tied hands, into the Norrstrom river.

Eric had inherited his mother's melancholy.   He saw hate and persecution around him, and in every man a probable enemy.   A look, a step, a word, even a movement, caused him to tremble from head to foot.   He ate and drank in fear of poison.   Subdued voices made him think the conversation must be about himself, a signal maybe for his death—a laugh caused him to imagine himself an object of ridicule.   He planted spies everywhere, and would often himself listen at doors in the castle. Meeting one day a servant of the Sture family who happened to be carrying a gun, he at once ordered the man to be tortured and hanged.   And when he discovered a conspiracy against him headed by Nils Sture, the old Count, with his only son and nobles, was thrown into prison, and the death sentence passed.   The King and his advisors sat in judgment on the carrying out of the death sentence, and when a messenger arrived bearing the news that Duke John had escaped from his prison, Eric became pale, his limbs trembled, he rushed into the street, and hurried to a room in the citadel where Nils Sture sat reading.   With a cry of ' Traitor ! ' he stuck a dagger through his arm and ordered his guards to complete the murder. But when he faced the old Count, Eric flung himself before him. "Cousin," he cried, "can you ever forgive me a wrong?" "All," replied the Count; "but if any evil has befallen my son, I summon you before God's judgment seat." "I thought so," shrieked the King; "you will never forgive me." He rushed away in a terrible state of agitation, tore off his clothes and put on a peasant's coat, and, with a few guards, rushed into the fields through hedges and ditches. There his old tutor found him and implored him to spare the other prisoners. But the King in his mad fury ordered them to be hanged. His wife Catherine at last induced Eric to return to the castle, but had great difficulty in convincing him that he was still King. Months passed by, and realising that his gruesome prophecies had not been fulfilled, Eric again took up the affairs of government. But at times he appeared filled with contrition for the many crimes he had committed and wishful to appease his enemies; the while he was plotting another way to avenge himself on those around him. When he met his brother John after his liberation, he fell on his knees and greeted him as 'King of Sweden.'

A general insurrection was headed by John and Charles. Eric, hounded by visions of his victims, and in a state of hysterical repentance, endeavoured to come to terms. Duke John, urged by the King's physician, promised his royal brother mild treatment and fair terms, so Eric abdicated without arranging any provision for his wife or children. In terror for his life, he only craved an honourable prison, but he was confined in a filthy room with barred windows. John's captivity had been in no way harsh, but he left his brother to the cruelty of his enemies. One of these, Stenbak, to avenge his own brother's death, seized hold of Eric fiercely, pressed him against the wall, and when he sought to defend himself, broke his arm with the butt of his gun, and left him lying alone.

In the year 1569, the trial of ex-King Eric opened. He defended himself with extraordinary eloquence, justi- fied many of his misdeeds, and found excuses for others. During the proceedings, John called out, " You are not in your senses ! " and Eric replied promptly, " I always have been except when I gave you liberty ! " [1]

But his enemies had long ago decided on his sentence. Eric was declared to have forfeited his throne, and ordered into perpetual confinement.   Books and writing materials were denied him, also light, heat, and a doctor's services ; his food, clothing, and bed were squalid and wretched. An unsuccessful attempt was set on foot by a few of Eric's old followers to replace him on the throne, and he was then taken to the island of Oeland and imprisoned in a narrow, dark room in Castleholm Castle ; later he was brought to Gripsholm where he had incarcerated his brother John, who gave an order that at the first sign of any insurrection, Eric should be at once put to death.[2]

On the late king's agreement to give his brother John the royal title, Eric's imprisonment was made less harsh, and, being a good musician, he was supplied with musical instruments, also books. He composed many songs, translated Johannes Magnus's historical works, and wrote psalms of repentance. His death was brought about by another unsuccessful attempt at his rescue, but it is not certain whether his murder was carried out by suffocation, by the opening of a vein, or by poison. The unhappy Eric was told of his coming fate and heard it with dull

[1] Flaux, l.c. p. 191 ; Celoins, l.c. i. 224.
[2] Flaux, l.c. p. 277, note.

indifference; he, however, received the Communion, and thus died at the early age of forty-four.

Charles IX of France (1560–1574) was so enthusiastic a huntsman that, when in pursuit of wild beasts, he is said to have evinced the savagery of the animals themselves. It is chronicled that he used to cut off the heads of donkeys and other animals, and was fond of disembowelling pigs and arranging their entrails in the manner of a butcher. One of his strange propensities was to hire ten young thieves and watch them rob his guests of their swords and jewels. Seeing the unconsciousness of the victims, or their indignant astonishment when they realised they had been despoiled, aroused the mirth of Charles, and he would laugh uproariously at his joke.

Don Carlos (born 1545), son of Philip II of Spain, had strange instincts even from his earliest infancy. He bit so hard and so constantly into his nurse's breasts that three out of the five who followed each other nearly died. For the first few years of his life he could not speak at all, and it was feared that he was dumb. At the age of twenty-one he had the ligament of his tongue cut, but even then his speech remained stuttering and often indistinct. Badoaro, in a description of Don Carlos at the age of twelve which he sent to the Venetian Senate, wrote : " The Prince is now twelve years old. His head is disproportionately large to the size of his body. He is physically weak and displays a tendency to great cruelty. I am told that when live hares or other animals are brought to him at hunting, he enjoys roasting them alive. He seems grave and desirous of pleasing the opposite sex. He cares to hear of nothing but wars, and will only read such books as deal with them."

After the death of his grandfather, Don Carlos gave

full vent to his vicious and peculiar inclinations. In 1562, descending a steep, dark, stairway to keep a tryst with the daughter of the castle warder, the Prince stumbled and fell on his head. Doctors and surgeons were summoned at once, but four days after he developed a high fever, which, however, ceased on the seventh day. He then complained of toothache, of a swelling on his neck, and that his right leg felt numb, and ten days after the accident his condition grew worse and he complained of violent pain. But although the doctors gave up all hope of his recovery, he left his bed after five weeks.

Carlos was evidently tormented by gloomy thoughts of death, and hated a number of people with an intense passion. He loved to inflict pain, and not only behaved with great violence to many persons of high rank and position, but made many personal attempts at murder. The first attempt was directed against Cardinal Espinosa, simply because that ecclesiastic had objected to the presentation of obscene dramas in which Don Carlos was interested. He was passionately attached to the Princess Anne of Austria, and when the negotiations for his marriage with her fell to the ground, he attributed the failure to his father's lack of zeal in furthering the contract, and the dislike for his parent grew into a terrible hate.

The Venetian Ambassador writes vaguely : " Too long have we considered him too chaste, but for some months he has shown signs of the contrary." His evident, though carefully concealed, meaning being, that the royal family dreaded the Prince's impotency rather than his purity. But if this were so, it is uncertain whether it was due to physical ill-health or to his recent violent debaucheries. His bad characteristics developed until his obstinacy, insatiable self-assertion, and wish to rule, became unbearable.

Finally, his father Philip, probably in self-defence and for his son's own welfare, had him imprisoned. He was forced to realise that Carlos could never rule a nation, since he was totally unable to rule himself. He died at the early age of twenty-three, and, evidently aware of his approaching death, he had made a will arranging for the disposition of large sums of money which he did not possess. Don Carlos mingled his cruelties strangely with acts of exceeding kindness. He was frequently guilty of intense brutality : he even maimed his own horses and ordered little children to be beaten.

In 1574 the Duc D'Alençon, afterwards Duc d'Anjou, looked upon his brother Henry III with a hatred which was fully reciprocated and led to the most puerile rivalry. The brothers vied with each other in such absurd follies as painting their cheeks, curling their hair to an absurd extent, and wearing enormous frills round their necks. Indeed Henry III carried his foolishness to the extent of sometimes donning female garb, and the favourites of Court, by following in the footsteps of the King and his brother, made themselves universally hated, and eventually perished at each other's hands.

Henry III used to amuse himself for hours with the game of cup and ball, and even played it whilst walking along the street. His pet aversion was a cat—indeed so violent was his antipathy to cats that he could not bring himself to remain in the same room with them. One of his favourites, Comte d'Epernay, was also possessed of a queer fancy. He fainted away if he saw a leveret, and yet the sight of a hare moved him not at all.

Queen Elizabeth had a great horror of anything deformed or ugly. She liked to surround herself with the young and handsome, and she very seldom consented to give an appointment to an ugly man. "Whenever she went abroad, all ugly, deformed, and diseased persons were thrust out of sight by certain officers whose duty it was to preserve her Majesty from the displeasure of looking on objects offensive to her taste." One of her most salient traits was her natural indecision, which caused many irksome, though often amusing, scenes. Her ministers were never sure what she would do next. As an example of her change of mind, a carter was ordered to go to Windsor one day to remove some of the Royal wardrobe. When he arrived there he was told that Her Majesty had changed the day. The man made a second journey—also a third, when, after waiting for a considerable time, he received a message saying that "the order for removal did not hold."

Queen Elizabeth's passion for dress is well known, and it is a popular saying that "she was the mistress of many million hearts and full a thousand dresses." Elizabeth was prone to amuse herself with the chimeras of alchemy, and when her doctor told her that as soon as he had perfected his discovery of the elixir of life he would be enabled, through the power of a foreign empiric, to bestow immortality and perpetual youth upon her, she implicitly credited the flattering prospect, as well as the prospect of endless riches, which Dr. Dee said he had discovered by transmuting the baser metals into gold. She always avowed the utmost contempt for prophecies and superstitions. But, one day Sir John Stanhope presented her with a piece of gold, "of the bigness of an angel," full of characters, which an old woman had bequeathed to her, alleging that so long as Her Majesty wore it on her body, she could not die. The Queen in confidence took the gold and hung it round her neck.

James I of England (1603–1625) had a love of mischief not untinged with petty malice. One of the royal chaplains, whilst preaching a sermon, made an opportunity to attribute the vices of which the advisers of James were accused to ministers of his Satanic Majesty, and he fixed his eyes upon Lord Cranfield. This nobleman, greatly perturbed and discomfited, kept his hat well over his eyes, whilst the King sat smiling, thoroughly enjoying his minister's humiliation. King James invariably shuddered when he saw a drawn sword, and Sir Kenelm Digby says that when the King knighted him, he nearly had the sword thrust into his eyes, because His Majesty turned away his face, so that he might not see the naked blade. James found his greatest pleasure in hunting, and Scaliger says of him, " The King of England is merciful except in hunting, when he appears cruel. When he is unable to find, he frets and cries ' God is angry with me, but I will have him for all that ! ' "

Queen Christina of Sweden (1633) had many rather unusual characteristics, though probably the most outstanding—her masculinity—was brought about by the fact that she was educated entirely under the guardianship of men, and grew up with a strong dislike for anything that was womanly. Her one endeavour was to be as like a man as possible, and her great delight was to wear men's clothes. For all womanly gentleness and refinement Christina had utter contempt. She swore like a trooper, and revelled in coarse conversation. She frankly owned that she was not nice of speech, and this lack of niceness was equally apparent in Christina's personal habits.

Manneschied, confessor to Quientelli, the Spanish Ambassador, writes of her thus : " She never combs her hair but once a week, and often lets it go untouched for a fortnight. On Sundays her toilet takes about half-an-hour, but on other days it is despatched in a quarter . . . her linen was ragged and much torn." To any suggestion on the subject of cleanliness, Christina would reply, " Wash ! that's all very well for people who have nothing else to do." She gloried in doing anything that might shock those around her. When on a visit to the Court of France, she threw her legs up on a chair in the presence of the King and Queen—in fact, Christina was extremely fond of exhibiting her lower limbs, probably simply because it was not considered nice or womanly to do so. She cared not at all for public opinion. But, notwithstanding her follies and peculiarities, she was an extremely clever and intelligent woman, with brain power quite *hors-de-ligne*.

Oliver Cromwell, in his early life, was not the ' Puritan ' into which he eventually developed. If we are to believe biographers and Cromwell's own letters, his youth was spent amongst depraved and dissolute companions. But through all those wild, early years, he never quite lost sight of the vision which had come to him in his boyhood—the vision of a figure of superhuman magnitude which threw back the curtains of his bed, and predicted to him that he would one day be the ' first gentleman ' in the land. He was a martyr to gout, which also probably partly accounted for his red-hot fits of temper. Towards the close of his life he had a constant succession of fits, which rendered him utterly prostrate.

Alfonso VI, King of Portugal (1656), wasted his time and ruined his health by indulging in every kind of infamy, and even when his country was in the greatest jeopardy he did not make any change in his ignoble life. He roamed at night along the highways, and " assaulted passengers, fired into the coaches of nobles, and routed religious processions at the point of the sword." He mingled in night orgies of the most depraved and repulsive character, and frequently brought back to his palace disreputable and garish women.

Alfonso was lost to all decent feeling, and utterly devoid of any spark of self-respect. Even when he was called to his dying mother's bedside, he amused himself so long on the journey that she had lost the power of speech before he reached her. He even violated the nunneries, subjected the terrified teachers to rough usage, and insulted them by fitting up a stage in the choir of the church at Alcantara, on which he had theatrical plays and indecent dances performed. He also " compelled the unhappy nuns to honour him with their presence." He was an extremely dexterous horseman, and so fearless that he once rode full tilt at a savage bull, but was unhorsed and nearly lost his life. One day, on returning from the chase, he charged the unoffending citizens, riding over many of them, sword in hand. Indeed he would have killed those whom he had trampled down but for the timely intervention of the grand huntsman.

The second son of the Emperor Ferdinand was known as Leopold the Angel. He delighted in rearing odoriferous plants, and, to mortify himself, denied himself the pleasure of ever going near enough to smell them. He imagined that by this continual act of self-mortification he was contributing another step to the ladder of good deeds " by which he hoped to scale Heaven."

Charles II of England (1660–1685), though by no means

an inveterate drunkard, always became the gayest of the company when he gave way to the temptation of joining an evening's debauch. And on one occasion, at such an entertainment, he smashed the windows of the maids of honour and attempted to force his way into their apartments.

Charles II of Spain (1665–1700) was frequently a prey to melancholy fancies. Sometimes he imagined himself to be suffering from the same malady as that of the wretched creatures in the New Testament who dwelt among the tombs. He then consulted a sorceress in the Asturian mountains. She told him that he had been bewitched by several persons, and recommended that the rite of exorcism should be performed, which was duly done. He was constantly disturbed by visions of demons, and kept monks and priests always near him to drive them out. He felt sure that he was a victim of some sorcery, and that he had been charmed with part of the brains of a corpse, given to him in a cup of chocolate, and to counteract the evil influence of this, a diet of hens fed on viper's flesh was suggested.

Not long before his death, Charles II was seized with intense funereal yearnings. He loved to go down into the royal mausoleums, open all the coffins and gaze upon the faces of his royal ancestors. Lighted by torches, he would proceed into the dark vault of the Pantheon, and order all the coffins therein to be also opened for him. Thence he passed to the Queens, and when the corpse of his first Queen was exposed to view, and he saw the form and perfectly preserved beauty of the woman who had for a short time illuminated the darkness of his life, he sobbed bitterly and fell upon his knees by the bier, crying out, "My Queen, before a year is past I will come to you."

He has been thus described by Macaulay: " With difficulty his almost imperceptible spark of life had been screened and fanned into a dim and flickering flame. His childhood, except when he could be rocked or sung into sickly sleep, was one long piteous wail. Till he was ten years old his days were passed on the laps of women, and he was never once suffered to stand on his rickety legs . . . the most important events in the history of his own kingdom, the very names of provinces and cities which were among his most valuable possessions, were unknown to him. In his youth, however, . . . he was not incapable of being amused. He shot, hawked, and hunted. He enjoyed, with the delight of a true Spaniard, two de-lightful spectacles,—a horse with its bowels gored out and a Jew writhing in the fire. The time came when the mightiest of instincts ordinarily wakens from its repose.

" It was hoped that the young king would not prove invincible to female attractions, and that he would leave a Prince of Asturias to succeed him. A consort was found for him in the royal family of France, and her beauty and grace gave him a languid pleasure. He liked to adorn her with jewels, to see her dance, and to tell her what sport he had had with his dogs and his falcons. But it was soon whispered that she was a wife only in name. She died, and her place was supplied by a German princess, nearly allied to the Imperial house. But the second mar-riage, like the first, proved barren. Meanwhile a sullen and abject melancholy took possession of his soul. The diversions, which had been the serious employment of his youth, became distasteful to him. Sometimes he shut himself up in an inner chamber from the eyes of his courtiers. Sometimes he loitered alone, from sunrise to sunset, in the dreary and rugged wilderness which surrounds the Escurial. The hours which he did not waste in listless indolence were divided between childish sport and childish devotions. He delighted in rare animals, and still more in dwarfs. When neither strange beasts nor little men could dispel the black thoughts which gathered in his mind, he repeated aves and credos, sometimes he whipped himself." At thirty-five he had lost his hair and eyebrows, and he died in 1700.

Queen Anne, wife of James II, always performed her toilet whilst her chaplain prayed in the room beyond. On one occasion her attendants thought it needful, for decency's sake, to close the door between the two apartments whilst the Queen was putting on under garments. The chaplain consequently stopped reading the prayers, and Her Majesty grew impatient at the pause, and enquired the reason. The chaplain called out through the closed door, " Because I will not whistle the word of God through the keyhole." Queen Anne performed the healing office with rings for ' touching for the evil ' in every town she halted in on her royal progress through the country.

James II (1633–1685) made a pretence of furthering national religious freedom of thought, although he made no secret of attending mass regularly, and certainly did all in his power to oust Protestantism and replace it by Popery. He was by nature cruel and cunning, and justified all his wrongdoings by alleging, "What the King doth, it is for the gods to examine, under whose ordinance he is, not for his men, whose overseer he is ! "

William III of Orange (1650–1702) hated the land over which he ruled. His drinking habits were well known, and the banqueting house at Hampton Court was, in his day, described as a gin temple. He used to say, " I will

defy anyone to quarrel with me as long as I can make the
bottle go round." He also behaved very oddly in church.
If his head happened to be uncovered during the recital
of the Liturgy, he put his hat on when the sermon
began.

Frederick William of Prussia (1688–1740) was much
addicted to practical jokes, and when at his club urged
foreign princes to drink and smoke until they were sick—
his jokes truly savouring more of unpleasantness and
cruelty than of merriment. He sent a monkey to be
placed by the side of Jacob Paul von Grindling, President
of the Academy of Sciences. He had the monkey dressed
in an exact copy of the dress worn by Grindling, declaring
that it was his natural son, and forced the unhappy man
to embrace the animal. The King's animosity for Grindling did not cease even after his death, for he ordered his
body to be put into a huge wine cask in his state dress.
Frederick William had a mania for recruiting giants, and
he instituted a man-hunt through the towns and villages
in order to form his giant regiment. Even during divine
service this hunt was carried on. If a petition were presented to him which he thought absurd or did not wish
to grant, he would draw on the margin an ass's head and
ears to signify his rejection. During the singing of a
hymn, " Naked shall I go hence," he interrupted the
singers, saying, " No, I shall be buried in my uniform."

George I (1660–1727) was warned by a French lady
astrologist to take the greatest care of his wife, because,
were she to die, he would not survive her more than a
year. This prophecy evidently impressed him very
deeply, for soon after his wife's death, when leaving for
Hanover, he told his son and the Princess of Wales that
he would never see them again.

George II (1683–1760) in moments of fretfulness or impatience was wont to vent his irritation by kicking his hat about the room, or by assaulting his own wig. A singular incident occurred one day to him as he was walking on the balcony of Windsor Castle. He suddenly drew his courtiers' attention to an amazing apparition in the clouds, where an armed Highlander could be distinctly seen fighting with a British Grenadier. The two men appeared alternately to be getting the better of the conflict, until finally the Englishman was victorious and the strange spectacle disappeared from the sky. A few days later despatches arrived, bearing the news that the Highlanders had been utterly routed at Culloden.

Frederick Augustus II of Poland (died 1763) thought of little else than dress. He had two large halls filled with clothes, and each dress had its own watch, snuff box, sword, and cane. Every costume was painted in miniature in a book which was brought to him every morning by his tiring-man. He had as many as 1500 wigs.

Queen Caroline (1683–1737), like Queen Anne, acquired the habit of listening to prayers whilst she was dressing. In the room leading out of her dressing room hung a large picture of a nude Venus. When Dr. Maddius was appointed as Her Majesty's chaplain, he looked whimsically at the painting, and said, "And a very pretty altar-piece is here!"

Louis XV (born 1710) spent his time between profligacy and devotional practices. He was in the habit of reading sermons to his mistresses, and he would kneel to pray with his victims. Also he possessed morbid tendencies, loved to discuss the symptoms of every malady, and to discourse on death bed scenes, tombs, worms, and epitaphs. He had such an intense passion for gambling that nothing could put him off a game. A guest at the royal table, M. de Chauvelin, was seized with apoplexy, and died on the spot. Louis looked calmly at him and said, " He is dead. Take him away. Spades are trumps, gentlemen ! "

Peter III (born 1728) had so vivid a keenness for militarism that he wished for a perpetual noise of cannon, that it might give him a foretaste of war. He gave orders that one hundred large pieces of cannon should be fired simultaneously, and was only dissuaded on the representation that such an explosion would shake the foundations of the town. He was seen to kneel before a portrait of Frederick of Prussia, and heard to exclaim, " My brother, we will conquer the world together."

Frederick II (1712–1786) had such a detestation of new clothes that he had only about three new coats during his whole life. He was a drunkard, as was Frederick V, father of Christian VII, who was grandson to George II and first cousin to George III. Frederick, Prince of Wales, was also a dissolute debauchee. Great was the rejoicing at the birth of little Christian VII (1749), whose mother, Queen Louise, daughter of George II, was adored by her people. Christian's childhood was one long punishment, even his education being intentionally put in the wrong people's hands. And the boy being highly strung and very sensitive, his spirit was almost crushed. He was moreover subject to epileptic fits, and even as a child was of a melancholy disposition. But withal, the young Prince had a keen sense of humour, a ready wit, and a charming person and manner, excelled in all learning, and was an excellent linguist and an elegant dancer.

Christian would frequently sit lost in thought, stare at his hands, and point to his stomach. It is uncertain if he felt any pain or discomfort, but when he roused himself again, he would ask Reverdil, his tutor, rude and extraordinary questions, and only many years later could Reverdil obtain a clue as to his bewildering conduct. Then he gradually discovered that Christian touched his stomach to feel if he were progressing towards a nebulous ideal of complete perfection which was floating in his mind. This Reverdil drew from the boy's own lips. It appears that the Prince, when five years old, had been taken to the Italian Theatre, and the actors in their wonderful clothes had seemed to him superior beings, which gave him the idea that there were supermen in the world whom he might some day resemble, after probably many hardships and metamorphoses. He was therefore continually watching his bodily progress, evidently thinking that a body invulnerable to pain would be a great step towards the ideal condition. For his position as a Prince he cared not a jot, sometimes he fancied and hoped that he was a changeling and might never be called to the throne. At times Reverdil found that Christian would learn better if he put books away and gave the lessons conversationally, but the governor of the castle did not approve of the Prince being taught without being shouted at or beaten, and would himself force him to repeat his lessons whilst pinching him and even striking hard blows on the child's head and hands. The same severity attended even his dancing lessons and physical exercises. He occasionally made a jest of his hard treatment, and said to Reverdil, " Yesterday's amusements were a terrible bore to my Royal Highness."

As he grew older, the page of the chamber, a vicious lad named Sperling, led Christian into the cunning and deceitful ways in which, though young, he was a past master, and corrupted the Prince's morals in every conceivable way. But Christian was never taught anything of his duties as a future sovereign. In 1757 Frederick V became ill, and the illness caused his temper to become still more violent. When he died in 1766, Christian was joyfully proclaimed King. He was then seventeen, and terrified at the thought of reigning.

But Christian all at once became seized with the longing to be a great soldier, even greater than Frederick the Great, and, as a King, he grew unbearably arrogant. His love for the fair sex and his religious fanaticism could not be reconciled, and he found no other way out of the problem than to drop religion. But his melancholy and bitterness increased. He displayed no eagerness for the marriage with the young Princess Carolina-Matilda, his first cousin, and sister of George III, but his friends and ministers pushed forward the negotiations for the nuptials in the hope that marriage with the beautiful princess might cause the young King to break away from his libertine habits.

Their hope was vain, for only a few weeks after the ceremony, Christian began to neglect his wife and spent both time and enormous sums of money on the most disreputable woman in Copenhagen. Her nickname was ' Milady.' Together they roamed the streets at night, broke windows and lamps, and he spent his days in wild rioting. Selfish ministers governed Denmark in his name, actuated merely by their own ambition. Christian had not the least consideration for his people, even his yearning for glory and admiration had gone from him. At last, when ' Milady ' led the King into excesses likely to ruin his health altogether, he was compelled by his ministers to sign an order for her imprisonment. The orgies of

Christian in his own castle took various forms.   At times he would ask Holck, his constant companion, to beat him, or he would lie on the ground, call himself a criminal who was being broken on the wheel.

His health at this time being very far from satisfactory, a journey through Europe was arranged.   But in every town through which he passed, Christian led the same wild life, of which the Queen, who had remained in Denmark, was well informed.   She, however, went to meet him at Roskilde on his return seven months after, and for a short while the King's behaviour appeared to amend. But, being surrounded by young libertines, he soon fell again into the old dissipated life and evinced an intense repugnance for any sort of public business, and when compelled to sign documents simply put his pen to them without even glancing through them.

His thoughts were totally uncontrolled, he spoke at random, often wildly, and showed great absence of mind, though a look from Holck would often pull him together. If annoyed or irritated, Christian flew into mad passions, but he remained most of the time in a state of dull lethargy. His son, the Crown Prince, ascended the throne during the King's lifetime, but Christian signed all papers.   At times he would refuse ; but if he heard the word ' abdication ' whispered, he trembled and obeyed. Even the knowledge that his wife, Queen Carolina-Matilda, was openly living with a lover, Count Struensee, who was in truth ruler of his kingdom, moved him not at all. He had become almost a prisoner in his own palace, and when Count Holck grew tired of humouring him, the King played with a negro boy and girl, and would run about with them smashing the windows, valuable china, and marble statues. Occasionally Christian seemed to become possessed by a dual personality, and from dull lethargy became almost bestial, and would grind his teeth and grin horribly, and endeavour to do someone a harm or injury. He would sometimes talk wildly, then would follow a spell of silence. But always he harped on his favourite topic—the metamorphosis which was progressing within him. During the next year the King grew still worse, his thoughts and speech frequently were homicidal or suicidal. The Crown Prince took up the reins of government, and Christian died in 1803.

Kotzebue chronicles that, being summoned into the imperial presence of Paul of Russia (1754–1801), the Emperor said to him in German, " I have often made rather a foolish exhibition of myself and have imposed upon myself a chastisement." He then handed Kotzebue a paper " to be inserted in all newspapers," and read him the contents, which were written in French to this effect : " The Emperor of Russia, seeing that the powers of Europe could not agree between themselves, and wishing to put an end to a war which had desolated it for eleven years, suggested a place where he would invite all the other sovereigns to meet and fight in a closed field, having with them, instead of pages and judges of the field and armed heroes, their most enlightened and clever ministers.''

Paul, the supposed son of the notorious Catherine II of Russia, ascended the throne when he was thirty-five. Whilst grand-duke his hobby had always been drilling his soldiers. He gave the utmost attention to every minute detail of the men's accoutrements, whilst completely ignoring the need that they should learn the use of their weapons. Paul stood on a terrace shouting out orders for his sentries to do up or undo a button, or stand a little more to one side or the other, or to perform some

such trifling and objectless detail. Contradiction of any
kind he could not endure. When driving through a
narrow, swampy road in a wood, Paul once ordered the
driver to turn back. The spot being impossible to turn
a vehicle, his order was not instantly obeyed. " Let the
driver overturn the vehicle, let him break my neck,"
shouted the infuriated Tsar, " but let him obey me and
turn the instant I command him." The unfortunate but
well-meaning driver was almost beaten to death on the
spot. Paul's orders were frequently so contradictory that
obedience to them was well nigh impossible, and he was
cruelly unreasonable in punishing the smallest deviation
from his pettily despotic orders. As he grew older,
his tyrannies were accompanied by the most violent
paroxysms of rage.

Charles III (1716-1788), the father of the Duke of
Mantua, enjoyed wearing the dirtiest disguise, and was
" accompanied by an escort of equally ill-clad bullies for
his defence." It was his great amusement to assail all
those he met in the coarsest terms, and if any one of them
should turn upon him, Charles returned the assault with
tongue and cudgel, and laughed uproariously, till his escort
came to the rescue. Sometimes he would enter shops
containing breakable articles, take up mirrors and glasses,
or any fragile article, and let it fall to the ground. He
would then derive great pleasure from the ruin he had
committed and the expressions of abuse that were
showered upon him.

Napoleon (1769-1821) was always more feared than
loved even from childhood. He was domineering, obstinate, fretful, bad tempered, and could not endure
contradiction or restraint of any kind. As he grew to
manhood, this temperament grew with him, side by side

with a complete disregard for the feelings of others. But, like most great men, his character was very contradictory —his smile could be as winning as his paroxysms of fury were frightful. He was a dullard at school, except for mathematics, in which he excelled, and he showed some interest in geography and history. He never could learn to spell, and his handwriting was execrable and almost illegible. He lived in a perpetual rush, and could neither wait for others to do anything nor to do anything himself. Even the operation of shaving was performed with such haste that he invariably cut himself.

His belief in his star is, of course, well known, and General Rapp, through Brierre de Boissmont, relates the following incident as to its origin : [1] " In 1806, General Rapp, on his return from the siege of Dantzig, having occasion to speak to the Emperor, entered his study without being announced. He found him so absorbed that his entry was unperceived. The general, seeing the Emperor continue motionless, thought he might be ill, and purposely made a noise. Napoleon immediately roused himself, and, without any preamble, seized Rapp by the arm, and said to him, pointing to the sky, " Look there, up there ! " The general remained silent, but on being asked a second time, he answered that he perceived nothing. " What," replied the Emperor, " you do not see it ? It is my star, it is before you, brilliant." Then, becoming animated, he cried out, " It has never abandoned me, I see it on all occasions, it commands me to go forward, and it is a constant sign of my good fortune."

Napoleon possessed many odd little tricks of manner. He " frequently gave an involuntary shrug of his right shoulder, accompanied by a movement of his mouth from

[1] Brierre de Boissmont, *Des Hallucinations.*

left to right." He also very often "made a movement
of his right arm, which he twisted while pulling the
lining of the cuff of his coat." He usually wakened in
a morbid mood, and sometimes with violent inward
pains, followed by sickness. During his campaign in
Russia his memory became confused, and he often fell
into fits of apathy.

He averred that the fate of battles was due to the
dormant thought of a second—"the decisive moment
appeared, the spark burst forth, and one was victorious"
(Moreau). He had a peculiar weakness for clinging to his
old hats ; indeed, he had such a fondness for them that
he wore a new one as seldom as possible. He suffered
from a twitch of the right shoulder and the hips. After
having come to high words during an interview, he remarked, " My anger must have been fearful, for I felt the
vibration of my calves, which has not happened to me for
a long time." Whenever he went through a street, during peace or war time, he felt himself irresistibly compelled
to count up all the rows of windows.

Napoleon, as a child, would endure no rivals, and be-
laboured with blows those who would not render him
homage, and then averred that his victims had beaten
him. " I am not a man like other men," he says of himself, " the laws of morality and decorum are not for me."
" Never," says Taine, " even among the Borgias and
Malatestas, was there a more sensitive and impulsive
brain, capable of such electric accumulations and dis-
charges, all his sayings are fire flakes." On one occasion
Napoleon knocked a Senator violently in the stomach,
and he frequently threw people forcefully out of the room.
Even a scarcely audible whisper would arouse his ever-
ready suspiciousness, and he construed it into a plot

against himself. He always threw into the fire any garments which were not a good fit, or did not please him.

One of his favourite amusements was to play blindman's-buff. He was also an ardent chess player, but could not bear to be defeated. If he thought his antagonist was likely to win, he would, with one sudden movement, sweep board and pieces from the table. Napoleon believed firmly in his ' star,' and it is also well known that he was frequently haunted by a spirit which he recognised as " the little red man." This spirit was always seen shortly before any great disaster happened to him.

Ludwig I, King of Bavaria (reigned 1825–1848), at the age of sixty, made the notorious dancer, Lola Montes, his mistress, and under her pernicious influence committed almost unbelievable follies ; in consequence of which she became such an object of abhorrence to the people that, stung to rebellion, they threatened to pull her house to the ground. Lola Montes, in angry contempt, insulted the people and flung a dog among them. Goaded on by her, Ludwig continued to perform the most outrageous acts of folly, until finally she dragged the wretchedly feebleminded King with her in her fall. He was forced to retire, and during his captivity one of his pet possessions was the velvety mattress stuffed with the moustaches and beards which the men of his father's old regiment had cut off expressly for the purpose.

Ludwig II, King of Bavaria (died 1886), was from childhood accustomed to seeing visions, dreaming strange dreams, and he delighted in romantic legends. Even when he grew to manhood the legends still exercised the same spell over him. His preceptors and tutors endeavoured to cram him with learning, but never thought to teach him self-control of any kind. Ludwig had a decided aversion for physical exercise, and to anything that did not appeal to him. He believed that at the castle of Hohenswangau, which was to him a place of great fascination, "Knights in armour spoke to him, Rhine maidens drew him into their arms—he saw his ancestors, the Wittlesbach heroes, seated upon their war horses, their swords drawn, fighting their way into Rome, or resting under palms by the banks of the Nile."

After the suggested marriage with Ludwig's cousin, Sophie Charlotte, had fallen through, he became still more melancholy. His days became nights, for he inverted the division of the twenty-four hours. He grew world-weary, lack of interest in life made him disgusted with living. Ignoring the gentlemen of the Court, his servants became his constant companions. One of his favourite beverages was champagne mixed with Rhenish wine in which violets floated.

CHAPTER III

THE CRUSADES

At the beginning of the tenth century, Pope Sylvester II obtained the Archbishopric of Rheims, and then the Papacy. When he asked the Devil how long he should reign, Satan replied, with *double entendre*, " If you never enter Jerusalem, you will reign a long time." After wearing the triple crown for four years, Sylvester was pontificating in the Church of St. Croce in Jerusalem, when it suddenly occurred to him that he had compassed his own fate by crossing the threshold of that church. Overwhelmed with repentance, he confessed his impiety to the congregation, and directed his attendants to sever his body in pieces, place it on a common cart and bury it wheresoever the horses stopped of their own accord. Divine forgiveness of the penitent sinner directed the footsteps of the horses to the Church of St. John Lateran, where he was buried. The memorial slab and epitaph still remain, and it is said that the rattling of his bones and the sweat with which his tomb becomes covered have always been a forewarning of the death of a pope.[1]

One of the first of the many ' end-of-the-world ' panics occurred in A.D. 999 and spread over all Europe through the preachings of a crowd of fanatics who sprang up in France, Italy, and Germany, and predicted that the

[1] J. Charles Wall, *Devils*, p. 89.

63

duration of the world, as set forth in the Apocalypse, was
to be one thousand years, and then the Son of God would
descend from Heaven and judge mankind.   As the last
and greatest judgment was to be at Jerusalem, pilgrims
commenced to journey thither in vast hordes, having sold
everything they possessed in order to defray the expenses
of their journey and to enable them to continue to live
in Jerusalem.   Buildings became so neglected that many
fell in ruins.   Of what use to build them up, or even to
repair those standing, when the world was so rapidly
nearing its end !

The pilgrims were a motley crowd.   Lords and beggars,
knights and serfs, saintly men and thieves travelled
together, often side by side, singing psalms as they went.
As they neared the Holy City their eyes turned constantly
to the sky, expecting that it would open and that they
would behold Jesus Christ in the clouds.   Each sudden
development of the elements sent many shuddering to
their knees, a thunderstorm would call forth fits of wailing,
and many indeed fainted, believing that the beginning of
the end had arrived.   Every meteor seen in Jerusalem
caused the entire Christian population to rush into the
streets and pray, and fanatical preachers did their utmost
to fan the flame of fear as long as they were able.

Two hundred years before Peter the Hermit urged on
the Holy War, pilgrimages were continually made to the
Holy Land by fanatics who longed to see with their own
eyes the place where their Lord had lived and died.
There were others too who took up the staff and journeyed
to Jerusalem—men of means, idlers who heard of the
wonders of the East, and who longed to be able to boast
of the great adventures they had (or had not) encountered
on their travels.   Loafers, and still worse, even men of

evil lives, made the pilgrimage, because it was generally believed that by so doing all their sins would be condoned. In spite of privations and much suffering the pilgrims plodded across Europe—the poorer ones begging their way. When in Palestine they met with no difficulties until the Turks resented the intrusion of so many pilgrims, and, fearing that they might become a menace and danger, they commenced to persecute and plunder them.

Tales of gross outrages, inflicted by the Mussalmans, were brought to Europe by those pilgrims who were fortunate enough to return in safety, and the indignation that they incited tended to swell the ranks of the pilgrims. Instead of being daunted by the prospects of such hardships, others were only spurred on to go quickly and render themselves pleasing in the eyes of the Almighty by visiting the Holy Sepulchre. Thus Peter the Hermit found the corn ripe to his hands, and he arrived on the scene at the psychological moment to gather the harvest. Although a bigot, he was a red-hot enthusiast, of dogged perseverance and amazing eloquence. In his youth he had served as a soldier, but gave up the accoutrements of war to don the cowl of a monk. Whilst on a pilgrimage to Palestine, Peter became so deeply moved by the daily, or even hourly, torments the Christians were forced to endure, that he determined to rescue his fellow-men and tear the Sepulchre of Jesus from the Turks. He sent to the Pope a detailed account of some of the flagrant evils of which he had himself been an eye-witness, and wrote letters to the most powerful Christian rulers of Europe, imploring them to go to the rescue of their fellow-believers. The Pope welcomed Peter's letters and, still more enthusiastically, welcomed Peter himself when the latter travelled to Italy to obtain his co-operation. His Holiness conferred on

Peter the full right to preach the Holy Crusade to all Christian nations.

Fabulous numbers responded to his call, and his marvellous eloquence roused them to a degree of excitement amounting almost to frenzy. Not alone the populaces of the countries through which the Hermit preached, but also the nobles, to whom war was the business of their lives, and whose only law was their own lawlessness, became eager to join. From France, Germany, and Italy he drew combatants in thousands, and the people worshipped him to such an extent that they even kept hairs, drawn from the mane of his mule, as priceless treasures. Barefooted, and clad in a long woollen tunic and cloak, Peter wandered far and wide, living chiefly on grain and fruit ; meat he never ate, nor even bread. Whilst he preached in every town and village that he passed through the Pope also made exhortations to the men who would lead the armies forward. The one great ecstatic idea, the one subject of conversation, the one thought in every mind, was the rescue of the Christians and of the Holy Sepulchre in Jerusalem. The Pope convened a great mass meeting in Rome, and came from the Vatican with his cardinals and bishops arrayed in the full magnificence of Romish ecclesiasticism, with Peter the Hermit beside them in his plain woollen garments, a figure of extraordinary dignity.

The wild enthusiasm of the crowd was with difficulty restrained whilst the Pope was delivering his eloquent address. He dwelt first on the piteous plight of the Christians in the East in such a way as to appeal to their humanity and chivalry, then he passed on to the spiritual progress which would touch the souls of all who joined in the Holy Crusade, after which he described to them the land of Palestine, the land overflowing with milk and honey, the land so dear to God Himself. And this land of wonder, continued the Pope, would come into their possession, and be divided amongst the crusaders. He promised that, before setting out, each man should receive full pardon for any offence he might have committed against God or man, and that in the future, in the world to come, everlasting glory should be theirs. The rapturous ecstasy of the people rose to an indescribable height, as with one voice they shouted " Dieu le veult " (God wills it). The Pope repeated the words, and " Dieu le veult " became the Crusader's war-cry.

Young and old, priests and profligates, rich and poor, fanatics and thieves, strong men and weakly—even women and children—joined the great army. By the order of the Pope, any debtor who enrolled himself was thereupon set free from his obligations, the ban of outlawry was removed, and the outlaw was restored to his rights as a citizen. The Church took under its protection the worldly property of every man who set out, and it announced the most dread punishments which would fall on all those who either refused or even hesitated to take the red cross. A ferment of wonder and excitement reigned everywhere, and all kinds of mystic rumours and omens were reported and received credence by the inflamed minds of the people. It was said that millions of stars had dropped from the skies, and that each star that fell implied the falling of a Turkish infidel. A monk had a vision of two mighty combatants on fiery steeds, fighting in the sky, the Christian eventually killing the Pagan with his flaming sword. These and hundreds of similar tales were regarded as prophecies of a sure victory. The women were not behind the men in the wildness of their enthusiasm ; they even entreated lovers and husbands to join the Holy Army, and many went with them. Some women donned male attire and went as soldiers, others burned a cross upon their arms and breasts, and stained the wound with red dye, whilst some actually burned the same symbol on the bodies of their children.

By the spring of 1096, every road was crowded with the Crusading armies, but only a few among the eager pilgrims had the slightest conception even of the direction in which the Holy City lay ; it might have been only a few weeks' journey or one hundred thousand miles away for all that the majority of them knew, and when they came in sight of each town or village on their way, the children cried out, " Is that the wonderful city ? "

Dread of derision, as well as spiritual fervour, was an important factor in the great crusading movement, for the ' conscientious objectors ' were frequently presented with such articles as knitting needles, and these contemptuous offerings speedily ended their objections. And it is a remarkable fact that in spite of the utter failure which had hitherto met the clergy's efforts to curb and soften the oppressions of the feudal chiefs, and thus lighten the burdens of the people, all the harshness and rapacity of these nobles became merged into the religious ardour of the crusading enterprise. Only this one idea seemed to possess the hearts of all, whether they beat under a coarse leathern jerkin or a velvet tunic.

The countryside of France was white with the tents of the pilgrims, who, on their onward march, however, led a life of wild license and debauchery ; it having been deeply impressed upon them that they would receive remission from all these sins as soon as they reached the Holy Land. Scenes of drunkenness, immorality, and obscenity were carried on openly and shamelessly by the leaders as well as by the common horde.

Like a pestilential torrent they rushed forward, carrying panic and often death with them, each man wishing to become a law unto himself. The first enormous army, led by Gautier-Sans-Avoir (Walter the Penniless), on entering Hungary were met with much good-will, but the good understanding with the Hungarian people was quickly ended when the Crusaders, instead of evincing any gratitude for the provisions and other things which were given to them, commenced to plunder, rob, and even murder. The indignant Hungarian people gathered a large army and attacked the vanguard of the Crusaders at Semlin, killing a large number and affixing their arms and crosses to the city walls. Walter the Penniless lost still more of his army when trying to force his way through Bulgaria, the cities opposing him with great force. By the time he reached Constantinople, half of his great army had been disseminated by sword, illness, and famine.

Peter the Hermit, at the head of a still more vicious multitude, soon followed in Walter's tracks, and, not being so impoverished as the latter's army, paid his way through Hungary ; but when Peter's army came in sight of the arms and crosses which the Hungarians had taken from their victims and hung over the gates of Semlin, their anger and rage were unappeasable. In spite of Peter's efforts the Crusaders made a violent attack upon the city, which they took by force, killing thousands of its inhabitants amidst all the terrors of which victory is capable. License of all kinds, every atrocity and every ill passion, were given full rein by this Holy Army. In vain Peter the Hermit preached mercy and peace and good-will; he had raised a storm which no effort on his part could quell.   It was only when the Crusaders began to dread reprisals that their ferocity abated and they departed from the ruined city of Semlin.   But the incensed and infuriated Bulgarians had no intention of letting them off so lightly.   A large army lay in wait for them by the Morava river, and attacked them with such ferocity that many of the Crusaders were either cut to pieces or drowned. As they approached Nissa, Peter exhorted his followers to peace ; but he might as well have endeavoured to keep the waves from rolling on.   Headstrong and aggressive, they attempted to scale the walls in the hope of taking the town by sudden assault, but the citizens of Nissa turned on the intruders and completely routed the offending army with terrible slaughter, and captured the women and children.

Peter the Hermit contrived to call together the scattered and fleeing remainder of his followers and led them to Constantinople, where their love of pillage and plunder reasserted itself in spite of his warnings and entreaties. In consequence the Emperor Alexius found guides to lead them into Asia Minor instead of entertaining them at his capital as had been his intention.   Peter, in despair at being unable to gain any ascendancy over his people, left them when they had joined forces with the reduced army of Walter the Penniless, and returned to Constantinople.   Immediately after his departure, quarrels hampered the movements of the two armies, and when Peter's followers had annexed the fortress of Exorogorgon, the Sultan Soliman burst on them with a huge army and laid siege to the town.   Scarcity of food, and still worse— want of water—caused the Crusading army much suffering. Their leader, with a few officers, turned traitors, and admitted the Sultan's men into the town.   The remainder of the Christian army, on their refusal to adopt the Mahommetan faith, were shown no quarter—so perished by the sword, or by worse torments. The multitudinous force that Peter the Hermit had led out with such enthusiasm was thus totally annihilated.

The army of Walter the Penniless, hearing of their comrades' defeat and massacre at Exorogorgon, craved to advance against the Turks, but Walter, whose qualifications as a leader were worthy of a better army, realised the futility of such a step and did his utmost to dissuade them. When, however, the Crusaders prepared to march without his leadership, Walter was too proud to hold back, so he, with his army, now reduced to twenty-five thousand men, advanced to utter destruction. Walter the Penniless himself, with twenty-two thousand of his men, fell in the ensuing encounter. The remaining three thousand were reinforced by a small force which, at Peter's earnest request, the Emperor Alexius had sent to the rescue, and conducted safely back to Constantinople.

Undeterred by the terrible calamities which had befallen the first two armies, a third was soon gathered together, and, led by a mystical German priest named Gottschalk, started out for the Holy Land. When they reached Hungary, however, the people, incensed by the cruelties and atrocities of the first two armies, as well as by the pillagings of the present band, attacked and slaughtered them almost to a man.

New multitudes poured out from Germany and France and a few from England, but though they bore the symbol of the cross, they practised plunder and massacre in place of peace and brotherliness. Their hatred of the Jews was so intense that they stopped in every town and village to slaughter all of that faith, torturing and mutilating the unhappy Hebrews before dealing the final death-blow. Believing in their gross superstition that geese and goats, being sacred animals, possessed divine intuition, they always took some with them.

Meanwhile these members of the Holy Army were living lives of utter and atrocious immorality. Vainly did the clergy endeavour to lead them to a sense of personal shame, and of mercy for their enemies. On their passage through Germany no less than seven thousand Jews perished at their hands—many taking their own lives rather than fall into the power of the Crusaders. A bitter retribution, however, awaited the Christian army in Hungary, where so great a number were slaughtered that the entire countryside was covered with their bodies, the river was choked up with corpses, and the waters were dyed with blood for many miles.

The soldiers composing the next Crusade were of a somewhat different calibre from those who had gone before, and they were led by men of cooler, if not of greater, courage —Godfrey of Bouillon, Robert, Duke of Normandy, Raymond of Toulouse, Bohemond, Prince of Tarentum, and the Count of Vermandois. Round their standard flocked the bravest nobles of France, Germany, Italy, Spain, and England. One hundred thousand horsemen and six hundred thousand foot went forth, not counting the women, children, and priests. By command of the Emperor Alexius, the Count of Vermandois was made prisoner immediately he entered Grecian territory. It must be admitted that the Turkish Emperor had much cause for grievance against the Crusading armies which had overrun his country with such aggressive arrogance. Their leaders sought his help and advice at all hours of the day and night. His apparent duplicity was, in a great measure, accounted for because fear was on him; he treated the Holy Armies with great kindness, amounting almost to ostentation, ere he allowed his natural animosity to assert itself.

When the news of the capture of the Count of Vermandois was brought to Godfrey of Bouillon, he sent messengers in all haste to Alexius, warning him that he would put the entire country to fire and sword if the prisoner were not at once liberated, and as this was not done, Godfrey commenced to carry out his threat. The Emperor, seized with panic, set Vermandois at liberty, but at the same time sought to force Godfrey to pay him homage just as he had compelled Vermandois to do. This being refused, Alexius declined to furnish food for the Holy Armies, although he made handsome gifts to Godfrey. The conditions in Constantinople became impossible to maintain without the outbreak of hostilities, and to avoid this the Crusading leaders crossed the Bosphorus as quickly as possible. It was not long before they encountered the Mussalmans, and during their first battle the most fiendish cruelties were indulged in both by Christians and infidels. Whilst the former were besieging Nice, the bodies of the Crusaders killed near the walls were drawn up by iron hooks let down by the beleagured Turks, who stripped and mutilated them, and then flung them back at their own people.

The besiegers, however, were well-nigh victorious, and indeed would have taken the town had not a body of soldiers from Alexius contrived to gain entrance and, by promises of rewards, induced the Paynim to surrender to them rather than to the Christians. Thus, in their almost victorious hour, the Crusaders beheld the flag of Alexius waving from the towers, so they retreated in much haste.

Dissension among the leaders caused the army to divide itself into two parts, and in July, 1097, the Sultan of Roum, at the head of a huge army in which cavalry predominated, attacked one party of the Crusaders and slew hundreds, not sparing women and children, nor even the sick or the wounded.   In the midst of the massacre, Godfrey de Bouillon made a timely arrival and put the Turks to flight, leaving their gorgeous camp in the hands of the Christians.   The Sultan in his flight burned and laid waste the entire country towards which the Crusaders were advancing, and as—with their usual lack of caution and wisdom—they had eaten up the luxurious store of food left in the Turkish camp, the Christians encountered terrible privations, and there being no grass, their horses fell dead beneath them.   The scorching sun produced insatiable thirst, and of water there was none. Every day hundreds of pilgrims succumbed.   In spite of all these experiences, as soon as the survivors reached Antiochetta and again found food and water in plenty, they returned to their former habits of luxurious waste.

When, a few months later, they besieged Antioch, their greed and extravagance were so great that their ample stock of food gave out quickly, and they were once more face to face with famine.   When the stock of animals had been exhausted, members of the Holy Army fell back on human flesh.   Pestilence and all kinds of diseases prevailed, and they were probably brought about by unwholesome food and by the bad odours from the marshes surrounding the city.   The Crusaders died in such vast numbers that it was hardly possible to give them decent burials.

The camp was full of Turkish spies, two of whom Bohemond ordered to be roasted alive.   Suspicion was rife everywhere, and the Christian leaders were driven to despair at the sufferings of their people. Help, however, was forthcoming at the crucial moment. A detachment of soldiers arrived from Europe with large quantities of food and necessaries. Unfortunately, however, these provisions were seized upon with such haste that no economy was possible, and famine again set in. To relieve the pressure, Stephen, Count of Blois, against the advice of Bohemond, retired to Alexandretta with about four thousand of his followers. The privations 'and length of the siege were wearying the besiegers ; they knew too that the Sultan was advancing against them with a still stronger force. Quick action was needed, and by bribing an Armenian who guarded one of the towers, the Crusaders contrived to enter Antioch and attack the inhabitants with a mad rage induced by all the sufferings they had undergone. The fight continued throughout the night. Men, women, and children were put to the sword, and had not the ' Christians' ' thoughts turned to plunder and loot not a human being would have been left alive. The Crusaders, however, were attracted by the wealth of which there was such abundance in Antioch, and left off killing in order to acquire gold, jewels, silks, satins, and velvets.

Of provisions they found but little, as the besieged had been as near famine as the besiegers, and before they were able to make plans for laying in fresh stores, the Turks and the Sultan of Persia with a great army descended on the city. Many of the Crusaders, dreading another siege, managed to escape to Alexandretta ; those who remained subsisting once more on vermin of any kind, which were sold only at fabulous prices. Fever and pestilence again set in, and sixty thousand discouraged and hopeless pilgrims were all that remained of the three hundred thousand who had raised the siege.

But all their courage and enthusiasm was suddenly restored by the device of a priest, named Peter Barthelmy, who told the weary Christians that two saints had appeared to him in a vision, and had bidden him to proceed to Antioch, where he would find a Holy Lance buried in a certain place. This lance he was to give to the Count of Toulouse, who would lead them on to certain victory. The lance was duly found by Barthelmy—the general idea prevailing among historians that only he could have found it, and that the whole scheme was planned by him and the Count of Toulouse. The incident met with immediate and amazing success, and this was enhanced by the visions described by other monks and visionaries, in which the apparitions had offered crowns of everlasting glory to all who were slain in the fight.

Superstition filled all with a valour so great that the tired, half-starved, and small army utterly routed the Turks, who were six times their number. It was another miracle, however, which completely turned the tide of battle and gave the victory to the Crusaders. Whilst the fight was raging fiercely, the Christians were beginning to despair when there came a terrific shout that the saints were fighting with them, and, looking up, they thought they saw fantastic white clouds hanging like shrouded figures above the far-off mountains. These apparently sepulchral forms were, as a matter of fact, caused by the smoke from the burning woods which had curled upwards and, in the absence of wind, hung on the brow of the mountain. One zealous fanatic started the belief that an army of white-robed saints riding on their white horses had come to the rescue. Faith was again instilled as all eyes turned upwards to gaze on the phenomenon. The Christians then fought with such intrepidity that the Turks fled after having lost over seventy thousand men.

The Crusaders next proceeded towards Jerusalem, and as the pinnacles of the Holy City loomed upon their sight the attitude of the men underwent a sudden and complete change. Their aggressive brutality turned to meek humility, many kissed the hallowed ground, many knelt down and prayed aloud, women and children " prayed and wept and laughed." They saw on the walls rudely constructed crosses which the Saracens had derisively fixed there, and as the advancing Christians drew nearer they pelted them with stones and mud and spat upon the crosses.

The siege was at once opened; but it was of short duration. By an ingenious ruse the Crusaders took the city, and, once inside, the slaughter was terrible. They showed no mercy, and massacred indiscriminately. The Saracens fled for safety to the mosque of Soliman, hoping to entrench themselves there, but as the invading army came immediately at their heels, two thousand Turks were killed in the mosque alone. The Christians already in Jerusalem rushed from their places of concealment to welcome their saviours; many of them who had seen Peter the Hermit during his previous pilgrimage kissed the hem of his robe, and worshipped him as their true deliverer.

The Crusaders remained in Jerusalem for fifty years, and during that time battles were frequent, in which they were sometimes victorious and sometimes not. Internal discords occurred frequently amongst the Holy Army, whilst the strength of the infidels increased in proportion. Many of the knights and soldiers of the Christian army

married daughters of their enemies even although they
made baptism a condition of the union.   Thus, in course
of time the Christian population felt little of the former
fierce hatred for the Saracens, and the chief battles waged
during the reigns of the later kings of Jerusalem were
against the Turks by the new Christian armies as they
arrived in their search for wealth and glory.

In 1145, when the strongly fortified town of Odessa was
wrested from the Christians by the Saracens, the clergy
were seized with panic lest the weakness and dissensions
among their people might enable the infidels to come once
more into possession of the Holy Land, and they sent
vigorous appeals to Louis VII of France, in consequence
of which he gathered round him the chivalry of France to
go and succour the Christians.   But enthusiasm, the
greatest factor in the preceding Crusades, was somewhat
lacking—though in Germany the number and excitement
of the Crusaders continued more marked than in other
countries.

A monk named St. Bernard was the great advocate of
the second Crusade.   A man of such a blameless and
virtuous life, as well as of unbounded eloquence, he had
no difficulty in stirring up much of the former enthusiasm,
although it is probable that many of the knights who
enrolled themselves under the banner of Louis VII were
not without hopes of retrieving the fortunes they had
squandered in riotous living.   An army of two hundred
thousand men was soon ready to take the field.   St.
Bernard was held in veneration so great that all believed
him to be imbued with the spirit of prophecy as well as
the power to work miracles.   It was reported of him that
devils vanished at his sight, and that his touch could
drive out the most malignant diseases.   Even in Germany,

where his language was not understood, thousands rushed to behold the holy man, and many German knights, including the Emperor Conrad himself, became seized with the contagious fanatic fervour. But although the monk himself was held in such high esteem, the masses of the people were not carried away by the religious ecstasy which had crowned the efforts of Gottschalk.

The first to start was the German army, with Emperor Conrad at its head ; Louis VII and his multitude followed. Both armies encountered innumerable difficulties and mishaps, notably at Constantinople, where the reigning Emperor resented the coming of the new hordes, yet was fearful of arousing their anger.

Arrived in the Holy Land, the siege of Damascus was soon raised, and had not the Crusaders wasted time by internal wranglings and disputes as to which among them should reign over the unconquered city, Damascus would have fallen into their hands. Meanwhile the Emir of Mousoul had hastened to relieve the city with so powerful a force that the besiegers sought safety by retreating to Jerusalem, and the two kings were only too glad to return to their own countries with as much of their armies as war and sickness had left them. All were weary and sick at heart, dejected and hopeless ; dead was the wild enthusiasm which had thrilled the start of the campaign.

When news reached Europe of the fierce battle of Tiberias, in which the Christians sustained a bloody defeat, and that Jerusalem and many other cities had been captured by Saladin, the clergy were seized with dread, and the Pope exhorted every God-fearing member to urge a third crusade to recover the Holy Land. The flower of the nobility throughout Europe made quick response to the call. Chivalry, a marked feature in this

Crusade, was not unmixed with the poetry of romance, for the nobles, as well as the people, had been influenced by the wave of culture which had spread over Europe during the century that had elapsed since the marching of the first Holy Army.   Much of this culture was the outcome of association with the people of the East who were civilised and learned, whilst even the European princes were little better than barbarians and savages.

Thus, when Richard Cœur de Lion and Philip Augustus of France, each with his train of knights, took arms for the Holy War, there was less of religious zeal and the glory of a martyr's crown in their hearts than a longing to distinguish themselves in the eyes of their ' ladyes.' Difficulties innumerable met them on the way—battles and violent storms.   Subsequently acrimony arose between the two kings.   Jealousy and suspicion usurped the place of good-fellowship, so Philip decided to abandon the Crusade and return to France, leaving only a very small number of his men to augment the host of Richard.

The English king, though eager to win back the Holy City, hesitated to advance, and remained inert for some months, until the news that Saladin had raised the siege of Jaffa urged him to move quickly forward.   He was only just in time to save the city, and after making a truce with the brave Saladin, Richard set out for his native land.

Other Crusades followed, notably the two under King Louis IX of France, who was persuaded to take the first in consequence of a dream which had greatly influenced his mind.   The second, in which he joined forces with Prince Edward of England, proved fatal to him ; he died at the age of fifty-four from the effects of plague.   The clergy tried to rekindle the energy and flame to promote further efforts for the recovery of the Holy Land, but the spark was entirely extinguished. Though bands of pilgrims with their staffs and wallets continued to journey to Palestine every spring and summer, their numbers were quite insufficient to attempt any kind of hostilities.

The fourth Crusade was devoid of even the romantic inspiration of the third, and was far more provocative of harm than of good, seeing that it ended in the recapture of Jaffa and the almost total annihilation of the army of the Cross, and consequently it still further embittered the Mussalmans towards the Christians of Jerusalem.

Foulque, Bishop of Neuilly, preached the fifth Crusade under the direction of the Pope, and his passionately inspired speeches aroused the slumbering ardour of the French nobles, who led a large army towards Jerusalem. The Christian army attacked Constantinople, and after a tumultuous assault they put to death every man who would not yield himself up, then sacked the city. At least two thousand people were massacred, and so sudden had been the onslaught that the Turks could wreak but little vengeance upon the invaders. As Constantinople contained a wealth of gold and jewels they were quickly annexed. In a sheer spirit of reckless destruction the Crusaders destroyed exquisite marbles and bronzes and other works of art. Baldwin, Count of Flanders, was chosen to reign as Emperor, and with him a new dynasty was inaugurated. The reign of the Christians in Turkey came to an end after sixty years.

The Children's Pilgrimage in the early Middle Ages was an intensely curious example of epidemic mania. When, in 1212, people were in grief and tribulation over the loss of the Holy Land, there appeared in Vendôme a shepherd boy, who affirmed that God appeared to him under the guise of a stranger, had eaten bread with him, and had entrusted to his keeping an important missive for the King. All the shepherd boys in the vicinity flocked to him ; he became the leader of thirty thousand children. Some of these, even at the tender age of eight, also became prophets, and either preached to the rest or worked miracles. These thousands of delirious children set out for Marseilles, notwithstanding the opposition of their parents and of the King, and resolutely facing all the terrors and hardships of the journey, they eventually arrived at the sea, but only to be the victims of the merchants, who sent them off in ships to the East, where the little fanatics were sold as slaves.

CHAPTER IV

WITCH MANIA AND SUPERSTITION

IN the twelfth century it was held that a sure exorcism for devils could always be relied on by the multiplication of gospels when recited after Mass. To use the words of Geraldus Cambrensis, " It is a good physic, and helps to drive away ghosts, especially the beginning of the gospel of St. John, because there is nothing devils hate so much as gospel."

It will thus be seen that the clergy were fully as prone as laymen to a belief in the supernatural. The popes and clergy denounced and punished all so-called sorcerers, wizards, and witches. But in most instances the crime of witchcraft was merely the pretext through which the Roman Church prosecuted those who would not embrace their faith. In this they were urged on by men in power who wished to rid themselves of their enemies.

To accuse a person of witchcraft was easy, to deny the accusation was hopeless, so that, knowing the inevitable and terrible penalty, reputed witches often not only confessed to their dealings with the Devil, but, under the torture of the rack, volunteered information which their tormentors never anticipated, in the hope that they would be released from torture and put quickly out of their misery.

Still more astonishing, however, is the number of those

who believed these witch tales. That they mostly did believe them there is no doubt, and the more witches who were arrested, the more human fires that were burnt, the greater grew the witch terror throughout Europe. A few there were who gave the tales no credence ; but to express pity for a witch, or even a doubt as to the justice of the sentence, would have been far too precarious to risk, for immediate arrest with torture and the stake would have been the sure consequence. Even the few who doubted ran with the tide and seemingly approved if their nearest and dearest were torn from them on a witch-charge. The trials for witchcraft, which were mere farces, became so numerous that scarcely any other crime was noted. Every man feared the work of the Devil through his imps and witches ; every man watched for it even while dreading it. Not a single misfortune or even worry could happen that was not attributed to witches, who in most cases were miserably poor, feeble-minded old women, though many young and beautiful girls and even children were also accused of holding intercourse with Satan, and burnt at the stake.

All Europe went mad over the witch mania. According to the then prevailing idea, if a witch or wizard renounced baptism and sold her or his soul to the Devil by a compact signed with blood, they were enabled to work any evil they had a mind to, on life, health, or prosperity. These compacts were made at the meetings which his Satanic Majesty held, usually in the night between Friday and Saturday, at a place where four roads met. And wherever the meeting place had been, the plot of ground became barren for evermore, the Devil's foot having consumed its fertility. Orders for these meetings were duly sent round to all the devilish satellites and witches ;

if they did not turn up, they were flogged with a rod composed of scorpions and serpents. The French and English witches were supposed to use a broomstick for their means of travel to the grand meeting, or the 'sabbath' as it was called; but in Spain and Italy the Devil, in the form of a pot which elongated or shortened according to the number of witches he wished to accommodate, bore them to the appointed place.

These witches left their dwellings through the keyhole, never by the door, and returned, broomstick and all, down the chimney. And in order that their absence should not be commented upon, some of the less high and mighty imps had orders to assume their form and take their places in bed, under pretext of illness, until their return.

The Devil himself is reported under an infinity of shapes and disguises. Sometimes he is described as having seven heads with ten horns and ten crowns, a mouth like a lion, a leopard's head, the feet of a bear and three faces. Another vision of him describes his face as terrible, his nose resembling that of an eagle, deep cadaverous burning eyes, wings of a dragon, hairy hands and legs and claw-like feet. The Devil was of course empowered to assume whatever form he chose, and he, as well as his millions of demons, could trace their pedigrees back to Adam, whom he himself seduced by assuming the shape of a lovely woman.

Some of the minor spirits of evil had the form of war horses with faces of men, lions' teeth, and hair like women; they wore crowns of gold and breastplates of fire and brimstone. All possessed tails pointed like those of scorpions, and the sound of their wings was as though multitudes of chariots and horses were rushing along. The tails of these imps, like those of their devilish master, had power to kill or poison. Sometimes the bodies of the inferior demons appeared to be composed of thin air, and they passed through wood, stone, or any solid substance without the slightest difficulty. Whirlwinds were invariably brought about when a quantity of these little devils gathered together, also terrible storms and earthquakes. Not only did these impish creatures multiply among themselves as humans do, but their number was also constantly increased by the souls of the wicked, of women who had died in childbirth, and of still-born children. The atmosphere was believed to be so impregnated with these imps that many people, in breathing, drew thousands of them into their mouths and nostrils. Lodging in their bodies they caused fearful dreams, and all sorts of pain, illness, and disease. Like Satan, they could at will assume forms of wonderful beauty.

The Devil is represented as having been bibulous as well as mischievous and wicked, and his love of mischief increased in his cups. One of his favourite amusements was to place his long invisible tail in the way of all who passed and trip them up by giving it a sharp whisk, also to scare folks out of their wits by giving unearthly quacks whilst in the shape of a huge duck in the long grasses. When paying the innkeepers for his drinks he always gave them gold pieces which changed into slate after a few hours. These were a few of his little playful ways, probably as mild recreation amongst his more serious work of causing plagues, fires, fruit and corn famines, spreading death and destruction, terror and vice. There are many instances when the Devil and many of his little devils assumed the form of extremely good-looking young men, hid their tails, and married lovely women, who bore them children. These children never throve or grew fat in spite of the fact that it took five nurses to suckle them.

At the great meetings the Devil was welcomed by all present with cries of " All Hail, Master ! " Before commencing his oration, a roll-call was held in order to make sure that all were present, and if any witch did not present herself a demon was told off to go and flog her with scorpions. Satan called no witch by her real name, nor was one permitted to designate another except by whatever name he chose to allot to her, such as ' Stick-at nothing,' ' Raise-the-wind,' ' Batter-them-down-Maggie,' ' Work-with-a-will,' etc.

Singing and dancing commenced at once, and was only held up at the entrance of any newcomer desirous of joining them. The fresh arrival was ordered to deny his salvation, to spit upon the Bible, and to kiss the master, whom he swears to obey implicitly. Thus, giving up his soul to the Devil, the new member obtained the privilege of his and his underling's services. He had but to express a wish to have it carried out, unless it happened to be a good wish. If he so far forgot his new character as to desire anything good, he was severely punished, and, needless to say, the order was ignored. When the company wearied of dancing, all seated themselves and gave an account to the Devil of all their wickedness since they had last met. If their deeds did not come up to his high standard of evil, he flogged them so brutally as to cover them with blood, and they could neither stand nor sit.

Satan then called upon ' his unclean spirits,' the toads, which rose up in hordes, and danced to his music of trumpet or hornpipes. These toads all possessed the gift of speech, and instead of asking the company for money they begged from the witches the flesh of unbaptised

babies. After receiving their promise, the toads disappeared at the stamping of the Devil's foot. A banquet
was next prepared, at which the most disgusting dishes
appeared and were eagerly consumed, and to those who
had performed deeds of transcendent evil, Satan gave
costly wines in crystal goblets and all kinds of luxurious
food. Dancing was again indulged in, and subsequently
the congregation started an ironical baptismal sacrament,
for which the toads were recalled and sprinkled with holy
water, the sign of the Cross being made by the Devil
himself. Sometimes, for a little extra excitement, he
ordered the witches to strip themselves naked and dance
for his entertainment ; whilst cats were tied round their
necks and bodies—the cat on the latter arranged to form
a tail. The hilarious entertainment continued until cock-
crow, then the meeting faded suddenly into thin air.

Such was the belief in the Devil and his powers, which
were of course equally vested in his servants—the wizards
and witches. The number of these poor creatures who
suffered death by burning was prodigious. As a natural
result of the violent persecution, the crime, or rather the
number of the supposed criminals, increased by leaps and
bounds. Although at the commencement of the indict-
ments it was the heretics who were chiefly victimised, the
latter believed as firmly in the crime of witchcraft as ever
the Catholics did, and the Calvinists and Lutherans became
fully as wildly fanatical over witch-burning as ever the
Catholics had been. The ' crime ' went on growing as the
fear of it grew, until many poor women prayed that they
might never reach old age, for the stake appeared to be
the inevitable end of all whose years and hard life had
rendered them dull of wit and memory.

Pope Innocent VIII, alarmed at the enormous increase

of persons who had dealings with the Devil, appointed
special inquisitors to deal with them.   These men became
known as the ' witch finders.'   They put each suspect on
the rack and, during the torture, asked each one the same
questions, the agony of pain invariably drawing out the
expected replies.   The inquisitors were armed with
complete power to torture and destroy, and thus exter-
minate as quickly as was possible the crime of witchcraft.   In Como alone there perished by fire one thousand
persons in the year 1524, and in many other towns the
burnings exceeded one hundred.   The populace looked on
complacently, even gladly, believing that every witch the
less meant greater safety for their own children, for themselves, and for their homes and prospects ; though to have
wept for a witch would, of course, have been at once
construed into confession of the crime.

In Italy, Germany, and France, the number of witches
convicted, and consequent number of burnings, increased
with extraordinary and terrible rapidity, and although
the persecution madness did not reach its height quite so
quickly in England, the campaign was carried on with
atrocious ferocity.   Men and women of rank, clergymen,
young and beautiful girls, and even children were among
the victims ; but the majority of the sufferers were aged
women, too poor and too ignorant, often too feeble even
to attempt to defend themselves, not that any defence
would have been of the slightest avail.   One of these
poor, simple women actually asked a Scottish judge if it
could be possible for a person to be a witch without knowing
it, and another, when her eyes fell on the lighted faggots
which were to consume her, held out her hands and cried
out, " See the bonnie fire ! "

About 1562 the public mind, again following the clergy's

lead, held only one seething desire—the extermination of witches, every man living in a state of terror lest he or his dear ones should come under their spell. Bishop Jessel, preaching before Queen Elizabeth, said, " It may please your grace to understand that witches and sorcerers within these last few years are marvellously increased within your Grace's realm. Your Grace's subjects pine away even unto death, their colour fadeth, their flesh rotteth, their senses become bereft. I pray God they never practise farther than upon the subject." So violently was the entire population smitten with the epidemic dread that many so-called witches died at the hands of the people themselves before they could be brought to trial.

In 1704 Janet Cornfoot was seized upon by an irate mob of fisher-folk at Pittenweem, who dragged her to the sea and ducked her several times, after which, as she lay unconscious, one of the brutes brought a door which he had taken from his hut and placed it upon her. The mob took great stones and piled them upon the door, thus crushing the poor woman to death. The witch-finders vied with each other, each one striving to outdo the other in the number of his arrests, indeed so obnoxious did this continual prying become that their name was changed from ' common pinchers ' to common nuisances.

If one of these witch-finders happened to pass a house which he knew to be occupied by one woman alone, and heard talking, the poor soul was at once indicted for holding converse with the Devil, even though she owned to a foolish habit of speaking to herself. During a period of thirty-nine years, the executions of witches amounted to 17,000. In England, during the first eighty years of the seventeenth century, the average number of execu-tions reached the terrific height of five hundred annually, so that about forty-two thousand witches were burnt in the presence of a delighted audience numbering thousands of people.

In the blindness and stubbornness of belief in witch-craft, the wisest and highest in the land were as ecstatically bigoted as the masses of the people. Though the intensity of the anti-witch campaign set in towards the beginning of the seventeenth century, the madness died very gradually, and even broke out rampantly again in Germany in 1740.

Of the latter part of the seventeenth century there are many strange tales told, not only in remote country districts, but also in many towns, more especially in Lancashire and Yorkshire, where a large number of witch-doctors profess to cure any disease of the devil's infliction, and not a great number of years ago, an old woman at Hastings, also a fisherman, were shunned and dreaded, being believed to have sold their souls to the Devil.

There are haunted houses even in the city of London, notably that in Hatton Garden, close to Bleeding-Heart Yard, once the residence of Sir Christopher Hatton and his wife, Lady Hatton, who is supposed to have signed a contract with the Devil, on the expiration of which his Satanic Majesty came to a room in the house (which is still pointed out) and carried her away and dashed her against a pump near by. He then tore out her heart with his fierce claws, and the spot on which it was found was called thenceforth Bleeding-Heart Yard.

A horseshoe has ever since been affixed to the house of the Hattons, and, as we all know, horseshoes are still accounted to bring good luck, which is but another form of expressing the old belief of their power of exorcism. This and other beliefs still extant are very minor follies in

comparison with those of the raving-madness of the
Middle Ages.

In Scotland, in the seventeenth century, civil rights of
the medical profession were set at naught by the Church,
as evidenced by the enactment " that no man should be
permitted to practise or profess any physic, unless he had
first satisfied the bishop of the diocese touching his religion."
Nowadays the medical profession certify beliefs in some of
the teachings of the Church as indications of insanity.
For having thrown some stones during a tumult, four
boys were scourged through the city of Edinburgh, burnt
in the face with a hot iron, and then sold as slaves to
Barbadoes. Cruelty was rife in Scotland during those
times. Sir William Bannatyne's soldiers bound a woman,
put lighted matches betwixt her fingers for several hours,
and caused such torture that she died. He also laid men
down to roast before great fires when he could not obtain
information or money from them.

In 1596 David Black, a Protestant minister, said in his
sermon that all kings were servants of the Devil; but that
in Scotland the head of the Court was Satan himself,
the members of the council cormorants, and the lords of
the session miscreants. In another sermon, preached in
Edinburgh that same year, the minister declaimed that
James was demented, that it would be right to lay hold
of the madman, and tie him hand and foot, that he might
do no further harm. Andrew Melville, in an audience
with the King, called him God's silly vassal. In England
Protestantism had gradually diminished superstition and
increased the spirit of toleration; whereas in Scotland
there still existed a reluctance to listen to the voice of
reason. John Knox was, in spite of his preachings, stern
and even brutal, as was evidenced by the giving of his

sanction to the murder of Archbishop Beaton in 1546. For this he himself was made to work at the galleys until liberated in 1549.

In 1678 armed Highlanders received from the English government an indemnity for every excess they might commit upon the towns and villages of Western Scotland. They stripped the inhabitants of their clothes and sent them out naked to die. Other horrible tortures and foul abuses were committed. In those days, iron shackles and thumb-locks (*i.e.* thumb-screws), were in vogue.

James II, the most cruel of all the Stuarts, fiendishly enjoyed witnessing the agonies of his fellow-beings. He was the ruler of millions, and, revolting as his conduct was, his actions were applauded by the Scottish bishops. In 1684 a new instrument of torture, the thumbikins, was imported from Russia. This was an arrangement of small steel screws whereby the whole hand could be compressed.

During the eighteenth century the ' true children of the kirk ' of Scotland regarded themselves as the excellent ones of the earth, all others being but slaves of Satan. It was generally believed that evil spirits were roaming about, with Satan at their head, and that these spirits assumed various forms, such as a black dog, or even a bull. As a consequence of the ravings from the pulpits the people were in a constant state of terror. They were told that the Deity was a cruel tyrant who would roast them in great fires, hang them up by their tongues, throw them into boiling oil, etc. He was held responsible for all the devastations, murders, and other crimes. It was held to be a sin to please either themselves or others. Some of the clergy, in drawing up regulations for the government of a colony, inserted the following clause : " No husband

shall kiss his wife, and no mother shall kiss her child on
the Sabbath day." They condemned cheerfulness, especially when it rose to laughter. Religious principles went
with sighs, groans, and tears, and jesting was incompatible
with a holy and serious life. Even beautiful scenery was
merely for the unconverted, for nature was well-nigh spent.
All pleasure was sinful and no person was allowed to be
joyful or happy. In order to avoid eternal wrath the
lusts of the flesh should be guarded against by a careful
and frugal diet. Man was debased even before he was
born, and to learn new words was a heinous sin. It was a
sin for any Scotsman to travel in a Catholic country ;
markets should not be held either on Saturday or Monday,
because both days were near Sunday ; no visits should be
paid, no gardens watered, no beards shaved on the Sabbath;
bathing and swimming were carnal practices ; all comforts
were sinful. Repression was the order of the day. All
pleasures were denounced by the arbitrary assumptions
of the Church, hence the delay in the evolution of the
feeling of well-being in the Scottish character. The
detestable tyrannies of the Scottish kirk equalled those of
the Spanish Inquisition, and it was not until theological
doctrines gave way to scientific reasonings that they came
more into line with the teachings of Kant, Hamilton,
Newton, and Harvey, and inductive methods of arguing
from the concrete to the abstract superseded the traditions
deduced from inspirations. Repression of thought gave
way to metaphysical speculation. The Scots have been
much indebted to Hutcheson for their emancipation from
the shackles of intolerance in thought and belief; and
certainly it is to his efforts that more mental freedom,
and even sympathy, has been attained. Adam Smith
contributed to the further expansion of the Scottish mind

when he pointed out that in order to form an opinion as to right or wrong we must first look abroad and consider the merits or demerits of others. His great practical lesson was that by enlightened selfishness of the individual the progress of the community becomes accelerated, *i.e.* self-realisation rightly conducted is beneficial.

Luther's credulity about the Devil, who was constantly visiting and worrying him, seems at first sight incompatible with the scholarly learning and penetrating intellect of this great man. But it must be remembered that superstition was rife in his times, and that of physical science he knew nothing. One day he was heard to say, " Idiots, the lame, the blind, the dumb, are men in whom devils have established themselves—and all the physicians who heal those infirmities, as though they proceeded from natural causes, are ignorant blockheads, who know nothing about the power of the demon."

In 1530 Luther wrote, " When I try to work, my head becomes filled with all sorts of whizzing, buzzing, thundering noises, and if I did not leave off the instant I should faint away. For the last three days I have not been able even to look at a letter. The day your letter came from Nuremburg I had another visit from the Devil. I was alone, Vitus and Cyriacus having gone out, and this time the Evil One got the better of me, drove me out of my bed, and compelled me to seek the face of man."

Luther, although he led a great religious movement, did not become the founder of a new religion, and there are no signs in any of his works that they were in any way influenced or affected by his remarkable delusions. He was frequently oppressed by a terrible anguish, from which he was unable to free himself. He believed this to have been brought about " by the anger of an offended God."

" Not seldom," he says, " has it happened to me to awake at midnight and dispute with Satan concerning the Mass."

The Stevingers (1234) received their name from a league which was entered into by a small band of Frieslanders, who, with an intuitive anticipation of representative government, held a lofty ambition to institute a free state with civil and religious liberty for all. The Church, and the tyrannical nobles, took umbrage, neither being wishful to resign from their long-held despotism, whilst the Stevingers were continually fighting against the incursions of the barons. The nobles then craved the intervention of the Pope, who was only too glad to punish the Stevingers for attempting to ignore his supreme authority. His Holiness denounced them as heretics and witches, founding the latter accusation on the fact that only the power of the Devil could have enabled so small a section of men to withstand the attacks of the barons, and concluded by urging all true believers to help in the good work of exterminating the Stevingers. A great army numbering forty thousand men marched into the little kingdom, which could not muster more than eight thousand, even when putting the sick and the aged into the field. They defended themselves to the last man, and the victors, infuriated at their splendid courage, massacred the women and children, and laid waste the entire country.

The Waldenses (1450), a party of religious devotees at Arras, were accused of witchcraft and subjected to torture, as was then the practise, the accusation lodging mainly on the fact that having a form of worship of their own, these people held their religious meetings secretly in the night. Nearly all these unfortunates, after inexpressible torments, suffered death by burning.

Charles, Comte de Valois, uncle to Louis X, had an

unshakable belief that if he made a wax effigy of an enemy and pricked and tortured it, the person it represented would become ill and die. But for the desired result to be certain of achievement, it was necessary that the making and torturing of the image should be carried out in most profound secrecy.

Louis XI of France set great store by astrology and superstition, although he would often pretend to gibe at both. He once sent for an astrologer and put the question to him : " You, who know everything, when will you die?" The astrologer replied : " Sire, three days before your Majesty." In spite of his pretended lack of faith in such prophecies, King Louis took the astrologer under his special care.

We are also told that although Louis gave no credence to the existence of a Heavenly Power, " he did believe in an invisible world of saints having exclusive power over the events of life." Burton writes of him that he was possessed of a fancy " that everything did stink upon him. All the odoriferous perfumes they could get would not ease him, but still he smelt a filthy stink."

Edward IV's extravagant and intemperate habits grew more confirmed with the passing of years, and utterly destroyed his health. Notwithstanding these pernicious leanings, Edward was a scholar and an enthusiastic believer in divination and astrology. Elizabeth of York tells us how her father, when one day studying a book of magic in his palace of Westminster, was extremely agitated, even to tears, and though earls and lords were present, none dared to speak to him but herself. She came and knelt before him for his blessing, upon which he threw his arms round her and lifted her into a high window. When he had set her there, he gave her the horoscope he had drawn,

and bade her show it to no one but Lord Stanley, for he
had plainly calculated that no son of his should wear the
crown after him.   He predicted that she should be Queen,
and the crown would rest with her descendants.

Ferdinand II, Grand Duke of Tuscany (1495), has been
nicknamed "The fool of his health."   Hebe Arnauld
writes of him : " I have frequently seen him pacing up and
down his chamber between two large thermometers, upon
which he would keep his eyes constantly fixed, employed
unceasingly in taking off and putting on a variety of skull
caps of different degrees of warmth, of which he had
always five or six in his hand according to the degree of
heat or cold registered by his instruments."

Sultan Bajazet (1512), being terrified at the approach of
a revolution, dreamed that he saw his son Selim ride up
to the front of the palace leading an immense force and
calling to him, "If you will yield, we will not touch your
life, but we will drag you by your robes on the points of
our javelins from the throne."   This dream impressed
Bajazet so vividly that, on the day following, he gave over
the throne to Selim, telling him that " It would be in-
jurious to resist such a sign."

Wyatt, in his *Memorials of Anne Boleyn*, writes that the
following incident occurred before that Queen's marriage
to Henry VIII.   She found one day a book in her chamber,
but could not discover how it had got there.   She read
the book and called her chief attendant, Anne Saville.
" Come hither, Nan," said she, " here is a book of prophecies.   This is the King, this is the Queen, and this is
myself with my head cut off."   And Saville answered,
" If I thought it true, I would not myself have him were
he an emperor."   " Tut ! Tut ! Nan," replied Anne
Boleyn, " I think the book a bauble, and I am resolved to

have him that my issue may be royal, whatever may happen to me."

The Anabaptists (1532) at Munster and in Poland were convinced that they saw luminous apparitions of angels and dragons struggling in the sky, and that they received from them commands to kill those whom they loved best, even brothers, and that they were also instructed to abstain from food for entire months, and that they had the power to paralyse large armies by a look or by their breath.

Catherine de Medici (1547) was a devout believer in everything appertaining to the occult arts. She was never without amulets and talismans upon her person, and ordered observatories and laboratories to be erected. She also had a mirror fitted up which she regarded as enchanted, and in it she saw reflected the fortunes of her descendants.

Gilles Garnier (1578), like Jacques Rollet and many others, was burnt to death on an indictment of being a loup-garoux, or were-wolf, and in that guise wandering in the fields and mountains and carrying away children, whom he was said to devour, sometimes taking part of the bodies home as a relish for his wife and family. No less than fifty witnesses swore to the truth of the accusation, and under the torture of the rack Garnier owned his guilt.

An extraordinary case happened in 1588 in Auvergne, when a huntsman, returning from the chase, caught sight of a friend as he was passing his house. The man called to him and enquired how he had fared, and the huntsman told him that a fierce wolf had sprung upon him, and with his hunting knife he had cut off one of its paws, whereupon the wolf limped away. " I have the paw here in my bag," continued the huntsman ; but when he drew the supposed member from his bag, he found to his horror that it was a woman's hand, and the third finger carried a wedding ring—to the other man's horror also, for he had last seen the ring upon his wife's finger.   He ran quickly to the kitchen where his wife sat by the fire, and noticing at once that one of her arms was concealed under her apron, he pulled it away and saw the hand was missing and the stump still bleeding.   He at once gave her into custody as a witch, and she was burnt at the stake.

Just before Henry IV was assassinated by Ravaillac, the Queen dreamed that " all the jewels in her crown were changed to pearls," and pearls were significant of tears. A night or so later, she actually dreamed that King Henry had been stabbed under the ribs with a knife, which of course really did happen within a few days.

Charles I of England (1625) was highly superstitious and frequently sought advice from Lilly, the astrologer, as did also Henrietta Maria his Queen.   The latter also often consulted Lady Eleanor, a lady in waiting and daughter of the Earl of Castlehaven, who writes : " About two years after the marriage of King Charles I, I was waiting on the Queen as she came from mass or evening service, to know what service she was pleased to require from me. Her first question was, ' Whether she could ever have a son ? ' I answered, ' In a short time.'   The Queen was next desirous to know what would be the destiny of the Duke of Buckingham and the English fleet which had sailed to attack her brother's realm and relieve the siege of Rochella. I answered that the Duke of Buckingham would bring home little honour, but his person would return safely, and that speedily. The Queen then returned to her hopes of a son, and I showed that she would have one, and that for a long time she could be happy.

' But for how long ? ' asked the Queen. ' For sixteen years,' was my reply. King Charles coming in at that moment, our discourse was interrupted by him."

King Charles had an odd fancy to bind himself to a certain line of conduct, and, looking upon it in the light of a secret obligation, he bound himself in writing solemnly to ensure its accomplishment. A case in point was, when, after signing the warrant for Lord Strafford's execution, Charles swore to perform public penance for this act of injustice. As was his custom, he swore it in writing and handed the paper to Dr. Sheldon, entreating him to remind him of the obligation at any time when he should be able to fulfil it.

It was during the reign of Edward I that the famous ' cramp-rings ' were first used. These rings, when blessed by the King, were looked upon as preservatives against epilepsy and cramp. They were discontinued by Edward VI, but Queen Mary must have brought them again into use, for there is an illumination still extant in a manuscript copy of the Order of the King of England's Household, which depicts Queen Mary kneeling, with a dish of rings on each side of her, waiting to be blessed by her. The ring for ' touching for the evil ' was believed in and used from the time of Edward the Confessor down to the reign of Queen Anne.

Dr. Johnson evidently attached credence to this superstition, for there is mention of him having been among those actually ' touched.' Charles II is reported to have ' touched ' nearly twenty-four thousand people for the King's evil. And so universal was the belief in its efficacy that many were crushed to death in the crowd seeking to apply for tickets which would entitle their children to be ' touched ' by the King.

Napoleon, Prince of Orange, heir-apparent to the King of Holland, always looked upon the second day of the month as his lucky day. He was also extremely superstitious about the numbers six and eleven, and by a strange coincidence he died on the eleventh day of the sixth month at eleven o'clock.

When we meditate on the many marvellous phases and phenomena of nature for which all our much vaunted modern science cannot even in this year of grace 1925 find the cause, the superstition and credulity of the Middle Ages, when knowledge and learning were possessed by a mere handful of the European population, can arouse no surprise. Tales of sorcery were frequent since Biblical days, but it was not until the year 1234 that persecutions for supposed witchcraft came to assume any important dimensions.

CHAPTER V

EPIDEMIC MANIAS AND ALMANACS

It has been said, and with undeniable truth, that " there is no sort of extravagance of which a wise man is not capable." That which is true of the individual must of necessity be equally true of whole communities, and at every age in the history of the world there has occurred some folly or delusion over which the people have gone mad in herds, and only recovered their senses after much suffering. All kinds and forms of frenzied excitement have been communicated, even more rapidly than contagion, from small villages to entire nations, from little children to aged men and women, alike to the most credulous and the most sceptical.

These contagions have taken the shape of wild rushes for the amassing of wealth, for pilgrimages, commerce with evil spirits, hero worship, search for the philosopher's stone and for the occult, for dancing, for fads of fashion, antipathy to sacred things, or more often religious fervour and prophetic enthusiasm, as in the Cevennes, when all the people of that district, women and children especially, read Divine commands in the skies, interpreted messages from the clouds and the sun, and sang psalms of worship and praise, even though their fanatic zeal was punished with death, hundreds of them being hanged.

Picard (1347) conceived the idea that he was a son of

God sent to earth as a new Adam to inaugurate the laws of nature, according to which it was incumbent to go naked and in the community of women. He gathered round him many believers and imitators, and founded a sect which he called the Adamites. The Hussites excommunicated these in 1347, but the sect was actually started again later under the title of Turlupins.

In 1374 a mania for excessive dancing broke out at Aix-la-Chappelle. It started in the wide thoroughfares and public squares. The dancing was accompanied by intense religious enthusiasm, the dancers believing that the heavens were opened wide, revealing all the blessed ones seated within. A curious feature of this craze was that the dancers had an intense aversion for the colour red. The mania soon attacked Cologne, Metz, Strasbourg, and other towns. And although the fever abated after some time, the craze for dancing has continued through several centuries, breaking out more violently now and again. And on the day of the Patron St. Vitus, thousands of dancers always gathered round his shrine.

The Tulip craze was another extraordinary example of epidemic mania. Conrad Gesner, who made it his boast that he brought tulips into fame, first saw one in 1559 at Augsbourg, and, being much struck with the flower, made enquiries about its origin, and found that it had come from Constantinople. He obtained some bulbs, but it was not until ten years later that they achieved any great popularity, when they became in such demand that the wealthy inhabitants of Holland and Germany obtained the bulbs straight from Constantinople at the most exorbitant prices. In Amsterdam especially, a collection of tulips was considered an essential adjunct to culture and refinement. From the aristocracy and wealthy burghers the craze soon spread to the merchants, the shopkeepers and all the middle classes, each man striving to outdo his neighbour in his rare specimens and the enormous outlay necessary to procure them. Men paid half their entire fortunes for one bulb, not at first with any idea of making profit by selling it again, but merely to possess it, and to know it to be admired and envied by their friends, or even by strangers. The thrift and prudence of the Dutch people went suddenly to the winds with 'Tulip fever.' Certainly, experimental cultivation had much developed the flower, for in its natural primitive state the tulip was almost entirely of one colour, with an altogether disproportionate length of stem. But even with its new pristine hues, it lacked the sweet scent of many other flowers.

By the year 1634 the craze for tulip possession had become such an obsession that the customary work and industries of Holland almost came to a standstill; the entire population, from the highest to the lowest, gave themselves up to the tulip cult. Prices went still higher in consequence, and the following year as much as one hundred thousand florins was laid out in bulbs. Of one very rare specimen, it was said that there were only two roots in the whole of Holland, one in Amsterdam and the other in Haarlem. Speculators were by this time becoming extremely eager and busy, and most anxious to obtain these two roots; for the Amsterdam plant, four thousand six hundred florins, a handsome new carriage, two horses and a new set of harness were delivered in payment. The Haarlem bulb was bought for the fee of twelve acres of extremely valuable building land.

We find in Blainville's *Travels* a humorous story of a sailor who returned to Holland at the height of the

' Tulip-fever,' and fell into a serious dilemma through his ignorance thereof. A rich merchant, very proud of his fine collection of rare tulips, was expecting a large consignment of goods, and news of its arrival was brought to him by the sailor. Much pleased, the merchant presented him with a red herring. The sailor was about to depart to enjoy the herring for his breakfast, when, among the silks and velvets on the counter, he espied what he took to be an onion. Onions were a particular weakness of his, and it seemed to him quite out of place for a common onion to lie amongst the handsome silks, so he found an opportunity to slip it into his pocket, and then hurried back to the quay. The merchant soon missed his precious bulb, which he valued at three thousand florins. A search was instituted, but without success. The unfortunate man was almost distracted. Then mention was made of the sailor. At once the merchant and his entire household dashed out of the house in the direction of the quay. There they found the sailor calmly seated on ropes chewing the last mouthful of his ' onion,' which he had much enjoyed in combination with the herring. But he did not enjoy spending several months in prison on a charge of felony which the merchant brought against him.

Soon marts were inaugurated on the Stock Exchange of all the important Dutch towns, solely for the sale of tulips, and gambling started in real earnest. Stock-jobbers, seizing on any chance for fresh speculation, used every possible means for making prices fluctuate, so that they had good opportunities to make large deals. Everybody was confident, everybody made money, everybody rushed to the tulip marts. People grew suddenly rich, many made fortunes. From every part of the world came demands for the popular flower, and any price that was asked was readily paid.

The Dutch people fondly visualised an Eldorado on the banks of the Zuyder Zee, imagining that the tulip craze would know no end. Men and women of every station and walk in life converted their property into money and invested all in tulips. And not only the Dutch—foreigners also caught the fever and poured money into Holland. The tulip trade operations grew to such an extent that a special code of laws to deal with them was compiled. The designation of ' tulip-notary ' took the place of public-notary, for scarcely any other business was transacted.

At last, however, a few of the far-seeing people began to realise that such a state of things could not last, the madness over a flower could not be indefinitely prolonged, so, instead of buying bulbs to retain, they sold them at once at a profit of at least cent per cent. Slowly but surely the doubt spread, confidence fell, and with it prices, and the dealers became panic-stricken. Day by day brought news of fresh defaulters. Crowds of people, who had believed that there could never again be such a thing as poverty, found that their only worldly asset was a few bulbs for which there was no demand at any price.

The careful few, who had managed to keep their suddenly acquired wealth, invested the money abroad and hid the knowledge of it from their neighbours ; hundreds of formerly rich merchants were now almost beggars, and many noble and ancient families were absolutely ruined. Actions for breach of contract were entered, but the judges, after a solemn conclave amongst themselves, decided that the law could not be called upon, as the debts

were occasioned through gambling, and gambling debts
were no debts in law. The whole commercial condition
of Holland received such an upheaval that it took many
years before the country quite recovered itself.

The 'Tulip-fever' took hold, though to a far lesser
extent, of London and Paris, and the jobbers in both
cities tried very hard to raise prices to the fanciful heights
they had reached in Amsterdam. They succeeded in
bringing the tulip into great favour, but did not fill their
pockets as they had hoped to do. Even nowadays, the
Dutch in their fondness for tulips will pay more for bulbs
than people of other countries, and it is of interest to note
that in 1836 a rare species was sold in England for seventy-
five guineas, and another was catalogued at two hundred
guineas.

The case of Dr. Valentine Greataks (1629–1683) is
another curious instance of epidemic mania. Greataks
was an Irish gentleman of considerable learning, who
became possessed of the notion that God had endowed
him with the power to cure the King's evil. The first
man he touched, a native of his own town of Cork, had
the malady in eyes, cheeks, and throat. Greataks prayed
ardently whilst stroking him, and the man improved
rapidly, and eventually, helped by other remedies, made
a complete recovery. Dr. Greataks became more than
ever convinced that he had a divine mission, also that he
could cure any other malady in a similar way. He
speedily became the wonder-man of the entire county—
everybody flocked to see the marvellous physician who
could work such miracles. The doctor himself relates,[1]
" Such great multitudes flocked to him from divers places

[1] See Greataks' account of himself in a letter to the Hon. Robert
Boyle.

that he had no time to follow his own business or enjoy the company of his family and friends."

Indeed the crowds were too numerous to find accommodation for in the adjacent towns and villages, and the authorities much feared that the congregation of so many sick people would cause contagion. Dr. Greataks declared that even the touch of his glove could expel pain, and that he once " cast out from a woman several devils or evil spirits which tormented her day and night." So great was the belief of all who came to be ' touched ' that some fell into fits on finding themselves in his radiant presence, but he soon brought them back to consciousness by prayer and by waving his wand before them.

The doctor fell foul of the clergy of the diocese, who could not stomach the working of miracles, and forbade him to continue the practice of " laying on of hands." Greataks had but little respect for the Church, but, deeming it prudent to leave Cork, he came to England, where his popularity quickly became very great, and in London his wondrous cures were the one topic of conversation. If a few doubted their genuineness and permanency, they never dared to say so. Greataks always adhered to his belief that his power was sent from Heaven, and that all illness and disease was brought about by evil spirits. To quote St. Evremond, " So great was the confidence in him, that the blind fancied they saw the light, the deaf imagined they heard, the lame that they walked, and the paralysed that they had recovered the use of their limbs."

Early in the eighteenth century a large band of sick people came to congregate round the tomb of their favourite saint, Paris, the Jansenist priest, where they practised the art of falling into convulsions. They relied upon their dear ' Saint Paris ' to heal all their maladies, and so great were the crowds of weak-minded and hysterical people who crowded to the tomb that they filled all the roads which led thereto. By inducing themselves into a frenzy of exalted excitement, they soon went off into fits, and some of those who were still conscious caused themselves enough pain and suffering to end their lives had they been in a state of normality. Atrocious scenes generally ended these convulsive orgies, scenes that baffle description and were a disgrace to religion and civilisation. Some fell on their knees and prayed aloud but incoherently, some gave vent to dreadful shrieking sounds, some writhed in convulsions, many in a state of convulsive excitement gave themselves up to gross indecencies. Some cried out to be beaten or trampled upon, some even attempted to crucify themselves. One slight, fragile-looking woman continued to cry for more even after she had been struck sixty times with a heavy sledgehammer. Another woman unflinchingly lay down on a glowing red brazier, for which she was always afterwards known as ' the Salamander.'

Many of the astrologers, alchymists, and fortune-tellers who abounded in London during the Middle Ages predicted in the summer of 1523 that on the first day of the following February the waters of the Thames would rise in such a way as to wash away most of the City of London. The prophecy was never doubted, and created such intense alarm that hundreds of people moved out to Kent, Essex, Croydon, or even the heights of Highgate. Rich and poor—in vehicles and waggons—migrated from the doomed city, taking all portable belongings with them.

So terrified was Bolton, the Prior of St. Bartholomew, that he had a building put up at Harrow-on-the-Hill, in the form of a fortress, and provisioned it for two months. He also got a number of boats ready on the Thames and engaged strong rowers. In the details given in the prophecy, it was said that the overflowing would be gradual, and large crowds came out early on the morning of the first of February, thinking that they would be able to get safely away before the inundations became perilous, but few waited long, for most of the watchers were seized with panic and made off whilst they had the chance. Even when evening arrived and the waters of the river still remained tranquil, the people who had remained feared to go to sleep, lest even yet the fateful prediction might come true.

In 1761 Londoners were again greatly terrified, this time by two earthquake shocks and a prophecy that there was a third to come which would destroy them all. The dread and alarm grew to such an extent that swarms of people hastened to take refuge in villages distant more than twenty miles from London. Between the first and second shocks there had been an interval of precisely four weeks—so that when a more than half crazy soldier made ranting speeches saying that the third shock would be at the same interval of time, the people became fully convinced that in another month London would cease to exist. As the dreaded day drew nearer, even many who had scoffed and laughed at the general exodus packed up their goods and took refuge in adjacent villages.

In the year 1736 the renowned prophet James Weston gave the date of October 13th as the day when the destruction of the world would take place, and vast crowds thronged to the fields near Islington and Hampstead and other places, so that they might get a good view of the destruction of London.

In 1806 another ' end-of-the-world ' panic occurred in Leeds, and was due to a strange cause. A hen in one of the outskirts of the town laid some eggs with these words inscribed upon them, " Christ is coming." Crowds hastened to examine the amazing eggs, and believing firmly that the Day of Judgment was in truth approaching, the people were overcome by religious fear. It transpired eventually, however, that the eggs had been lettered with corrosive ink and forced into the body of the unfortunate hen.

The Almanac craze, like most other epidemics, enjoyed extreme popularity, and for a longer time than any other fad or mania, and although people do not—in every perplexity or doubt—resort to their almanac as they did fifty years ago, its use is still, in a minor degree, practised. In early days the Bible and the almanac were the chief ' literary refuges ' of the rural communities. Though primarily inaugurated as a calendar and astronomical guide, the almanac speedily enlarged its field, and from merely containing a list of all movable functions and festivals, and predicting the weather from astronomical data, it became an absolute encyclopædia of information upon all subjects—political, social, domestic, agricultural, etc., as well as an exposition of innumerable quack medicine men, who, through its multitudinous pages, pushed their wind pills, their stomach bitters, their magnetic rings, their galvanic belts, and countless remedies for every real or imaginary ill.

Mother Shipton (1488–1561) takes second place only to the legendary Merlin amongst all English prophets. Even to this day many of her prophecies are not only remembered with credence, but there are still many people who quake with dread over the misfortunes that will befall this country when London and Highgate are completely united by continuous houses. This was one of Mother Shipton's last predictions before she died. Her fame was remarkable; people of all ages, all ranks, flocked to consult her, and whatever their doubts happened to be—love, jealousy, poverty, fear of treachery, or grave matters of State—she solved them all, and, according to her traditionary biography, " all returned wonderfully satisfied with the explanations she gave to their questions."

Regarding her prophecy of the Great Fire of London, a story is told by an eye-witness of the fire, which proves the implicit faith with which Mother Shipton's words were relied upon. This eye-witness, who went each day with the Duke of York through the burning districts, tells us that they were extremely hampered in their endeavours to prevent the fires from spreading by the people themselves, who—because Mother Shipton had prophesied that London would be burned to the ground—considered that any attempt to check the flames would be quite futile. Sir Kenelm Digby's son, who had inherited his father's gifts for prophecy and alchemy, assured the people that they were wise, and that no earthly power could stem the conflagration, because the utter destruction of the great city was marked in the book of fate. Thus, hundreds who could have rendered the work of the few volunteers far easier and more successful and saved whole districts from ruin, stood with folded arms and watched the deadly progress of the fire.

Her mother, Ursula Sontheil, had been left an orphan, and at fifteen years of age was compelled to beg for her living. One day a handsome young man noticed her sadness and enquired its cause; further meetings followed,

and soon the young girl realised that her love for the
stranger would involve her good name. He thereupon
informed her that he was a spirit and not a mortal man,
and, in recognition of her love, he could endow her with
supernatural powers. It is said that once, being tired of
the neighbours' constant inquisitiveness as to her means
of living, she called the wind to her aid, to bear them to
their own homes. Other instances also led to Ursula
being arrested on a charge of witchcraft, which, however,
she very cleverly disproved.

In 1488 her child was born, and she gave it her own
name of Ursula Sontheil, a child with a marvellous brain
in a misshapen body. Leaving it in charge of the
parish nurse, the elder Ursula sought peace in a convent.
The little Ursula was so unmanageable that as soon as
possible she was sent to school, where the rapidity with
which she imbibed knowledge astonished her teachers.
But when teased and annoyed by her fellow pupils, who
jeered at her deformities, Ursula retaliated so violently
that she was expelled from the school. In her twenty-
fourth year she married Toby Shipton, and was ever
afterwards known as Mother Shipton. Her power of
foretelling the future soon spread, and men and women
came from far and near to secure help and advice on
every matter.

The following is one of her first attempts at prophecy :
" When the English lion shall set his feet on the Gallic
shore, then shall the lilies begin to droop for fear ; there
shall be much weeping and wailing among the ladies of
that country, because the princely eagle shall join with
the lion to tread down all that shall appear in defence of
the lilies ; yet shall they not prevail, because the dull
animal of the North shall put them all to confusion, and,

though it be against his will, yet he shall cause great
shame unto them."

Every word of this was soon verified. For, in 1513
Henry VIII (the British Lion) landed in France. There
was much fear in France, whose national emblem is the
lily, and " much weeping and wailing " among the ladies.
Maximilian of Germany (the princely eagle) joined forces
with Henry, and they gained a complete victory over
the French, in spite of the courageous stand made by the
French cavalry (' the Saggatories '). The English cavalry
(" the dull animal of the North ") won success " against
his will " in this way: as the battle was beginning, the
horse of King Henry, being struck, bolted in the direction of the enemy, and the cavalry, believing that their
King was charging, led an onward rush and overcame the
enemy.

With the exception of her prophecies that the world
would soon come to an end, Mother Shipton's predictions
came true.

> " Great London's triumphant spire
> Shall be consumed by flame of fire.
> The crown then fits the white King's head,
> Who with the lilies soon shall wed ;
> Then shall a peasant's bloody knife
> Deprive a great man of his life."

—this being, of course, the marriage and beheading of
Charles I, who was dressed in white on his wedding day.

> " Over a wild and stormy sea
> Shall a noble sail,
> Who to find will not fail
> A new and fair countrie,
> From whence he will bring
> A herb and a root
> That all men shall suit."

—obviously Sir Walter Raleigh's discovery of tobacco !

" All England's sons that plough the land
  Shall be seen book in hand ;
  Learning shall so ebb and flow,
  The poor shall most learning know."

Tunnels under rivers, carriages without horses, and
many other happenings were foretold by Mother Shipton.
She also predicted rightly the day and exact hour that
she would die. In spite of the general opinion that she
was a witch, the old woman was greatly esteemed by all
who came in touch with her, and her memory is revered
to this day in her native county of Yorkshire.

The 'Clog' (Wood Log) Almanac was in general use long
before printing had been invented, and it was still very
popular in many parts of England up to the start of the
eighteenth century. It was composed of a four-sided
stick, the corners of which stood for the four quarters of
the year, each edge having a notch to denote the conse-
cutive days.

Information from these almanacs was given to the
people by the priests and monks. The 'Clog' was covered
with symbols, each of which denoted the coming festivals,
dates of which could be read by the astronomical signs.
It was a ' Perpetual Calendar,' comprising a lunar cycle
of 235 lunations. The symbols, representing all Church
ceremonials, were duly appropriate—all ceremonies con-
nected with the Blessed Virgin being marked by a heart,
Epiphany (Old Christmas) by a star, St. John the Baptist
by a sword, and so forth. At times agricultural dates
were shown, but the priests did not encourage secular
advice in the ' Clog.'

Edward the Confessor, or 'St. Edward' as he was called
on account of the piety of his life and the miracles performed by his corpse after death, figured on the almanac

in the form of the inverted figure of a knight—which position can only be accounted for by the doubt which existed as to the manner of his death, believed to have been brought about by crucifixion in an inverted position. Some of these quaint Clog Almanacs are still in existence —heirlooms in a few ancient families, or they can be seen in the libraries at Oxford and Cambridge.

Old Moore's Almanac is one of the oldest and most relied on of all English almanacs, and is, in fact, a continuation of the *Vox Stellarum* of Francis Moore (born 1637), which bore the reputation of being the most renowned of all predicting almanacs. It is also a fountain-head of every kind of information as well as a complete farmer's almanac, and gives a full list of all the astrological signs and portents for the month.

Poor Richard's Almanac (1732), of which Dr. Benjamin Franklin was the author, is almost the most celebrated of all American almanacs, and it obtained an enormous following of those whose faith in its predictions was as great (probably sometimes more so) as in their Bible. The interest and esteem in which *Poor Richard's Almanac* was held is the more remarkable owing to the fact that Dr. Franklin did not earn any renown as a scientist until long after he had published his almanac.

Zadkiel's Almanac (1874), compiled by R. C. Smith and James Morrison, is full of general information and predictions of all kinds. Both make much of their verified prophecies of the preceding year—indeed they must all have been verified, seeing that there is never a word of any that failed. The weather for the entire year is also fully set forth in both these almanacs, but the farmer is advised to be heedful always of the sign in which the moon finds itself before deciding when to sow his various crops.   This heed-the-moon instruction is still, to a very large extent, believed in and followed.

Josh Billings' Farmer's Almanac is, more than any other, a calendar of weather 'Prognostics,' some being somewhat of a humorous nature, such as, in the prediction, " Perhaps rain, perhaps not."

Hicks' Almanac was for thirty years universally read and believed in.   This almanac boasted of being constructed on a scientific method of predicting the weather meteorologically, and so completely did it arouse the credulity of its readers, that the government meteorologists were continually pestered by people who could not understand why that body could only issue forecasts of the weather for a day, considering that Hicks was able to make a sure prediction for an entire year.

The World's Encyclopaedia is a formidable volume, containing 850 pages of information and 35 of advertisements ;   invaluable no doubt as a book of reference, but as an almanac it might perhaps suit its purpose better were it confined to the twenty-six pages which is all the space occupied by its calendar and astronomical information.

CHAPTER VI

THE ALCHEMISTS

ALBERTUS MAGNUS, Count of Bollstädt, was born in Swabia in 1193. In his boyhood he entered a Dominican convent, but his brain was so dull, that although he longed for knowledge, he almost gave up the hope of acquiring it. This continued until he was thirty years of age. Then suddenly his mind appeared to expand, and he found himself able to learn anything with consummate ease. This change he attributed to the kind intercession of the Holy Virgin, who, he said, appeared to him and asked him whether he would rather succeed in divinity or philosophy. She was mildly reproachful when he chose the latter, but promised that he should in due course be the ablest philosopher of his age.

Albert studied so assiduously that his fame quickly spread over Europe. But whatever branch of philosophy engaged his attention, he continued his search for the philosopher's stone and the elixir of life. Though neither he nor his assistant Thomas Aquinas ever discovered them, it was asserted that he must have unravelled something of the secret of life, as he and Aquinas were said to have given animation to a brazen statue. It took master and pupil many years of work, under proper conjunction of the planets, to achieve this result ; but when they at last succeeded they found that owing to some little defect in the machinery, the statue was so loquacious, and its chatter so incensed its creators, that Aquinas, infuriated by the continued noise, smashed it to pieces with a huge hammer.[1]

Albertus had the reputation of being able even to change the seasons. At one time he was most anxious to erect a monastery near Cologne, and the plot of land which he desired for the building was owned by the Count of Holland, who could not be induced to part with it. Albertus, however, we are told, did obtain the ground in the following strange manner. Hearing that the Count was passing through Cologne, he invited him and his retinue to a sumptuous entertainment. It was mid-winter, snow and ice covered the outside world. When the Count and his court reached Albertus's house, they found, to their surprise and horror, that the banquet was arranged in the garden, and they wished to remount their horses and depart at once. Albertus, however, begged the Count and his followers to sit at the table, and as soon as they had done so, the clouds passed and the warm sun shone out. A mild breeze taking the place of the biting northern blast, the snow melted, the streams flowed once more, and the green leaves unfolded themselves from the bare trees, flowers bloomed, and birds sang. The Count was so entranced at the transformation that he at once offered the philosopher the coveted ground. As soon as the banquet was concluded, Albertus gave the word— snow again fell, the leaves dropped from the trees, clouds gathered over the sun, and it became mid-winter once more.

When Roger Bacon (born about 1214) had completed his studies at Oxford and became a doctor of divinity, he joined the order of St. Francis as a monk. His erudition

[1] Naudé, *Apologie des Grands Hommes accusés de Magic*, chap. xviii.

was so remarkable that many of his contemporaries could only account for it on the ground that he was possessed of a devil. Bacon was a firm believer in the philosopher's stone, and searched for it assiduously during his entire lifetime. During his researches and experiments, however, he made other valuable discoveries and inventions, notably gunpowder, the magic lantern, the telescope, and burning glasses.

Pope John XXII. (1244–1334) is said to have learnt the hidden secrets of alchemy from Arnold Villeneuve, to whom he was pupil and friend. He carried on the art of transmuting baser metals into gold with such enormous success that he piled up a colossal fortune. He was the author of a famous book on the subject of transmutation, and his laboratory at Avignon was renowned. He took infinite pains not to give away even a breath of his secret, and guarded it just as jealously as every other hermetic philosopher has done through all the ages.

Nicholas Flamel, a native of Pontoise in the fourteenth century, chanced to buy a wonderful old book, in which the text was written upon the barks of trees with some kind of implement of sharp steel. He discovered it to be a comprehensive treatise on the transmutation of metals and the correct seasons for successful experiments. But the one great secret, the prime factor in the work, eluded all his close study. He fancied it must be enshrined in the allegorical pictures which appeared on every third and fourth leaf, and invited all the alchemists and wise men of Paris to discover the mystery.

For twenty-one years Flamel continued his close study of the pictures, then decided to seek further knowledge by travel; so, leaving his treasure-book with his wife, he went to Madrid and Leon. At the latter place he met a physician named Cauches, and to him he described the book. The doctor was ecstatic with joy when he heard its title and nature, and told Flamel that it must have been written by Abraham and handed down from him to Moses, Joshua and Solomon, and that if his surmise were true, it was the most marvellous and precious book in the whole world, and contained all the hidden truths of alchemy as well as of other sciences. Cauches begged to be allowed to return to Paris with his new friend, as he was crazy to verify the book. Unfortunately, he was seized with illness on the journey, and his one sorrow when dying was that he could not see the wonderful volume.

Flamel returned to his home, and for another two years endeavoured to read the pictured secret. At last a ray of light shone through his darkness, which, united to a phrase spoken by the doctor, led him to understand where his experiments had diverged from the right road. With redoubled energy he started again, and in a year's time, by making a projection on mercury, he procured ' very good silver,' and also transmuted a quantity of the same metal into ' gold.' His joy was indescribable; he felt that he did indeed hold the great secret. If this was an actuality, the assertion of his friends that he had also found the *elixir vitae* seemed well founded, for although eighty years of age, Flamel was strong and healthy. He made an immense amount of gold, but lived in a simple way in his former humble lodgings, where an earthern vessel sufficed to contain his meagre meal of porridge. So far as his great secret was concerned, Flamel was as impenetrable as all his famous predecessors in the art had been. He endowed hospitals and churches, built chapels, and died at the age of one hundred and sixteen years.

Cornelius Agrippa (1486–1534) asserted that every spirit of the air, as well as all the demons of the earth, were ruled by him and ready to obey his least command, and that he had the power to transmute metals at his will and merely by a word. His assurance was so vivid that it conveyed itself to the people, who, one and all, wondered at and admired but never doubted his extraordinary gifts. He was held in the highest veneration by all the contemporary great scientists and other learned men, and was the recipient of a succession of honours which fell thickly upon him.

Agrippa described himself as a clever physician, able philosopher, sublime theologist, and a great alchemist. His career, which began so brilliantly, was, however, marred by the defects of his own personality—his presumption, lack of stability, and argumentativeness, amounting to aggressiveness. By these characteristics he turned his friends into enemies, and thus alienated his best and most influential patrons. He brought upon himself much worry and anxiety, and died in a condition of great poverty at the early age of forty-eight. It is chronicled that the gold with which he paid for his wares had a strikingly brilliant colour and lustre, but always turned to lead after twenty-four hours. He is supposed to have made enormous quantities of this false gold with the devil's help, which leads one to the conclusion his satanic majesty was far from being a good alchemist.

Montanus (1488–1523) the German monk, through long solitary meditation, became possessed of strange fancies. At one time he imagined himself to be a grain of wheat, and dreaded that he might be swallowed by birds. It is recorded that Bishop Münster's absent-mindedness was so great that when he saw a notice on the door of his ante-chamber—" The master of the house is out "—he sat down and patiently awaited his own return.

Loyola (1491–1556), after being severely wounded, became impressed with religious fervour, and believed firmly that in all his projects he received the personal help of a virgin, whose heavenly voice urged him to perseverance.

Haller (1492–1536) was fully convinced that he was an object of persecution. He believed that all men, and even God Himself, were against him because of his wickedness and heretical writings, and he lived in a state of abject terror, which would only be calmed by long discourses with priests, and by incessant and heavy doses of opium.

Paracelsus (1493–1561), as he called himself, though his real name was Theophrastus von Hohenheim, asserted that he possessed the wisdom of the world, and that nearly all other physicians both in and out of the universities were merely quacks. If long words and classic utterances are a sign of wisdom, Paracelsus may have had some reason for his boast, for he certainly made continual use of them in his lectures, and, probably because they were too complex to be understood, he was regarded by his hearers as a man of almost superhuman power and intellect, and he gained an extraordinary influence over them. Indeed they believed his assertion that he was the king of medicine. Without going so far as this, however, he may be regarded as a pioneer in new fields of knowledge, and as the first to discover some of the powers in the magnet. He may also be said to have paved the way for the theory of animal magnetism, as it was called more than a century later. Although Paracelsus propounded the existence of magnetic properties in the human body, his system was crude and gross, founded as it was on fanatical mysticism. Dr.

Lawrence [1] writes : " These irregular practitioners, however impetuous and ill-balanced, were pioneers in opening up new fields of knowledge and in exploring new paths, which facilitated the progress of their successors in the search for scientific truths."

It appears as though Paracelsus, in his joy at discovering so much undreamt of power in the magnet, sincerely believed it to be the much talked of, and longed for, philosopher's stone, and though it could not transmute iron into gold it could and did ease human suffering and stem decay. He also believed much in spirits—one of these, which he called Azoth, he kept in a jewel which he named after the spirit. Followers and imitators crowded round him, and hung on his words. He affirmed that he could transplant disease from the body into the ground by the power of his magnet, and that he could cure wounds which had been caused by any metal. This latter idea spread with such amazing rapidity and obtained such credulity, that it was considered possible that the mere magnetising of a sword would heal any hurt which that weapon had inflicted. And in this lies the fundamental idea of the weapon-salve, of which Paracelsus gave the recipe, and which was accredited with some miraculous cures.

If the fame of this clever but boastful physician increased with great rapidity, his ill-fame spread with even greater when it became obvious that sobriety was not his strong point, and that he also indulged freely in the arts of sorcery, boasting of the hosts of spirits who obeyed his will.

Cardan (1501–1576) the great Italian physician, mathematician, and author, who, in addition to many dis-

[1] *Primitive Psycho-Therapy and Quackery*, Appendix.

coveries and achievements, was the founder of a new era in algebra, summed himself up as a " stammerer, impotent, with little memory or knowledge." He refused to include fire among the elements, and looked upon saints and witches as insane. He heard cocks talking to him with human voice ; and saw Tartarus before him full of bones. Any object which passed through his imagination, he fancied he could see in real and solid form. From the age of nineteen to twenty-six a kind of genius watched over him and advised him in all things. He averred it was the same genius which had assisted his father. But even after that age, when deprived of his invisible ally, he still imagined that he received ' help,' as when, having made a mistake over a prescription, the paper on which it was written " rose to his table to warn him of the error he was about to commit " (*De Vita propria*, ch. 45).

Cardan believed himself to be afflicted with every malady and disease possible to humanity ; from which he was cured not with medicine but by a prayer to the Holy Virgin. At times he detected the smell of sulphur or wax in his soup, and saw phantom figures and flames rise from terrific earthquakes. He recounted these to his friends, who, of course, had seen nothing. He also believed himself to be surrounded by enemies, and that he was being persecuted by every government. In his thirty-fourth year, virility came to him in a dream, in consequence of which he married the daughter of a brigand whom until that dream he had never met. In all matters he kept his blind faith in dreams. One day he thought he heard very sweet harmonies in a dream. He awoke and found he had resolved the question of fevers, why some are lethal and others not, a question which had troubled him for twenty-five years. Even his medical consultations were

carried on under their advice and direction. He possessed
so distorted a state of sensibility that, in order to feel at
his ease, it was essential for him to be under the stimulus
of physical pain, and if nature did not provide this, he
bit his arms or finger tips until he drew blood. " I sought
causes of pain," he said, " to enjoy the pleasure of the
cessation of pain, and because I perceived that when I
did not suffer, I fell into so grave and troublesome a
condition that it was worse than any pain."

At one time he was convinced that he had been poisoned
by the professors at the University of Pavia, and that he
owed his escape only to the grace of the Virgin of St.
Martin. He had a son to whom he was passionately
attached, and longed for a grandson who must resemble
him. His son, however, was condemned on a charge of
poisoning, and Cardan, almost distracted with grief,
sought to distract his mind either with gaming or by more
strenuous work—then returned to his old ' safety valve '
of biting or striking himself. But all to no purpose ; he
could find neither distraction nor the peace of sleep.
Feeling that he must either die or go mad, he offered up
a prayer that God might take him away from life. After
this prayer he fell asleep and heard the approach of someone whose face " I could not see, but a voice said : ' Why
grieve about your son ? Put into your mouth the precious
stone which you bear suspended from your neck, and as
long as you carry it there, you will not think of your son.
On waking up, I asked myself what connection there could
be between forgetfulness and an emerald. I put the
emerald into my mouth, and then against all expectation,
everything that recalled my son vanished from my
memory. It was so for a year and a half. It was only
during my meals and at all public lectures, when I was

unable to keep the precious stone in my mouth, that I fell back into the old grief." [1]

Cardan was, in his own estimation, the seventh physician since the world was created, and asserted his full cognisance of all things, both before and above us, as well as those which will follow after. There is no doubt that in spite of all his vagaries, he left the tree of knowledge the richer; in some of his remarkable discoveries he anticipated the work of Rénan and Dupuis. He predicted the day and hour of his death, and it has been suggested, though there is no foundation for the suggestion, that he even forestalled it so that there should be no doubt about his horoscope.

Dr. Dee (1527–1608) was from boyhood extraordinarily studious, and only happy among his books. Indeed he allowed himself but little time away from them, never giving himself more than four hours for sleep and but scanty times for meals. And his intellectual power being commensurate with his capacity for study, he quickly rose to the front rank as mathematician and philosopher. But to the disappointment of the University and his College at Cambridge, and to the disgust of the town authorities, Dee soon threw himself heart and soul into the study of the occult, and commenced to practise astrology, alchemy, and magic.

Whispers quickly went round in which sorcery and his name were linked together, and as at the time sorcerers received short shrift, Dr. Dee deemed it advisable to leave England for a time, and went to France. He received a warm, eager welcome at the University of Louvain, and

[1] Jewels in sleep are symbolical of sons, also of messages of joy : in Italian ' Gioire ' means ' to enjoy.' Cardan had, as is evidenced in many of his works, a rooted belief in the virtue of precious stones. *De Somnis*, p. 338.

there pursued his search for the philosopher's stone. After a few years he returned to his own country, where the kind influence of a friend procured for him a gracious introduction to the Court of Edward VI. He remained in London, casting horoscopes, telling fortunes, advising, in his astrological capacity, as to lucky numbers, lucky days, etc.

Dee miraculously managed to exonerate himself from a charge of sorcery, and just escaped being burnt at Smithfield. He was received with much favour by Elizabeth on her accession to the throne. She frequently sent her courtiers and retainers to consult him upon her affairs. On one occasion her spokesman was Robert Dudley, Earl of Leicester, and she went once in person to consult him at his house at Mortlake.

But whilst Dee practised fortune-telling and astrology in order to ensure himself a livelihood, all his interest was fixed on alchemy—the discovery of the philosopher's stone and the elixir of life. He persuaded himself so entirely into the belief that, as a great alchemist, he would be able to hold intercourse with angels, that he at last truly believed that one of these angels had deigned to appear and had assured him of his friendship and help through life. Dee tells us that " one day when engaged in fervent prayer, the window of his museum suddenly glowed with a dazzling light, in the midst of which, in all his glory, stood the great angel, Uriel. Awe and wonder rendered him speechless, but the angel, smiling graciously upon him, gave him a crystal, and told him that whenever he wished to hold converse with the beings of another sphere, he had only to gaze intently upon it, and they would appear in the crystal, and unveil to him all the secrets of futurity.

Dr. Dee took the crystal, but in order to procure the appearance of the spirits, he found it essential to devote all his powers of concentration to such an extent that he was never able to remember the words and messages which they had given him, and for this reason it occurred to him to admit a third person into his great secret, so that he might write down all the spirit's sayings which this other person drew from them in conversation. Dee chose as assistant Edmund Kelly, who was also imbued with a great longing for the mysteries of alchemy, though he possessed none of the genuine earnestness of his master and only desired knowledge, or the pretensions thereof, for the purpose of amassing money, no matter how fraudulently. Kelly's previous life would not by any means bear inspection, and even Dee was entirely ignorant of the fact that the oracularly solemn skull-cap which completely covered his head and reached to his cheeks, was worn solely to conceal the fact that its owner had lost both ears—a punishment for forgery in earlier days.

The suggestion that he should consult the spirits by means of the crystal exactly fitted in with Kelly's deeply laid plans. Rumours of the marvellous happenings in Dee's museum at Mortlake soon flashed from one end of the kingdom to the other, and even spread abroad, and moreover he let it be known that the secret of the *elixir vitae* was in his possession. Ignoring and forsaking astrologers whom they had hitherto consulted, crowds came from near and remote parts to take advice and ask help from the famous Dr. Dee. He might have been an exceedingly rich man, had he not spent so much money on his transmutation experiments. These were so costly that he was in constant need of money, and when the Count Palatine of Siradz, Albert Laski, came to England

and sought him out, Dee was soon persuaded by Kelly to make of this stranger a source of revenue—an easy task since Laski was himself an alchemic enthusiast. He begged to be admitted to their angelic conferences, but permission was not at once granted. Dr. Dee said he doubted whether the presence of a third person might not be inimical to the spiritual revelations ; but, after making the Count's eagerness the keener for the hesitation, he was at last given entrance into the ' holy of holies.' The spirits, according to the interpretation of Kelly, looked with much favour on Count Palatine, and predicted that for him were reserved the honour and glory of the discovery of the philosopher's stone, that he would in due course ascend the throne of Poland, and by his magnificent victories over the Saracens, that he would be renowned throughout the entire universe ; also that his life would be prolonged through centuries. The only stipulation the angels made, said Kelly, was that Laski must take him and Dr. Dee and their wives and families back with him to Poland and treat them *en prince*.

Laski readily agreed to do this, and after a long journey the party arrived at Cracow, where the Count's estates were situated. In the gorgeous palace, Dee lost no time in renewing his experiments, helped by the Count's money as well as by his knowledge of alchemy ; but the philosopher's stone seemed as far off as ever. Laski, however, continued to pour out money, owing to his firm belief in the power of transmutation ; but the only thing transmuted was the Count's personal property, which speedily diminished to such an extent that he became compelled to sell part of his heavily-mortgaged acres, and even continued in his blinkered dream to find money for Dee's crucible, until he found himself face to face with ruin.

Then he woke up and decided to free himself from his costly guests, and in order to avoid any unpleasantness, he gave them letters of recommendation to the Emperor Rudolf at Prague.

Thither the accomplices journeyed, realising that they could make nothing more out of Count Palatine. The Emperor Rudolf was not unwilling to attach some credence to the visionary idea of the philosopher's stone, but the Pope's nuncio happened to get wind of the scheme, and warned the Emperor against encouraging the ' heretic magicians,' who were thus compelled to make a hurried departure.

With Count Rosenberg of Bohemia, Dee and Kelly found a luxurious abiding-place for four years, the Count being greatly interested in alchemy, and eagerly following all their work. It was at this time that Kelly, who had always been jealous of the greater respect and attention bestowed on Dee, became more actively inimical to his former master, and let fall threats of leaving him. The doctor, immersed in his one chimerical thought of trans-mutation, had become as wax in Kelly's hands, and was panic stricken at the mere thought of being left alone without his spirit-medium and fellow worker. But Kelly was merely playing a deep game, its object being no less than the possession of Dee's wife. His own spouse was bad-tempered and plain of face, whereas the doctor's lady was attractive and charming, and he had formed a plan whereby it would be possible to attain his desire even without hurting Dee's moral sense or arousing his jealousy. He appeared to be almost horrified when next communing with the spirits, and even told the doctor that he could not bring himself to repeat their words. At last, after much apparent unwillingness and Dee's firm insistence, he yielded and told him it was the spirit's wish that he and the doctor should have their wives between them ; he asserted that the suggestion had so shocked him that he had even asked if there could be no compromise, or if a general and true friendship would not suffice. But to this the spirits had replied that nothing except the liberal interpretation would satisfy them.

Kelly, however, was far too clever to appear to jump at the project, so he told Dee that only evil spirits could so decide, that the idea was impossible to him, and with that he took his departure. But not for long ; he left Dee just long enough for him to suffer much anxiety and distress as to whom he could secure in Kelly's stead for the spiritual conferences, he even attempted to get his boy of eight to fill the breach. The child, however, only strained his eyes, till he burst out crying, and said he could " see nothing."

Kelly, who had never gone far away, waited his opportunity, and came back and began to confer once more with the unseen world. The project, referring to the ' wives in common,' was repeated ; but this time it came as a command. Kelly threw out his hands to Dee in a well-feigned semblance of forced obedience to higher orders, and the doctor, in a tumult of joy at the return of his fellow worker which would enable his work to continue unbrokenly, consented humbly to the matrimonial mix-up. The unusual *ménage* continued for some months, but Kelly's naturally quarrelsome nature re-asserted itself, and a final separation was the result. Dee never saw his former pupil again, for Kelly foolishly went back to Prague, where he was arrested as a sorcerer, and in attempting to escape from prison he was killed.

When he returned to England, Dr. Dee was welcomed with much kindness by Queen Elizabeth, but she did not offer him the pecuniary help of which he was sorely in need. Her Majesty probably thought that a man who boasted the power of turning iron into gold could never be in need of money. She, however, secured him a post, and he worked untiringly among his furnaces ; but his crystal had lost its value, the spirits would not answer to his call. The scanty emoluments of his post were soon burned away in his crucibles, and the once famous Dr. Dee died in poverty.

During these times men of all ranks, character, and nationality had become smitten with the alchemist mania, the great goal being the finding of the philosopher's stone and the *elixir vitae*. Many of the philosophers who spent their lives searching for this will-o'-the-wisp believed firmly in its existence ; many, on the other hand, were charlatans who merely traded on the credulity of their fellow-creatures in order to fill their own pockets. Each, in his turn, had evolved a different theory and a different way of working, which he believed would succeed where others had failed. The science of chemistry owes a great debt of gratitude to the many valuable discoveries which have resulted from that prolonged search for the un-attainable. In Europe, nowadays, we seldom hear of the study of alchemy, though occasional mention is made of one of its devotees. It is hardly likely that anyone now-adays would even consider the idea of transmuting iron into gold, but enthusiasts still seek an elixir capable of endowing centuries of life. In the East, however, in China, Persia, Egypt, Arabia, and parts of India, the art of alchemy is still much practised.

Sir Kenelm Digby (1603–1665) gave up much of his life to the study of alchemy, and was an ardent believer in all the wildest fantasies of that science. Apart from this belief, which was sincere, he was one of the ablest scholars of his time. Digby was a close student of the methods of the famous alchemists who had preceded him, and, having read that Villeneuve prescribed a meal of capons fed on vipers for the preservation of life and beauty, he gave his wife this dish, so that her loveliness should not wither for a hundred years.

He became a strong supporter of the ' weapon-salve ' theory, and performed cures, sometimes without even seeing the sufferer. On one occasion Digby asked a patient, who came to him suffering from a sword-cut, whether he would consent to be treated in this way, and, to use Sir Kenelm's own words, the man's reply was, " The many wonderful things which people have related unto me of your way of achievements, make me nothing doubt at all for its efficacy, and all I have to say unto you is— let the miracle be done, though Mahomet do it.' I asked him for anything that had blood upon it, so he presently sent for his garter wherewith his wound was first bound, and I called for a basin of water. . . . I took a handful of powder of vitriol . . . and presently dissolved it. As soon as the bloody garter was brought me I put it into the basin, observing in the interim what Mr. Howell did, who stood talking to a gentleman in a corner of my chamber, not regarding at all what I was doing. He started suddenly as if he had found some strange altera- tion in himself—I asked him what he ailed. ' I know not what ails me, but I feel no more pain. Methinks that a pleasing kind of freshness, as if it were a wet, cold napkin, did spread over my hand, which hath taken away the inflammation that tormented me before.' I replied, ' Since you feel already so much good of my medicament, I advise you to cast away all plasters, only keep the wound clean and in a moderate temperature betwixt heat and cold.' After dinner I took the garter out of the water, and put it to dry before a great fire. It was scarce dry before Mr. Howell's servant came running, and saying that his master felt as much burning as ever he had done, if not more, for the heat was such as if his hand were betwixt coals of fire. I answered that although that had happened at present, yet he should find ease in a short time, for I knew the reason of his new accident and would provide accordingly. . . . Thereupon he went, and at the instant I did put the garter again into the water, thereupon he found his master without any pain at all. To be brief, there was no sense of pain afterwards, but within five or six days the wounds were cicatrised and entirely healed."

Pretensions to this mode of cure were made by many practitioners of Sir Kenelm's time and after, some of whom thought it was not essential to use the weapon-salve, nor even the powder of sympathy, to ensure successful treatment. They merely magnetised the sword with their hand in order to remove whatever suffering that sword had brought about. But the movement of their fingers on the weapon had to be upwards, then the injured man would be relieved at once, whereas a downward movement would cause him intense pain.

Joseph Francis Borri (1616–1695) was one of the chief members of the Rosicrucian Brotherhood, a fraternity of visionaries which is said to have been founded in the fifteenth century by a German philosopher named Christian Rosenkreutz, who, when seriously ill in the East, was cured by a party of Arabs through the instrumentality of the philosopher's stone, in all the mysteries of which they inspired and instructed him.

When Rosenkreutz returned to his own country, he

trained a few of his great friends in the science he had just learnt, making each man swear not to divulge the secret for one hundred years.   There exists some doubt as to the veracity of this, but if it be true, it quite accounts for the fact that the Rosicrucian Brotherhood did not come into any prominence until 1605, when their doctrines were spread far and wide by means of placards affixed to the walls of the towns.   It was not long before a large number of alchemists and philosophical dreamers joined the fraternity.

The creed and the declarations of the Rosicrucians were extraordinary beyond words.   They affirmed that " the meditation of their founders surpassed everything that had ever been imagined since the creation of the world, without even excepting the revelations of the Deity—that they were destined to accomplish the general peace and regeneration of man before the end of the world arrived . . . that they possessed all wisdom and piety . . . all the graces of nature, and could distribute them among the rest of mankind according to their pleasure ; that they were subject neither to hunger nor thirst, nor disease, nor old age . . . that they had a volume in which they could read all that ever was or ever could be written in other books till the end of time ; that they could force to, and retain in, their service the most powerful spirits and demons ; that by virtue of their songs they could attract pearls and precious stones from the depths of the sea or the bowels of the earth ; that God had covered them with a thick cloud, by means of which they could shelter themselves from malignity of their enemies ; that they could thus render themselves invisible from all eyes ; that the first eight brethren of the ' Rose Cross ' had the power to cure all maladies," etc.

These visionary enthusiasts gathered round them large numbers of followers throughout Germany and in Paris. Their books had an enormous sale—in these they proclaimed that the brothers had no recourse to the help of magic, and no dealings with the devil, that they had found happiness, had already been on earth for over a hundred years and would go on living for several more centuries.   They further declared that all human creatures were surrounded with " myriads of beautiful and beneficent beings, all anxious to do them service."

It is remarkable how well the Rosicrucians kept their identity veiled in mystery—nobody, to their knowledge, had ever seen a member, nor did anyone know even the meeting places of the fraternity.   Although the doctrines never gained a vast number of adherents in France, the brotherhood had a good muster in England and other countries and thousands of followers in Germany, and even at the end of the seventeenth century the Rosicrucians still flourished, but their ideas and tenets had become much more modified and less fantastic.

But to return to Joseph Francis Borri, whose life was later on so much influenced by his connection with this fanatical sect.   He commenced his studies in the Jesuit College at Rome, and had such a remarkable memory that learning came to him easily.   But his love of excitement and his uncontrolled temper made him continually at loggerheads with his precepts and with the police.   As soon, however, as he left college, he commenced his career as a physician, but after a short time turned his attention to alchemy, which had such an attraction for him that he resolved to search for the philosopher's stone.   He did not, however, change his mode of life, was constantly implicated in vulgar street brawls, and consorted always with gamblers and bad characters of both sexes until he reached the age of thirty-nine. Then, with inexplicable suddenness, Borri appeared to have become a changed man. No longer a debauchee and a scoffer, he wore the manners of a philosopher and allowed it to be understood that his altered demeanour was the result of a higher agency. He gave out that beneficent spirits had become his friends and companions, and that they disclosed to him the mysteries of nature and even the secrets of Heaven. Followers gathered eagerly round him in large numbers and gladly took the oath of poverty which his 'new communion' exacted; they also gave up all their worldly goods to Borri for the benefit of the great fraternity.

"Whoever shall refuse," he said, "to enter into my sheepfold, shall be destroyed by the papal armies of whom God has predestined me to be the chief. To those who follow me all joy shall be granted. I shall soon bring my chemical studies to a happy conclusion by the discovery of the philosopher's stone, and by this means we shall have as much gold as we desire. The sylphs and elementary spirits fly to the uttermost ends of the world to obey me and those whom I delight to honour."

Borri also asserted that the Archangel Michael had presented him with a heavenly sword. Finding such a large army of followers gathering round him, he became possessed of the belief that he would eventually become a second Mahomet and inaugurate a new era, a new faith, and a monarchy, with himself as prophet and king. So obsessed was he with this idea that he actually formed a project to seize the town, by taking the guards prisoners, and to them proclaim himself the ruler and king.

But his project was discovered, and several of his adherents were arrested. Borri himself escaped, and, after a short stay in Switzerland and Strasbourg, journeyed to Amsterdam, where he presented himself with the title of Excellency, and commenced to live in a style of much grandeur, probably aided in this by the funds handed to him by his wealthy disciples of Milan. He soon became famous, as much for his marvellous cures as for his splendour of living; but his continuous alchemic experiments were so costly, that, after having reduced his living expenses to a minimum, he found himself compelled to quit the Dutch capital under cover of night, taking with him some diamonds which had been brought to him because he averred he could remove the flaws that were in them.

At Copenhagen, Borri found that Frederick III was an enthusiast in the transmutation of metals, and easily prevailed upon him to give him money to continue his work. He also became physician to the King, and for six years remained at the Danish Court; but the end of that time found him no nearer to the philosopher's stone. Borri then conceived the idea of going to Turkey and becoming a Mussalman, but was arrested on his journey and charged with being implicated in a recently discovered conspiracy. He gave his real name to the authorities and vowed he was innocent, but he was nevertheless taken to Rome and incarcerated, by the Pope's order, in the prison of the Inquisition and condemned to lifelong imprisonment. He would indeed have been put to death had he not made " a public recantation of his heresies."

In his old age Borri's sentence was lightened; he was given a laboratory, where he recommenced his futile experiments, and where he was often visited by Christina, the ex-Queen of Sweden, who talked with him of chemistry and alchemy and of the tenets of the Rosicrucians, she herself being an ardent believer in the existence of the philosopher's stone.

Cagliostro (1743–1790), whose true name was Joseph Balsamo, was sent to study in a monastery at the age of fifteen, but, being of an indolent disposition and the possessor of ungovernable passions, he made little or no progress. After some years in the monastery, where he was looked upon as too dissipated to make use of the natural talents he undoubtedly possessed, he joined the well-known fraternity which, in France and Italy, bears the name of ' Knights of Industry,' and in England, 'The Swell Mob.' Balsamo often found himself in prison for theft, for counterfeit, and for various other crimes. People came to look upon him as a sorcerer, whose soul had been bought by the devil, because he had found the secret for supplying himself with gold by means of transmutation. And once this belief had gained ground, Balsamo, or Cagliostro, as he preferred to call himself, encouraged it by every means in his power, and continued his depredations under cover of his supposed power of magic.

To escape being called to account for these, he went to Medina, and there won the friendship of a Greek scholar named Altotas, an ardent alchemist and a man who understood the languages of the East. For a short time Cagliostro worked as his assistant, but speedily made himself his partner, and persuaded the old man to turn some of his valuable discoveries to profit. One of these, upon which Altotas had stumbled quite accidentally when experimenting in chemicals, was a substance which, used with flax, gave to it all the softness and glimmer of silk. By the sale of this ingredient, the Greek and Cagliostro profited exceedingly in Alexandria and other Egyptian towns, then went to Turkey.

Returning thence, stormy weather drove the two men into Malta, where the Grand Master of the Knights, who was himself a great alchemist, invited them to use his laboratory for their experiments in transmutation. The three worked together for some months, but Cagliostro, who possessed none of the earnest faith of Altotas and the Grand Knight, secured from the latter some letters of introduction to influential people in Rome and Naples, and, armed with these, he left the other two to continue their search.

During his travels he had not only completely dropped the name of Balsamo, but had taken several other names whenever his questionable actions made it advisable for him to disappear. He called himself Count de Cagliostro when he arrived in Rome, declared that he possessed the secret of transmuting all metals into gold, and affirmed that he had been chosen to restore Rosicrucian philosophy. He also said that he had the power to make himself completely invisible, to cure any and every disease, and that he had discovered the elixir of life.

The Count's faith in himself quickly attracted the faith of others, and he was soon besieged by patients, on whom he performed very many ' miraculous cures.' He wooed, and soon won, the beautiful Lorenza Feliciana, a highly born but fortuneless lady, whose charm Cagliostro felt sure he could turn to good account, all the more so because Lorenza was utterly unprincipled and possessed of a fund of imagination.

' The Countess ' speedily grasped all the secrets of her husband's ' business,' and learnt to call up angels and genii, sylphs, or demons, as might be required. The

' Count and Countess ' visited all the chief cities of Europe, selling their elixir, and telling fortunes. So successful were they that they brought with them to London a considerable amount of valuable property in jewels, plate, etc.

The ' Count ' now engaged a Portuguese lady as his interpreter, who soon spread reports of his marvellous power. Vitellini, a gambling teacher of languages, soon replaced the Portuguese lady, and he, on becoming convinced that the ' Count ' had indeed discovered the great mystery, praised his powers publicly and with more forcefulness than she had done. He declared that the ' Count ' was a marvel and a perfect adept, that he could make of lead, iron, or copper, as much gold as he wished, and that he possessed, in consequence, a stupendous fortune.

As a result the ' Count's ' consulting rooms were invariably crowded ; but he, in his turn, became for a time the dupe of a swindling gang, headed by a man named Scot—Lord Scot—who, under pretence of expecting a large legacy, borrowed a large sum of money from the ' Count,' whilst consulting him and his ' Countess ' on lucky days, numbers, etc., which he predicted with unfailing success. Scot believed implicitly in the ' Count's ' occult powers, and he and a female accomplice gave the ' Countess ' valuable presents, bought with the money Cagliostro had lent him. When, however, the ' Count ' discovered Scot to be an impostor and ordered him out of his house, Scot turned the tables on him by getting him arrested for a debt which he swore that the ' Count ' owed to him, and also preferred against him and the ' Countess ' an accusation of sorcery.

When Cagliostro was remanded on bail, after many weeks in prison, Scot, accompanied by an attorney, broke into his laboratory, holding in his hand a loaded pistol and vowing to kill him if he did not explain to him his method of transmuting metals and prophesying lucky numbers.

During Cagliostro's imprisonment, he was robbed of many manuscripts and a box of powder, with which Scot had hoped to discover the great secrets himself. The ' Count ' reminded him of this, but promised to forego all the money of which he had been swindled if Scot would return the manuscripts and powder. Scot and his friend the attorney angrily rejected the offer, and swore to be revenged. They then instituted a further action against the ' Count and Countess ' for the return of the presents they had given to her, which they affirmed had been stolen. Cagliostro made a long speech in his defence, but although he was innocent of the present charges against him, and indeed much injured and persecuted by Scot, the story of his life as set forth in his defence was so wildly and obviously a fabrication that it told rather against him than in his favour, and during the trial he was unlucky enough to be recognised by someone in the court as the iniquitous Joseph Balsamo of earlier days. This last fact showed him the advisability of leaving England in all haste, even after he had been declared not guilty of Scot's accusations. He and his wife went hurriedly to Brussels, with scarcely anything remaining to them of the wealth they had brought to England, but by selling enormous quantities of the *elixir vitae* in Belgium, Russia, and Germany, they soon again amassed a lot of money.

At Strasbourg, a great reception awaited the ' Count and Countess.' Cagliostro became again noted for his wonderful cures and marvellous predictions, as well as for his kindness to the poor, to whom he gave free treatment, as well as monetary help. The ' Countess ' added to their joint fame by speaking of her eldest son, who, she said, was a naval captain and twenty-eight years of age—she herself being at the time twenty-five ! This, of course, brought all the women, young and old, to their consulting rooms, to buy the wonderful essence which could make the ' Countess ' look like a lovely young girl and yet be the mother of a son of twenty-eight. Men also thronged to the rooms, but it is probable that the wonderful beauty and glorious eyes of ' Countess ' Cagliostro drew them even more than the mystical powers she was believed to possess. In Strasbourg the Cardinal de Rohan, who was on a visit there, became much interested in the ' Count ' and urged him to travel with him to Paris.

Shortly after his return, Cagliostro's success and popularity commenced to decline—he had remained too long. The people had begun to realise that the elixir did not keep death away, nor decay, nor old age, so they called him a devil in human form, the anti-Christ, the man of fourteen hundred years. At Bordeaux—their next resting place—history repeated itself. At first a tremendous sensation and success, which speedily faded out. Next they wended their way to Paris, where the Cardinal de Rohan introduced the ' Count and Countess ' to all his highly born friends.

Upon all the most learned men of the time Cagliostro made a deep impression ; he was believed to be the most wonderful magician of his or any day. This is perhaps hardly to be wondered at, since the ' Count ' declared that, like the Rosicrucians, he could at will hold converse with any of the elementary spirits, call from their graves the mighty dead, and transmute all the baser metals into gold. Lucretius, Alexander, Hannibal, Cæsar, Socrates, and many other great spirits were thus brought into communion with those who craved a word with them. Sometimes the charge for these visitations rather startled Cagliostro's patrons, but, as he said, " such spirits could not rise for nothing ! "

But Paris was Cagliostro's undoing. When the trouble arose about the valuable necklace of which, through the intervention of Madame de la Motte, the Cardinal de Rohan desired the Queen Marie Antoinette to become possessed, Madame de la Motte and he were arrested. The latter affirmed that she had given the necklace to the ' Count' and his wife, and that it was Cagliostro who had planned the Cardinal's ruin and forced her to fall in with his vile plan by casting his evil spells over her mind, and accused the ' Count' of being a sorcerer as well as a thief. The four persons accused of obtaining the necklace by a forged signature from Marie Antoinette lingered in prison for six months and were then brought to trial, Cagliostro being the first to be tried. He absolutely denied ever having had or ever seen the necklace ; but the over wordy story he told in his defence convinced his hearers that he was an impudent charlatan, although guiltless of the present charge against him. Cardinal de Rohan and he were both acquitted, it being proved that Madame de la Motte had invented the vile conspiracy against them both. She paid the penalty, and was publicly whipped as well as being branded on the back with a red hot iron. When the ' Count and Countess ' came back to their apartment after being liberated from the Bastille, they found many papers and a great deal of their property had been removed. They tried to recover the missing articles, but on receiving orders that they must leave Paris within twenty-four hours, Cagliostro and his wife departed hurriedly, impelled by their recent associations with the Bastille, which, if repeated, might end yet more hazardously.

Returning to Italy, the ' Count and Countess ' were suddenly arrested by order of the Government. He was charged with being a heretic, a sorcerer, and a freemason, and he and his wife were sentenced to death. The sentence was wholly unjustifiable, and, in the case of Cagliostro, was commuted to lifelong imprisonment. The ' Countess ' was permitted to seek seclusion in a convent and thus escape the more severe penalty. Cagliostro's vicissitudes, however, had told considerably upon his health and spirits, and death soon released him from his captivity.

CHAPTER VII

BEDLAM

ONE year after Pope Innocent IV had met Louis to have a little talk (the First Parliament) it was deemed advisable and even necessary to provide shelter and a safe retreat for the poor, the stranger, and the pilgrim, and to afford succour to all Christians in any other affliction. The Pope, who was in exile at Lyons, gave Geoffrey, bishop-elect of Bethlehem, a special circular letter to found an institution which has since come to be known as ' Bedlam.'

Three years later (1247) Bedlam [1] was founded in spite of national resentment, and it is recorded that when the proctor of the bishop-elect of Bethlehem called to collect the emoluments of Long Itchington he received not only a good beating, and fracture of two of his ribs, but also his horse's tail was cut off, and both servant and horse were tied to a stall. The circular letter of appeal of Innocent IV was responded to with reverence by Simon FitzMary, alderman of the City of London, who made a deed of gift whereby Bedlam was founded.

Previous to this there had existed many colonies of Bethlemites in Europe. There are records of Bethlemite hospitallers in Padua in 1186 and at Pavia in 1210, whilst in 1227 there were eight hospitals and seventy churches served by Bethlemites. As early as the time of Jerome

[1] E. G. O'Donoghue, *The Story of Bethlehem Hospital.*

148

(384-420) St. Paula built a hostelry for pilgrims close to the basilica of Bethlehem, and, according to O'Donoghue, the order of the 'hospitallers' existed throughout the Middle Ages, Bedlam itself being founded for the entertainment of the sick and poor. Simon FitzMary probably thought more of the salvability of his soul than of conferring protection for the afflicted in mind. In those times the classes consisted of wealthy aristocratic burghers, whilst the masses were traders and artisans. One of FitzMary's friends, Osbert, rector of St. Mary Bothaw (on the site of which Cannon Street Station now stands), witnessed the donation in 1248. It is on record that a member of the FitzOsbert family was hanged at Smithfield as a martyr of public rights in 1196. The people held him to be a saint, and subsequent miracles of healing by contact with his chains and clothes were said to have occurred.

John of Gaddesden (1320), the Court Physician of Edward II, used to wrap small-pox cases in red to prevent any marks of it from remaining. He prescribed pounded beetles for the stone, the heads of seven fat bats for diseases of the spleen, a magic necklace for epilepsy, and brandy for palsy of the tongue. As a 'ladies' doctor' he ingratiated himself by divulging the secret of a new perfume and hairwash. In 1337, John Arderne, the famous surgeon, said he was able to extract gold from quartz, and, whilst compounding his remedies, used to repeat psalms or paternosters. In 1377 William Langland (Long Wille) wrote the vision concerning Piers the Plowman, who used to wander along the roads with Tom o' Bedlam, and who when his mind was unbalanced, refused to make obeisance to ecclesiastics, which so upset his ' Wyffe Kytte ' that she sometimes " wished he were in heaven."

' Long Wille ' wrote of wandering lunatics : " They care not for cold, and they reck not of heat ; they carry no money, nor even bags to beg with ; and they salute no man by the way, reverencing not even a mayor more than another. They are all more or less mad according to the age of the moon. But surely they walk the roads in the spirit and guise of the apostle and disciples of Christ. Does not the Holy Book teach us that we ought to receive into our houses the poor and the wanderer ? Ye rich are ready to entertain fools and minstrels, and to put up with all they say. Much more should ye welcome and help lunatic lollers, who are God's minstrels and merry-mouthed jesters. Under his secret seal their sins are covered." To what extent these pathetic remarks apply to the present day it is for the sympathetic reader to consider. In Morocco and other Mohammedan countries there prevails a spirit of sympathy and toleration towards the mentally perverted who are regarded as inspired, or under the special protection of Allah.

Referring to conditions within Bedlam about this time, O'Donoghue conjectures that the patients would be suffering, for the most part, from acute mania, and their treatment would be drastic. "Some of them, however, would be termed, in the scientific language of the modern text-book, cases of hallucination, whether of sight or hearing." The monastic annals furnish us with many illustrations of these and other forms of insanity. O'Donoghue also suggests that Matilda of Cologne would find her place in a refractory ward to-day. Her language was foul, she tore her clothes to pieces, and struck at everyone who tried to remove her. She had to be tightly trussed, and, thus bound, she raved on for four or five hours. By degrees she came to herself, and said that she had seen in a dream the " Martyr clothed in pontifical vestments with the blood streak across her face."

" The treatment of patients in the Middle Ages," says O'Donoghue, " was not quite as absurd or inhuman as it may appear at first sight. The ducking of maniacs, their confinement in a church all night, and the use of ligatures and whips were calculated to exhaust their fury, and to instil into them that sense of terror which tames a wild beast." In the days of ' The Canterbury Tales ' wandering friars and physicians alike used to purge the ' possessed ' of their black bile by natural means, or the unfortunate sufferer had the devil cast out of him by being held over pans of smoking brimstone, until he had vomited up the ' evil spirit '—or the bile. Such fumigations are referred to by Shakespeare and Bunyan.

At a mediæval aldermanic dinner (1346), with music and dancing between each course, the Mayor of London, Richard Lacer, took for a toast : " May the order of the Blessed Mary of Bethlehem, which was the first order of the Church Catholic created next after the order of Christ and His apostles, and descends, as originally created, directly from that order, for ever flourish by means of this house among all the orders of the Church Catholic, and may it fulfil the aims and objects for which it was at first introduced and instituted from such ancient times by so many holy men and for such holy ends."

The chronicler (O'Donoghue) suggests that as the loving cup passed round from mayor to master, and from monk to citizen, the men who wore on their capes and mantles the red star of Bethlehem, with its centre of azure blue, were vouchsafed a vision of the days to be. That these visions have been realised through the centuries of evolution of methods of care and treatment of the mentally afflicted is beyond dispute, and Bedlam has served as a haven of refuge and rest for thousands who have been unable to battle against the agencies of the outside world.

During the reign of Henry VIII, Sir Henry More (*circ.* 1522) alluded to the madness of sin. O'Donoghue has found evidence for the belief that the ' scourge,' ' wire,' or whip was in daily use in Bethlem about the time of the renaissance of the learning brought about by the importation of Italian books and manuscripts. These methods of treatment were used to instil fear in the minds of the afflicted. O'Donoghue suggests that as whipping was the universal punishment and panacea for mischievous conduct or for offensive speeches, no doubt More had often seen chastisement administered as a sort of medicine—the dose to be repeated as often as necessary. One man who was habitually guilty of very disgusting behaviour in various churches was bound to a tree and constables striped him with rods till they waxed weary. The treatment was in this instance successful, and O'Donoghue suggests that there is perhaps more virtue in the medicine of the ' cat ' than we imagine. The loosening of the bonds of control may be arrested in some cases by such drastic treatment, but, unfortunately a flogging for the horse which has escaped control is foolish, whereas an adequate punishment for the factor or factors which left the stable-door open is reasonable. So it is with regard to many of the ill-results accruing from outside influences on thought and conduct, and but seldom is a corrective administered to the main factors of causation.

Skelton said of Wolsey :

> " Such a mad bedleme
> For to rule this realm."

In *The Hyeway to the Spyttel House*, R. Copeland (1536) wrote that the only thing which stands between nagging wives and an attack of madness is the chance of getting a bed at St. Bartholomew's Hospital.

> " We have chambers purposely for them,
>   Or else they should be lodged in Bedlem."

It is recorded that George Boleyn, Viscount Rochford, brother to Anne Boleyn, was the governor of Bethlem from 1529 until he was beheaded in 1536. His body, together with that of his sister, Queen Anne, remained beneath the chancel of St. Peter's church within the Tower until they were exhumed and examined by permission of Queen Victoria.

In 1561 one of the Egertons of Cheshire, found wandering with beggars and drunkards, was probably " Whipped from tithing to tithing ; " but he preferred the open road to the chain and iron collar in castle or court house. In some districts a Tom o' Bedlam was made to stand with his back to a river, then he was knocked backwards into it, and ducked, until exhaustion had taken all the fighting and violence out of him.

In 1574 a man was charged with sending his wife to Bethlem without cause, her defence being that for six weeks previous to her committal she had been tied down in bed by her husband and another till she was " well-nigh famished." O'Donoghue refers to another case in which the Wisdom of Solomon was eclipsed : " As she seemed to be mad " she was first whipped, and then sent to Bedlam.

In 1538 Bethlem was pillaged by Henry VIII " from the highest of motives," and under the guise of diplomacy. Henry accused the citizens with being ' pynche-pence ' (stingy) on the question of ransom, and it was not until

March 1547, some seventeen days before he died, that the charter of the Hospital's second foundation was ratified. Another historical coincidence is to be found in the records of the ' Chequer ' inn in the neighbourhood of Bedlam, then situate in Trafalgar Square and in close proximity to the sites of the National Gallery, the Union Club, and Royal College of Physicians.

In 1543, grave complaints were made by convocation against the " ungodly solemnisation of marriages of the sane in the hospitals of Bethlehem," and, in view of the present-day practice of solemnising marriages of the biologically unfit, it gives one furiously to think as to how far the Church and Bedlam have interchanged their relative functions as custodians of principles of eugenics.

In the sixteenth century, Shakespeare possibly obtained much of his knowledge of mental disease from Dr. Timothy Bright, who wrote a book on *Melancholy* in 1586 ; and O'Donoghue suggests that Shakespeare's knowledge may have been enhanced by clinical demonstrations at Bethlem. Shakespeare refers in *King Lear* to a religious maniac who was " bound on wheels of fire." Another is " led by the foul fiend through fire and flame, over bog and quagmire," and Flibbertigibbet "mops and mows at him." "He has delusions of persecution, and every man seems his enemy." O'Donoghue suggests that Shakespeare scientifically isolated in a group those who have lost all the sensibilities of humanity. They "eat the swimming frog, the tadpole, mice, and rats "—not to mention more loathsome carrion—and they " drink the green mantle of the standing pool," and so dead to pain were they that they stuck pins, thorns, and sprigs into their " mortified, bare arms." Many Toms o' Bedlam had perforce to wander as mendicants on the King's highways, for mental hospitals as such did not exist.

In 1619, James I was denounced by one of his subjects in the following terms : " Stand, O King ; I have a message to deliver thee from God. I brought thee out of a land of famine and hunger into a land of abundance. Oughtest thou not, therefore, to have judged my people with a righteous judgment ? But thou hast perverted justice, and, therefore, God hath rent the kingdom from thee." The speaker was consigned to Bethlem forthwith.

In 1637, Richard Farnham,[1] a Colchester weaver, was confined to Bethlem as a prophet who identified himself with biblical characters. " Farnham, with whom was associated ' John Bull,' announced that he was one of the ' anointed witnesses ' of the book of Revelation ; that he should be slain in the streets of Jerusalem, where he was to receive the ' gift of the holy tongue ' to make himself understood ; and that he should rise again on the third day as priest and king."

" These delusions," continues O'Donoghue, " were inspired by the mystic visions of John the Divine. He proceeded—with the sanction of Hosea, as he supposed— to tempt a wife away from her husband. Hosea—if we interpret the book with Western eyes—was commanded by God to marry an unfaithful woman, or to retain a wife who had become unfaithful, as a sign to apostate Israel. The woman's husband—not a mystic student of prophecy but a plain, blunt sailor—indicted his wife for bigamy. As a result of the trial Farnham was committed to Newgate and afterwards to Bethlem. I have hunted out two entries in the Court books of 1638, from which it appears that in March the governors were unwilling to part with

[1] O'Donoghue, *The Story of Bethlehem Hospital*, p. 169.

him, whereas in June they implored Archbishop Laud to remove him. Dr. Meverall, physician to the hospital (c. 1634–1648), asked by the lords of the council for a report on the case, recommended that he should be discharged on probation.

" Farnham—so impregnable was his faith or so deep-seated his delusion—confidently prophesied that the plague should have no power to hurt him : he interpreted quite literally and in his own favour the text, ' The plague shall not come nigh thy dwelling.'   Nevertheless, towards the close of 1641 he sickened (hard facts give the mystic many a knock-down blow !), and died at a disciple's house in the beginning of the following year, John Bull dying ten days later.   His followers refused to admit that he was dead, and some of the women-folk, hysterical or mendacious, actually testified to a resurrection of Farnham on the 8th of January, 1642.   Indeed, the sectaries used to drink to both their dead friends, saying that they were still alive, and had gone in ' vessels of bulrushes ' (Revised version—papyrus) to convert the lost tribes of Israel."

Subsequently several Tom o' Bedlam prophets made their appearance, e.g. Robins the ranter, who claimed to be God and to raise the dead, and Tannye, the ' Lord's High Priest,' who, however, died ' within ' in 1677. Lady Douglas the prophetess also spent seven years of her life in Bethlem.   The ' Blessed Ladie,' as she sometimes rather presumptuously styled herself, after her release from Bedlam in 1643, or thereabouts, published a dozen or more incoherent treatises which prove that her malady was incurable.   In 1644 she managed, after the fashion of Jeremiah, to get a ' testimony ' conveyed to Charles I, but he, like another Jehoiakin, proceeded to burn it in the presence of his courtiers.   She also presented

Cromwell some four years later with a tract, *The Armed Commissioner*, based on the text ' Behold He cometh with ten thousand of His saints,' on which Oliver remarked with a spice of dry humour, " I'm afraid we are not all saints."

Since about the middle of the sixteenth century Bethlem Hospital has reflected faithfully the sentiments and methods of the world outside, and it does not appear unwarrantable to go further and say that the outside world has reciprocated and reflected the sentiments and methods of Bedlam only too well. The heartiness of the reciprocation, as evidenced in religion, art, science, literature, music, etc., has been so noteworthy that to the critic there is oftentimes no perceptible difference between them. Certain it is that ' Toms o' Bedlam ' have established a cult, and a lucrative one, for their appeals to charity have met with a ready response. In early days Tom o' Bedlam had his imitators, who derived pecuniary benefits from the simulation of crankeydom, just as at the present so-called artists, musicians, poets, writers, and others trade upon the stupidity of the public. To protect the public from such imposture the governors of Bethlem issued a notice in 1675 and 1676 that they never sent patients out to beg, and that no brass plates, or other marks of any kind, were ever attached to patients either during their residence or after their discharge. The seventeenth century toast " God save the King and the governors of Bedlam " has not entirely lost its significance.

Christian was not the only pilgrim who heard ' Bedlam ' shouted after him in Vanity Fair. The ' Inner light ' led George Fox into paths of righteousness and sobriety. With the help of the Bible, and his theory of the atonement, Bunyan climbed up out of the mire, and the burden

fell off his back at the foot of the cross.   But the poisonous
fumes, exhaled by the mystical treatises of Ranters,
Muggletonians, and fifth Monarchy Men, ate away the
sanity of such men as Daniel, Cromwell's porter, who was
admitted into Bethlehem Hospital in 1656.   In the course
of his studies in mystical divinity Daniel had collected
quite a large library of books and pamphlets, which he
was allowed to keep in his cell when his malady was
recognised as incurable.   Conspicuous amongst these was
a large Bible, presented to him by Nell Gwynn.

The Rev. C. Leslie, in his *Snake in the Grass* (1696),
describes a visit paid to Daniel, who is mentioned in
Hudibras as having " filled Bedlam with Predestination."
" He could quote scripture as fast and as little to the
purpose as either Fox or Muggleton, nor did he want his
disciples.   I was one day making a visit to him, when
upon a grass-plot before his window at the east end of the
building I saw some women very busy with their Bibles,
turning to the quotations with sighs and groans, as he
preached to them out of the window.   I had the curiosity
to speak to one of these women, a grave, sober-like matron,
and I asked her what she could profit by hearing such a
fellow.   She, with a composed countenance, and as pitying my ignorance, replied that Felix thought Paul ' beside
himself '—which made me reflect what ill-luck some had
to be closed up, while others were about the streets."

In 1907 some works of Prior, the poet, were published
for the first time by Mr. A. R. Waller : they had been
lying for many years among the manuscripts at Longleat.
Among them were four *Dialogues of the Dead*.   One was a
conversation in the next world between Sir Thomas More
and the Vicar of Bray—a very tantalising situation—and
another between Cromwell and his porter, Daniel. " From

a porter I raised myself to be a prophet.   I was the senior
inhabitant of old Bethlem, prince of the planets, and
absolute disposer of everything.   I excommunicated, or
blest, as I thought proper, and, when the palace of Bethlem
was on fire, I forbade the people to quench the flames, and
told them the day of judgment was come, and uncon-
cerned I read on."

Oliver affects to pooh-pooh the grandiose rhetoric of
his former servant as the emanation of the crazy brain
of a man who had been " so many years locked up in a
little cell with no other furniture but the torn leaves of
three or four Bibles."   " I was, indeed, mad," rejoins the
imperturbable Daniel.   " For that matter every mortal
man is more or less mad—when he is in love, for example,
when he becomes a miser, but, most of all, when he is
ambitious.   Your madness, however, was worse than
mine, for you set the world on fire.   Men bring even to
this place some germs of their former madness, and the
truth is—between friend and friend—that you are very
far gone, and you must take a course of Lethe waters for
six months at least."

In the seventeenth century Thomas Dekker, the poet,
said of the inmates of Bethlem :

> " There are of madmen, as there are of tame,
>   All humoured not alike ; we have here some,
>   So apish and fantastic, play with a feather,
>   And, though 'twould grieve a soul to see God's image
>   So blemish'd and defac'd, yet do they act
>   Such antics and such pretty lunacies
>   That spite of sorrow they will make you smile.
>   Others again we have like hungry lions,
>   Fierce as wild bulls, untameable as flies.
>   And these have oftentimes from strangers' sides
>   Snatch'd rapiers suddenly, and done much harm,
>   Whom, if you'll see, you must be weaponless."

Inspired by the calmness of mind shown by a patient in captivity, he said :

> " The best of men
> That e'er wore earth about him was a sufferer.
> A soft, meek, patient humble, tranquil spirit,
> The first true gentleman that ever breathed."

At Whitsun in 1677, Lord Gerard, on visiting Bedlam, addressed a virago who was standing on the steps as " my good woman." This ' vile innuendo ' was followed by a scene of violence which resulted in Lord Gerard being carried within. As a result of his experiences therein the conclusion was arrived at that the people within Bethlem are not so bad as those without. O'Donoghue claims this to be the boast of Bethlem to-day, " for many are the uncaught."

Owing to the efforts of Pepys, John Carcasse was charged with having misappropriated certain funds, and ten years later he was admitted to Bethlem, where he posed as a " minister of God's most holy Word." He believed himself to be inspired by the " heavenly fire, born in Bethlehem " and, fired by religious exaltation, he sought to convert Dissenters to the Church. In his volume of poems *Lucida Intervella* dedicated to Charles II, he wrote : [1]

> " I'm a minister of God's most holy Word ;
> Have taken up the gown, laid down the sword,
> Him I must praise, who open'd hath my lips,
> Sent me from Navy to the Ark by Pepys.
> By Mr. Pepys, who hath my rival been
> For the Duke's favour more than years thirteen.
> But I excluded, he high, fortunate ;
> This secretary I could never mate.
> But Clerk of th' Acts, if I'm a parson, then
> I shall prevail : the voice outdoes the pen."

[1] O'Donoghue, *op. cit.* p. 220.

Dr Edward Tyson (physician to Bethlem, 1684–1708) is referred to by Elkanah Settle, the laureate of the city, in his *Threnody on the Death of Dr Edward Tyson*, which contains the following lines : [1]

> " O Bethlem, Bedlam, with a grinning smile
> Let sneering fools thy glorious rise revile,
> As if Augusta too profuse they saw
> To raise such costly walls for beds of straw,
> The lazar lodg'd ev'n in the Dives' roof.
> 'Tis charity that builds, and that's enough !
> Then let thy walls magnificently shine,
> When founded in a service so divine."

Hogarth scratched the letters LE on a plate representing walls of a ward in Bethlem, in *The Rake's Progress*, and this refers to Nathaniel Lee, the dramatist, who was under the care of Dr. Tyson for four years.   Dryden relates that when a visitor remarked to Lee that it must be very easy for him now to write like a madman, Lee replied, " No, Sir, it is not so easy to write like a madman ; but it is very easy indeed to write like a fool."

During the eighteenth century Defoe took an active part in severely criticising private asylums which had multiplied in number during the reign of George III.   In those days such institutions were not subject to adequate visitation or inspection, and this defect afforded material for journalists and novelists, such as Defoe, Henry Cockton, and Charles Reade, to write upon.

Dean Swift was elected a governor of Bethlem in 1714, and as a result of his visits to the hospital he suggested the theory that great conquerors, founders of religion and political schools " have generally been persons whose reason was disturbed."   He asked if it would not be worth while to appoint commissioners to search Bedlam

---

[1] O'Donoghue, *op. cit.* p. 226.

for suitable persons to command regiments during war,
to carry out the less agreeable researches of the laboratory,
or to bawl and wrangle in the pandemonium of a law
court or a contested election ? O'Donoghue refers to
Swift's whimsical fancies in *A Tale of a Tub* and in *A
Serious and Useful Scheme to make an Hospital for
Incurables* (1733). The incurables were to include fools,
rogues, liars, the vain or envious, etc.

George Whitfield and John Wesley were caricatured and
ridiculed with malevolent satire in connection with their
Evangelical Revival, and they were subjected to many
innuendos as to their being worthy of Bedlam. Wesley
himself went to see a young woman in Bedlam, but, being
forbidden to enter, noted in his diary : " So we are forbidden to go to Newgate for fear of making them wicked,
and to Bedlam for fear of making them mad." O'Donoghue believes " there to have been some justification for
the ban pronounced against John Wesley by physician
and committee, for wherever he preached there were
extraordinary outbursts of contagious hysteria." At his
meetings many women and some men would suddenly
fall, as if mortally wounded, to the ground, where they
writhed and howled in an agony of pain or terror. Meanwhile the singing and praying proceeded without inter-
mission, and just as suddenly, in the course of ten minutes
or an hour, these very same persons would break out into
hymns and ecstasies of joy. They were then ' converted.'
Such emotional outbursts in connection with ' revivals '
have always been prone to occur. Wesley advised—in
acute cases of mental excitement—that water should be
poured from a kettle on the head of the patient, or the
patient may be placed " under a great waterfall " so long
as his strength will bear. Dr. Monro, the physician of

Bethlem, treated similar cases by the application of blisters. Nowadays, outbursts of excitement are sometimes treated ' without ' by a hose, and ' within ' by an aperient.

In 1750 London was disturbed by earthquakes, which were regarded as warnings from God. One ' prophet,' a Lifeguardsman, was sent by Horace Walpole to Bedlam as being crazy, believing, as he did, that not only was he the cause of the earthquakes, but that he had a ball of fire in his body, and a sword which would cut devils in two. The trend of public thought is always apt to follow some form of emotional excitement, and those who are emotionally unstable tend to imagine themselves to be participators in the event. Thus, ' Jack the Ripper ' has had many imaginary counterparts in Bedlam. So it is with every instance of revolting crime recorded by the press. It must be remembered, however, that the records are not in themselves the cause of the mental aberration, but merely the objects to which the already unstable minds direct their attention. It is, nevertheless, by unsound mental diet that precedents are formed, and thoughts are directed towards the commission of similar special offences, as is evidenced in cases of murder, lust, and many other forms of crime. Such records are, therefore, of very doubtful utility in the prevention of crime. Certain it is that knowledge of the ' psychopathia sexualis ' and the ' cult ' of Freudism is to be discouraged, rather than enhanced by publicity.

Were we to attempt to define our beliefs pertaining to religion, science, art, conduct, or to formulate a creed of almost any description, our verdict on the result would be either ' found wanting,' ' of no fixed idea,' or, if formed, ' paranoia,' or ' delusional insanity.' Indeed there appears to be no getting away from the fact that our brains are

strewn with mental nebulae, and that the more expansive
our mental horizon the dimmer the visibility.   Christopher
Smart, the poet, was confined to Bethlem on several
occasions, and possibly wrote his *Song of David* there.
O'Donoghue [1] refers to Smart's disjointed lines and stanzas
scribbled on the walls of one of the cells.   Dr. Johnson,
whose mental outlook was more comprehensive than most
of his contemporary thinkers, thought that Smart ought
not to have been shut up.   " His infirmities were not
noxious to society.   He insisted on people praying with
him ; and I'd as lief pray with Kit Smart as any one else.
Another charge was that he did not love clean linen ; and
I have no passion for it."   Intolerance of intemperance in
religion is indeed a paradoxical relationship with which
the alienist is familiar.   That Dr. Johnson was familiar
with Bethlem appears evident from the records by Boswell.
On one visit, accompanied by Murphy, the dramatist,
and Foote, the comedian, he appeared to sympathise with
a Jacobite patient who was banging his straw under the
delusion that he was chastising the Duke of Cumberland
for his cruelties after the battle of Culloden.

In 1807 Sir G. O. Peele reported to the Home Secretary
that there was hardly a parish without some unfortunate
creature who was either chained in a cellar or garret of a
workhouse, fastened to the leg of a table, tied to a post in
an outhouse, or shut up in an uninhabited ruin ; or he
would be left to ramble half-naked or starved through the
streets or highways, teased by the scoff and jest of all
that is vulgar, ignorant, and unfeeling.   No wonder is it
that such unfortunates were driven mad by such circumstances, and it was due to intolerance without that they
were afforded sanctuary within.

[1] *Op. cit.* p. 266.

CHAPTER VIII

VISIONARIES

MOHAMMED (A.D. 570–632), the great prophet, who raised a gigantic religious movement not only throughout Arabia and the East, but even as far as the banks of the Loire and the Oxus, held that the grand truth and simplicity of his system was conveyed to him by Divine revelation, and as each revelation came to him he set it down, and so gradually completed the wonderful work embodied in the Koran. Mohammed was a man of good position in Mecca, by trade a travelling merchant, and until his forty-second year there seemed nothing to differentiate him from other men of his calling. He was an upright man and a good husband to a wife many years his senior, much liked by his friends, and respected even by his enemies. But that an amazing, inspired work like the Koran should have been the child of Mohammed's own thoughts and heart and brain is difficult of belief, indeed almost incredible ; yet his own conviction, his sure faith that he was a messenger from God, and consequently the medium through whom all Divine truth should be transmitted to the world, leaves us still more wondering.

"Mohammed's revelations," according to Sprenger, "began with visions in his sleep as bright as the dawn of the morning. Then a love of solitude came upon him. He used to live alone in a cave on the mountain Hira, where he spent several days and nights together in prayers and devotional exercises . . . until suddenly the truth came to him. An angel came to him and said, ' Read, in the name of thy Lord who has created you. He has created men from blood. Read, the Lord is the greatest who has taught men. He has taught man by writing what he did not know.' " Mohammed went back to his wife in a state of great agitation and told what he had seen both to her and her uncle Waraka. The latter became envious of what he looked upon as Mohammed's marvellous good fortune, and that he should be chosen among all men for so great a destiny. " Oh, that I were you ! " he cried. " Oh, that I should be in life, when thy people persecute you." " What ! " broke in the prophet, " Will they persecute me ? " Until that moment Mohammed had not realised that the great truth he had been given to bring to the world would also bring enemies. It has been recorded that in his revelations Mohammed heard stones and trees welcoming him as a ' messenger of God,' and that the angel Gabriel appeared to him many times. The prophet described his revelations thus : " Inspiration descendeth upon me in one of two ways. Sometimes Gabriel cometh and communicates the revelation unto me, as one man unto another, and this is easy—at other times it affecteth me like the ringing of a bell, penetrating my very heart, and rending me as it were in pieces, and this it is which grievously afflicteth me."

Mohammed's wife said that, as verse after verse of the Koran was revealed to him, his eyes became fixed on the heavens and then to the right side, his lips moved—then he would look to the left, and big drops of sweat covered his face. Some traditions tell us that when he received a revelation he sank into a condition of torpor almost resembling drunkenness. It has been recorded that these trances—or hallucinations, as some historians describe them—were due to epilepsy; but it seems well-nigh unthinkable that epilepsy could cause a man of wisdom, as he undoubtedly was, to believe in his own prophecies so completely as to form them into the vast faith which brought all the peoples of the East under its teachings.

Mohammed invariably came out of his trances with a rhymed verse of the Koran complete and ready; there was none of the semi-confusedness about his returned consciousness such as is customary with epileptics. But it is true also that there are cases of epilepsy in which the intellectual powers are greatly stimulated, but these are extremely rare. It is possible that Mohammed's highly strung condition amounted almost to a nervous disorder; this, and his dislike to the prevailing idolatry and polytheism of the people of Mecca, may have made him see and hear both pictures and words which convinced him that he received direct messages from God. It was only but natural that, when once he felt certain himself, and had impressed others with the divinity of his inspiration, he should look upon all his impulses, dreams, and omens as messages from Allah.

It must be remembered that Mohammed was a deeply religious man; his sincere fervour, combined with his reasoning mind, had led him far beyond the idolatry of his fellows. He had read of the angel forms which had appeared to the Hebrew prophets, and he himself believed in the existence of good and evil spirits. His intellect and powers of organisation were quite exceptional, as was also his skill in warfare, and an unfailing tact in dealing with his enemies. It is certain that the Koran evolved a religion which spread not only with amazing rapidity,

but has endured through all the generations.   Even now
the missionary strength of Islam is gathering millions of
new adherents from among the natives of Africa.

Possibly the prophet's victories as a martial leader may
have conduced somewhat to his success at the onset of
his great campaign ; he also doubtless re-aroused all the
warlike instincts of paganism in direct contradiction to
the teachings of the early Christian Church, which held
that the love of women was an unholy stain upon the ideal
life of sanctity.   Monks, nuns, and hermits abounded in
Syria and Egypt, and they had the belief that they were
fulfilling a sacred duty which made them superior to those
who responded to the call of nature.

To counteract this ascetic life of incompleteness,
Mohammed brought all the strength of the life-forces,
and, far from considering it sinful to indulge to the full,
actually predicted that, for all true believers, such a life
would continue in Paradise.   There is a sledge-hammer
simplicity in the creed taught by Mohammed's revelations,
which, in spite of the forbidding of wine and threats of
judgment and hell, forced its stern way into the Oriental
mind.   It made an irresistible appeal to human nature
as it was in the prophet's time, and it still exists.   Whether
they were in truth ' Heaven-sent ' messages and revelations, or merely the inspired thoughts and impulses of an
extraordinary man, the outpourings of the Koran are
undeniably full of divine wisdom, combined with a
wondrous understanding of the human soul.

Francis of Assisi (born 1182) was the most popular of a
merry company of young men who paraded the streets at
all hours of the day and night.   His genial manners had
so much charm that with the citizens he went by the name
of ' the flower of youth.'   His character was of the noblest

and most cultured, indeed he seemed more like the son of a great noble than of a merchant. Even when during a skirmish between the burghers of his own and a neighbouring town Francis with several of his friends was taken prisoner, he kept up their spirits by his cheerful courage. He always gave liberally and gladly to all who were in poverty or trouble. Stricken with a severe illness when twenty-four years of age, he was compelled to remain in bed for a lengthy period. As soon, however, as he was able to walk, although feebly and with the help of a stick, he wandered out into the country; but its beauties did not bring to him the former delight. Mingling less and less with his gay companions, he grew pensive and sad, and spent many hours in solitary meditation in a cave.

His illness was followed by a great deal of pain, for the relief of which he prayed earnestly. He had a vision of Christ nailed to the cross, and felt the passion of Christ impressed even upon his bowels, upon the very marrow of his bones, so that he could not keep his thoughts fixed upon it without being overflowed with grief.[1] After this vision, Francis wept so much that he was asked if he were ill. " I am weeping for the passion of my Lord Jesus," he replied. His friends then advised him to think of marriage. " Choose a wife," they said to him. And Francis answered, " Yes, I am thinking of a lady, of the noblest, the richest, the most beautiful lady that was ever seen." To the disgust of all who knew him, he clad himself in a beggar's cloak, and cast aside all his fine clothes. They drove him away with gibes and stones, but he bore his self-imposed cross with patience and suffered meekly the mockery and cruel handling.

[1] Bonghi, *Vita di F. Assisi*, 1885.

An ascetic from this time forward, he held, perhaps subconsciously, some thing in his soul which had nothing in common with asceticism, *viz.*: a wide, far-reaching humanity which embraced all and forgave all.   Whereas ascetics shun nature and human affections, Francis preached the love of nature, sympathy, mutual affection, and work.   Instead of looking upon all the beauties of the world as works of the devil, he preached and fostered the true revelation—that everything beautiful is from God, and he praised and gave thanks to God for it.   With these thoughts in his heart, " The Song of the Sun " was given forth direct from his impassioned heart.   This song, the most benign ever written, is full of beneficence ;   all living creatures, human and animal, and even inanimate objects, are joined together in tender unison and brotherhood.   And with it, Francis made the first onward step to devout poetry in the native tongue.   Round the song he wove a beautiful musical melody which was sung by his disciples.

Cola di Rienzi, son of a water-seller, was born at a time (1313) when Rome was in a chaotic state of disorder.   In the absence of any firm government, the city and the entire country was given over to the lawless tyranny of the barons, who were little better than robbers and bandits. As a boy, Cola worked in the fields, then studied as a notary, and showed profound interest in gleaning knowledge relating to the history of his country and its ancient laws and customs.   When he read of the former glories of Rome, and compared them with the condition of things of his time, it brought tears of grief and rage to his eyes, and he would cry out, "Where are the good Romans of the old time ?   Where is their justice ? " Having seen his brother murdered by the so-called governors of the city, the event only served to embitter him more against their tyranny and oppression, and he felt within him an irresistible impulse to test for himself the thoughts and plans he had evolved from books.

As notary Cola undertook the protection of widows and orphans, and gave himself the title of consul, in accordance with the then prevailing custom when watchmakers, cloth-workers, and every guild had consuls at their head. He was chosen, on account of his eloquence, to go to Avignon as spokesman of the people at a time when revolution was in the air, and his eloquence was so great that the prelates gave him the appointment of notary to the Urban chamber.

On his return to Rome, he bestowed upon himself a still bigger title, and called himself 'Consul of Rome.' It has been written that, during the early part of his life, Cola had always "a whimsical smile upon his lips." But he inveighed against the barons in no measured terms, referring to them as " the dogs of the Capitol." He even addressed them in the Senate house, exclaiming, " Ye are evil citizens, ye who suck the blood of the people." After this open accusation, Cola deemed it wise to work more circuitously—he made paintings symbolical of the miseries of Rome, and showed them to the people. In these paintings, apes and cats represented murderers and all other criminals, foxes stood for unjust judges, and wolves and bears stood for the nobles.

Cola went to an exhibition dressed in a German cloak and white hood. His hat also was white, and bore on it several crowns, the topmost of which was cut through the centre by a small silver sword. He made long speeches to the people, exhorting them to remember the greatness and prosperity of their country in the bygone days, and he went so far as to tell the nobles how, " when I am emperor or king, I will make war on all of you. I will have such an one hanged, and such another beheaded." He made it plain that he would spare none of them.

With increased power in his political career Cola developed a love for money and pomp, also for extraordinary garments and symbols. He painted a picture of a dove carrying a branch of myrtle to a small bird; the dove, he said, represented the Holy Spirit. But the picture bore the inscription, " The day of justice is coming—await the moment." The nobles smiled indulgently, indeed they looked upon him at first as a harmless lunatic, and he was thus able to continue uninterruptedly his campaign and work the people's mind into a state of ferment. In this way he started a revolution, obtaining funds for the purpose from the revenues of the Apostolic Chamber. Cola then called himself Tribune, and took over the entire lordship of the city. He not only executed severe justice on the nobles, but even upon members of the populace for the slightest violation of his laws. Nor did the monks escape scot free; some of them the new ' Tribune of the good State' put to death after having accused them of secret murders and other crimes. He allowed no escutcheons of the nobles to remain on palaces or banners —there must not be in Rome any lordships except the Pope's and Cola's.

One day when Cola was exhibiting one of his symbolic pictures to the people, a dove alighted by his side—this happening rendered him still more convinced that his every thought and act was conceived through and done by the Grace of the Holy Spirit! He believed that he referred all matters to God, and that he heard within himself God's voice advising and counselling him. In his own mind he compared himself to Christ. He took his bath in the porphyry basin of Constantine, to whose power he imagined he had succeeded. With supreme autocracy he issued mandates to Pope Clement IV and his Cardinals, and to the reigning Dukes of Bohemia, Bavaria, Saxony, and Brandenburg, commanding that " they shall appear before us in person at the date appointed, failing which we shall proceed against them."

The Roman nobles, who had hitherto been merely amused at what they considered Cola's colossal conceit, began to plot against him and even sent an assassin to attempt his life. The Tribune, however, escaped and put the would-be assassin to the torture. From that time Cola's attitude became as suspicious as it was aggressive, and he adopted a tyrant's tactics to rid himself of some of his enemies. He invited them to the Capitol, nominally to a banquet or conclave, and ordered their arrest. For their trial, the huge hall of the Capitol was decorated in white and red, as was the custom in the case of pronouncements of death sentences. Suddenly and inexplicably the Tribune changed his mind, and not only acquitted the prisoners, but even made long speeches in their praise and honour. This was followed by another change of mind, for, shortly after their liberation, he again summoned them to his august presence, and ordered pictures to be painted, representing some of them hanging head downwards. The infuriated nobles marched against the tyrannical Tribune and took from him the town of Nepi. But Cola merely ordered the drowning of two dogs in revenge—the dogs being intended to represent the nobles, or his opinion of them.

After many objectless marches, Cola returned to Rome and had himself crowned again with even more pomp and

grandeur than before. The ceremony included his consecration as ' Knight of the Holy Spirit.' In addition to
the public coronation, he crowned himself with six wreaths
of leaves, taken from different plants, to which he added
the mitre of Trojan king, and another crown of silver. In
one of his letters, Cola said : " There should be but one
shepherd and one faith, and the new Pope, the Emperor
Charles, and Cola should be, as it were, a symbol of the
Trinity on earth. Charles should reign in the west, and
the Tribune in the east."

With his stupendous self-aggrandisement, Cola's better
nature became merged in selfishness and even ferocity.
He no longer befriended the widows and orphans, but even
forbade the former to grieve for their dead. His atrocious
deeds earned for him the contempt of his former adherents
and of all honourable men. No longer temperate, Cola
lived a life of actual drunkenness. His mind was continually changing, he had violent paroxysms of joy, ending
in depression and weeping. His intemperate habits he
excused to himself and others as resulting from " the
effects of a poison which he believed to have been administered to him in prison." Even the people turned against
him, and Cola was eventually overthrown by them.

Joan of Arc (1411–1431), the Domrémy peasant girl,
ploughing the fields—ignorant, unlettered, but religiously
devout at the age of thirteen years, heard strange voices
and chiming bells, and saw brilliant lights which seemed
to come from the same direction as the voices. Angels
and saints sang to her, and the words she heard were,
" Fille de Dieu, va, va, va, je serai à ton ayde, va ! "

Joan had three brothers and a sister. One day, when
she was running a race with her girl friends, one of them
told her that she ran so swiftly as to appear almost to be

flying along. When the race was over, Joan fancied she heard a boy's voice telling her to go home to her mother. She went back at once, believing that her own brother had bidden her to do so. But her mother was surprised to see her, saying she had not sent for her, and that she should not have left her sheep. Joan was surprised at her own mistake, then all at once a bright, misty cloud appeared before her and a voice within the cloud spoke and said, " Joan, you must lead another life and do wonderful actions, for it is you whom the King of Heaven has chosen for the succour of France, and the help and protection of King Charles expelled from his dominions. You will put on male attire, and, taking arms, will be the leader of war. All things will be ruled by your counsel."

The angel Michael, accompanied by St. Catherine and St. Margaret, came to Joan with the next visions. She kissed them, and in obedience to their entreaty, promised to keep her life pure and unsullied. When at her trial the girl was requested to describe minutely these saints and angels, she sometimes said she had been forbidden to speak. But it is quite possible that in every question Joan was afraid that her captors were setting a snare for her. In her belief as to the reality of the figures she had seen she never wavered, and she told the judge that they were as plain to her as he himself. How and where Joan learned her equestrianship has never been elucidated. It is said that she took horses to water whilst staying at Neuf Chateau, but even if that were so, it would hardly have made her an Amazon.

There is no doubt that the voices grew more and more insistent, and when Joan was eighteen she heard them bid her go to the Commandant, Robert of Baudricourt, at Vaucouleurs. At last she entreated her uncle to take her

to him, but he attached little credence to her tale.   The
voices however, continued their urging, and the citizens
of Vaucouleurs, in their anxiety as to their country's
peril, were inclined to believe in Joan's sincerity.   They
gave her a horse and male clothes, and the Commandant
at last gave way to her pleadings and sent the soldier-girl
to the Dauphin at Chinon with a small escort.   She
arrived there in May 1429, and although she had never
seen the Dauphin, she picked him out from among his
crowd of courtiers, with the help, she said, of the friendly
voices.   We are told that Joan was graceful and good
looking, with dark hair and a sweet voice, inclined to be
emotional, but ordinarily very cheerful.   The King, to
test the genuineness of her story, had her kept under close
supervision, but gave her every opportunity to mingle
with people of every class.   When asked to give some sign
of her divine mission, Joan told the King she would show
it at Orleans, but that it was not the wish of Heaven that
she should do so before.

She wrote to the priests asking them to seek for a sword
which they would find close to the altar of St. Catherine
of Fierbois.   The sword was found—a rusty one, but the
rust fell off as though by magic.   Joan used the sword
until, during the siege of Paris, she broke the blade when
striking a courtesan who was waylaying her men at arms.
When asked about this sword at her trial, she replied that
she had once passed through the chapel of Fierbois, but
she did not disclose how she had discovered that arms
were concealed under its pavements.   If she guessed the
fact, it was indeed a good guess, and well located.   She
entered Orleans riding on a white horse and clad in full
armour.   Her standard was also white, and on it was an
image of Our Lady and two angels, each holding a lily.

This, and Joan's own purity, earned for her the name of the ' Lily Maid.' She rode at the head of the nobles and soldiers. The wearied and besieged citizens rushed to meet her, believing that in her they saw the Almighty Himself, and their joy was great if they might touch her.

In ten days the English besieging army was in full retreat. All the fighting men of France gathered to fight under the holy maid. In spite of her extreme youth, Joan took part in all the councils of war, and upheld the power of the voices she heard against all the plans and projects of the French leaders. An old chronicler records that she rode always in as complete armour as that of any captain of the time, and when one spoke of war or of putting troops in order, she made it to be heard and seen that she knew what she was about. When the cry of arms was sounded, she was the first and readiest, whether on foot or horseback. She might have been a soldier for twenty years, so skilful was she in the disposition of artillery.

She told Jean d'Aulon, who had been ordered by the king to watch over her, that from her council of three advisers, she always received instructions. One of these was ever beside her, one came often to visit her, and the third consulted with the other two. When the French were repulsed at St. Pierre le Monstier, Jean found Joan left with only four or five men, and when asked why she had not joined in the retreat, the maid replied that fifty thousand of her people were still with her, and she would stay and take the town.

All historians agree that Joan was of a highly sensitive nature. When she received an arrow wound in the breast at Orleans she was afraid, and cried. She also wept for the souls of the English soldiers who were wounded.

She endeavoured always to prevent gambling, plundering, and profane language among her men, and, as far as she could, discouraged the girls who sought to follow the camp.

Acting in accordance with her predictions gained from the voices, and adhered to even against the experienced generals, Joan fulfilled her promise and led the Dauphin to Rheims to be crowned. After she had completely routed the English army and taken seven cities, she was wounded in an assault upon Paris, and, though anxious to renew the attack on the following day, the King decided to retire. It was the soldier-maid's first check, and it weakened the faith in her divine power. Her forces were reduced, and many of the King's courtiers and ministers, who were envious of her popularity with the people and of the wonderful success she had achieved, sought to compass her downfall.

At Compiègne, then besieged by the Burgundians, she was surrounded and taken prisoner by John of Luxembourg. Joan was kept in irons for six months, scoffed at by the women who came to visit her, and insulted by some of the men. Finally she was sold to the English, King Charles making no attempt to ransom her in spite of all she had done on his behalf. When she heard what had happened, she attempted to kill herself by throwing herself from the Tower, rather than fall into the hands of the English. The unfortunate girl was taken to Rouen and subjected to the most vile treatment. Her ankles were loaded with chains fixed to a beam, and the men placed to guard her were coarse and brutal, even endeavouring to shame her by violation. She became ill, but the Earl of Warwick sent doctors to attend upon her, saying that it would be displeasing to the King of England if she should die, since he had decided that she should be burned.

It was essential, however, to give Joan a trial, and this farce lasted four months, although from the first the outcome was never in doubt. For six hours every day she was made to endure most trying cross-examinations, worded with the most obvious desire to force her into some fatal admission. In all the assembly she had not one friend, and yet nothing could shake her or make her deny the truth of her revelations or the voices which came to her while still in prison. The visions did not come to her so much, but the light still accompanied the voices. The voices told her how to reply to the questionings—she had but to pray and they spoke to her at once. They spoke to her cheerfully and said, " Do not distress yourself about your martyrdom, you will come at last into the Kingdom of Heaven."

Joan certainly showed much wisdom in fencing with her questioners ; she declined to reply to irrelevant queries, or to be examined more than once on the same point. Taking into consideration the simple upbringing and lack of education of this peasant girl, this fact is at least remarkable. A woman named Catherine of Rochelle had once told Joan that she had seen a white lady robed in gold who had bidden her ask the King for heralds and trumpeters to collect money for the maid's soldiers, and Joan stayed one night with Catherine and remained awake to test the truth of the vision, but saw nothing. Catherine of Rochelle, incensed against the maid for doubting her ' voices,' denounced her as being in league with the devil. She herself, however, also fell into the hands of the English, and was accused of witchcraft. Under the severe interrogations of the Court as to why her claims should receive more credence than those of Catherine, Joan was drawn into making a vague statement about a special sign which had been vouchsafed to her when she was at Chinon. She said she had been visited by a group of angels who had guided her to the royal castle and into the King's chamber, and these angels had handed a golden crown to the Archbishop of Rheims to place upon the head of the King.[1]

Though unable or unwilling to give any minute description of her visions, Joan adhered inflexibly to the fact that she heard voices and the ringing of bells, and that the apparitions appeared to her both clearly and definitely, sometimes singly, sometimes in large numbers. It is chronicled that once she was heard to say that her visions must be bad spirits, since they had allowed her to be delivered into the hands of her enemies.

The sentence of the Court being that Joan must renounce her ' errors ' or be at once burnt at the stake, she made a vague recantation, and was condemned to lifelong imprisonment. Instead of being cared for by the Church and by persons of her own sex, she was incarcerated in her former cell, and treated with the same brutality as before. She resumed her female garb, this being one of the conditions of her reprieve ; but the voices reproached her for her weakness and told her to be firm and strong in all the things they had taught her. Urged on by ' voices,' she again put on the male attire which had been left in her prison. The English seized upon this slight pretext, and on the 30th May, 1431, Joan was burned as a ' witch '

---

[1] In some additional notes made by several judges who visited the Maid before her death, they state on oath that Joan confessed that she, and no other, was the angel who brought the crown to King Charles. When questioned as to the reality of the apparitions, she answered, " Whether they were good or bad spirits, they appeared to me."

in the old market place of Rouen. Even in her last
moments, she was heard to invoke St. Catherine and
the Archangel Michael, and to testify to the truth of
her revelations. The executioner afterwards asserted
definitely that he was for ever damned, because her heart
would not consume, and he had burned a ' holy woman.'
An Englishman who had helped to heap up the faggots,
sobbed in bitter repentance, for he had beheld a dove
come forth from the flames.

In considering the Maid and her visions, it must be
remembered that she was deeply distressed by the misery
of France, and that it had been prophesied that France
would be made desolate by a woman and restored by a
virgin. Joan was heard to quote this prophecy, and
perhaps she pondered over it until her mind, simple and
earnest as it was, became attuned and ready to read
signs of the supernatural in everything. In spite of all
her visions and dreams she showed a power of organisation
and a strength of purpose wholly beyond her years and
simple upbringing. What determined her success was not
so much her valour, or her visions, as her good sense. She
endeavoured to cut the knot which men of little faith
could not unravel. She declared in God's name that
Charles VII was the true heir, and she set him at ease as
to his legitimacy, of which he himself had doubts. That
legitimacy she sanctified, and took her King straight to
Rheims. There is not the shadow of a doubt that Joan
was idolised by the people, who believed implicitly in her
warnings and prophecies. They asked her to lay her
hands on the sick, to pray for their recovery, to say prayers
for the dead. It was even said that birds would fly from
the heights at her call, and that soldiers, whose lives she
had warned would be short, were killed in battle, whilst

others, to whom she had promised life, came safely through the fray.

Savonarola (1452–1498), a Dominican preacher and writer, was criticised by Villari, who wrote: "This is the singularity of his character, that a man who had given to Florence the best form of republic—who had dominated an entire people, who filled the world with his eloquence and had been the greatest of philosophers—should make it his boast that he heard voices in the air and saw the sword of the Lord." From his early youth Savonarola believed, through a vision, that Christ had sent him to rescue the nation from the corruption into which it had fallen. In another vision the calamities of the Church were made manifest, and a voice bade him make the facts known to the people. He saw the prophets of the New Testament and had a vision of the Apocalypse. Once, during Advent, he saw the Sword of the Lord turned earthwards. Darkness ensued, and a rain of swords, fire, and arrows was followed by famine and pestilence. After this vision Savonarola prophesied the coming of the pestilence.

A few years before his death he desired strongly to preach a gospel of faith and spiritual reform, and to leave all political matters out of his sermons; but, he said, "I watched all Saturday, and the whole night, but at daybreak while I was praying, I heard a voice say: 'Fool, dost thou not see that God will have thee go on in the same way?'" In another vision, he saw himself, as Christ's ambassador, journeying to Paradise, and there having discourse with saints and the Virgin. He even described the throne on which she sat, and the jewels with which it was set.

Savonarola gave much thought to his dreams, and

endeavoured to decide which of his visions were guided to him by angels and which by devils. In one of his writings these words occur: "To feign oneself as a prophet in order to persuade others would be like making God Himself an impostor," from which it would appear that the great preacher had no doubt as to his own sincerity. And yet in a previous work he had written: "I am not a prophet, neither am I the son of a prophet; it is your sins that make me a prophet perforce." With remarkable absence of egotism he was often heard to say that he felt the glow of fire within his bones which forced him to speak, and borne along by the terrific power of delirious ecstasy, he carried his enthusiastic audience with him into his wonder-world of thought and rapture.

Christopher Columbus (1445–1500) heard distinctly a voice speak to him when he was shipwrecked off Jamaica. It urged him to have more faith in his Heavenly Father and not abandon himself to grief. The voice then added: "What happens to you to-day is a deserved punishment for having served the master of the world, and not God. All these tribulations are engraved on marble and are not brought about without reason."

Tasso (1493–1569) was constantly sad, weighed down with troublesome thoughts, haunted by visions and phantoms, and worried by his faulty memory. "I am frenzied," he said in a letter to Gonzaga, "and I am surprised that they have not written to you of all the things that I say in talking to myself—honours, the good grace of emperors and kings which I dream of, forming and reforming them according to my fancy." He also told Cattaneo: "I have much more need of the exorcist than of the physician, for my trouble is caused by magic art. I will tell you about my goblin—how he carried away letters. The little thief has robbed me of many crowns, he puts all my books upside down, opens my chests, hides my keys—so that I do not know how to protect myself from him. One day a loaf was taken from me, beneath my eyes, towards three o'clock. Thus I possess a certainty that these wonders must be attributed to a magician."

Tasso was, as he himself said, always unhappy ; he travelled much, but his sorrow, his suspicion, his dread of poison, his ceaseless remorse for the heresies of which he imagined himself guilty, went always with him, even from country to country, so that he found no peace. He was subject to fits of rage, and in one of these he drew a knife and attempted to kill a servant. Sometimes he saw lights sparkling, sometimes he heard awful sounds—hissings, the sound of bells and the striking of countless clocks. " When I am asleep," he wrote, " I seem to see a horseman throwing himself upon me and casting me to the earth, or else I imagine that I am covered with filthy beasts. All my joints feel it, my head seems heavy, and in the midst of so many pains and terrors, sometimes there appears to me the image of the Virgin, beautiful and young, with her son, and crowned with a rainbow." This apparition cured him of a violent fever, and he penned a sonnet to the Virgin to evince his gratitude. He firmly believed that he not only spoke to his ' genius,' but that also he touched him, and received from him new and beautiful ideas for his work. Tasso, whilst working out his inspirations, was like a man possessed, his eyes grew feverishly bright, his whole frame trembled with enthusiasm and excitement; but when the inspiration was over he appeared to have no consciousness of the beauty of the work. He owned in a letter, " I do not deny that I am mad, but I believe that my madness is caused by intoxication and love, for I know that I drink too much."

San Juan de Dios (1495–1550) was from early childhood possessed with a craving for adventure, and when only eight years old he ran away from home and became a shepherd. After tending sheep for seven years he enlisted as a soldier. Army life was then very wild and corrupted —the officers even leading the way to plundering and looting. For losing some booty which an officer had entrusted to him, Juan was condemned to death, but eventually reprieved and dismissed from the army. He returned for a short while to his old work as a shepherd, but later on he re-enlisted and fought in many wars. Later he lost his memory and could not even remember his father's name.

Whilst serving as a shepherd in Andalusia Juan imagined himself to have been called in a dream, and in consequence he dedicated his life to God and to the poor. The pirates of Barbary at that time constantly landed in other countries which they knew to be ill-defended, and seizing many of the inhabitants, sold them in the slave markets of Fez, Tunis, and Algiers. Juan resolved to attempt to end this horror by collecting alms for the ransom of the Catholics who were being sold in this way. With this object he obtained employment as an artisan with an exiled Portuguese family at Ceuta, thence he went to Gibraltar, where he sold relics and other sacred objects, and, with the money thus realised, he opened a shop in Granada.

Juan was then forty-three years of age, and, whilst in Granada, he heard a sermon preached by Juan d'Avila and afterwards burst into a fit of wild devotion, loudly confessed his sins, threw himself in the dust, pulled out his hair, tore his garments, and then dashed frantically

through the streets entreating God's mercy. Reaching
his library, he destroyed every secular book, distributed
the sacred ones, as well as his clothes and furniture, to all
who came along, and remained, clad in his shirt, beating
his breast and entreating that all should pray for him.
Juan d'Avila, the preacher whose sermon had caused this
extraordinary and sudden conversion, listened to the
unhappy man's confession and endeavoured to advise and
console him. But Juan threw himself on a dung heap
immediately afterwards, and again declared his sins in a
loud voice. He was hooted and hissed by most of the
crowd, but some few, out of pity, led him to the Royal
Hospital, where the authorities treated him with " binding
and scourging," as was the custom, " to deliver him from
the evil spirit supposed to possess him."

After being released from the Hospital, Juan made a
vow that he would go on a pilgrimage to the Virgin's
shrine at Guadalupe, and commenced his journey in the
midst of winter, barefoot and penniless. When he arrived
there, after much difficulty and suffering, he had a vision
of the Virgin. She stood before him holding out to him
the child Jesus, naked, but giving him clothes to cover
him. He read in this the meaning that to him was
entrusted the work of pitying the weak, sheltering the
destitute, and clothing the needy. An Hieronymite monk
gave Juan a white robe, and with a pilgrim's staff in his
hand he returned to Aropesa and sought admission at the
poor-house, with a view to studying the necessities of its
inmates. He begged alms for them and sold faggots in
the streets, slept in stables, and gave all that he gained to
the poor.

A notice posted in a public square, " House to let for
the Poor," put the idea into his head of making it into an

asylum. To put this project into practice he begged from the rich, obtained sufficient to lease the house, and bought the most necessary articles of furniture. There he sheltered and cared for forty-six crippled and sick paupers. To obtain food for them, he walked the streets during the dinner hour, endeavouring to collect the leavings of the meals of the rich. He cried out as he went, " Do good, my brethren, it will return in blessing to yourselves." Many volunteers gathered round him, and the little band of ' mercy-workers ' grew until it became the great congregation still in existence. It was at this time that Juan took the name of Juan de Dios, by which he became known throughout Spain. He continued to collect funds, and from a journey to Granada, returned with a goodly supply of funds to continue and increase his mission.

Although worn out with exposure and hard work, he treated himself nevertheless with more than Spartan austerity. He fasted continually, and imposed upon himself strenuous and difficult exertions. He journeyed always shoeless and hatless, his sole covering consisting of a single grey garment, whilst of body linen he allowed himself none. Over and over again he risked his life to save children from drowning, or dashed through fire to rescue the sick and helpless.

When Juan felt that his end was near, he sent for his first disciple, Antonio Martin, and commended the work to him, and at the last he rose from bed to offer up prayers, and died whilst he knelt in supplication. In his asylum, Juan de Dios instituted very radical and much needed reforms, which, until then, had never been thought of. He placed one patient only in each bed, and divided the sick into classes ; he was, in fact, the originator of the modern hospital, as well as the founder of casual wards.

St. Francis Xavier (*born* 1506), called the apostle of the
Indies, was born at a time when all the thinking minds
of Europe were more or less weighing and considering the
teachings of Luther.   Whilst studying and delivering
lectures in Paris, Xavier fell under the influence of Ignatius
Loyola, a humble and unlearned Jesuit, who prevailed on
him to join his order.   Xavier and Ignatius, with one
other Frenchman, three Spaniards, and a Portuguese, took
the four vows, *viz.* : poverty, chastity, a pilgrimage to
Jerusalem, and the promise to convert infidels.   Thus
started the society of Jesuits.

In Venice, Xavier attended the patients in the Hospital
for Incurables.   He fasted assiduously and practised the
severest austerity of life.   Thence he went to Portugal,
and at thirty-five years of age set sail for the Indies, where
this apostle of the creeds and maxims of the order of
Loyola found corruption in all its worst forms to be rife
among the natives, who were chiefly Portuguese.   According to Xavier's biographies, " each Portuguese had several
native concubines.   Assassination was common, Justice
was sold in the tribunals, and the most revolting criminals
were punished only when they had nothing wherewith
to corrupt their judges."   Wealth ruled everything—
religion was forgotten.

Soon after Xavier commenced his preachings, however,
a religious revival followed his wanderings.   He himself
was tall and lean, with a bright, cheerful face, dark hair
and kind blue eyes, and he possessed courage that nothing
could shake.   This courage, combined with his absolute
self-forgetfulness, gave him great power as a leader.
He wore only one garment as dress and mantle, and often
a morsel of bread was his only meal.   This he frequently
obtained by begging, and he never allowed himself more

than four hours of sleep. During that short rest he saw visions. In all weathers, and at all times, he continued his own preachings, and superintended his disciples' work.

In India, Xavier found that not all his eloquence or persuasive power, or intuition of gaining ascendancy over his hearers, could avail him until he had learned the Tamil language, of which, however, he soon obtained sufficient knowledge to enable him to hold converse, though he could not discourse publicly. His manner of conversion was of the simplest. He had the creed and other parts of the catechism translated into Malabar, learned them by heart and repeated them to his listeners, who were at once baptised if they owned to their belief in them.

Xavier himself was assured that the powers of Portugal over the Indies had been assigned by Providence for the furthering of the Christian faith, and, thinking that the officials were too slack, he appealed to the King of Portugal. As a result of this appeal, an inquisition was established in Goa and the island of Lalsette, and it was decreed that all idols must be destroyed, idolaters punished, all revenues to the mosques given to the Christians, and no Pagan was to continue in office. It was further ordained that no slaves should be sold to heathens, and that Xavier was to have a free hand to place the pearl fishery trade in the hands of Christians. It must be remembered that the Apostle was in earnest in believing not only that his Church was infallible, but that all unbelievers were doomed to everlasting torture after death. The same belief has lived through all the ages, the same conviction that the rite of baptism can save even an infant from damnation still prevails.

Xavier, although he employed and directed numerous Jesuit missionaries, himself always undertook journeys to the places which had not yet been visited by preachers of Christianity. Whilst Mohammedanism was being voluntarily, or forcibly, impressed upon the natives of Malacca and the island of the Moluccas, the Jesuit apostle won over many of the chiefs who dreaded the law of Islam.

In 1549 Xavier sailed for Japan, and gloried in the manifold perils of the voyage. Arrived there, he was again faced with the difficulties of the language, and forced to learn the elements of Japanese grammar. As soon as was possible, he commenced his great mission, and in an interview with the King of Satsuma he obtained an edict by which the King's subjects were accorded full permission to discard the old Buddhist faith and embrace the Christian. After the first year he had made about one hundred converts, but the King of Satsuma began to fear that because the Portuguese vessels now sailed to Firado he would lose the trade which had always enriched his own port of Kagosima, so, acting on the persuasions of his ministers, he commanded that any man who received baptism should be killed.

Xavier was forced to depart for Firando, where he made a few converts, thence to Amanguchi, where he met with no success. From there, he set out for Kioto, where there was a renowned and large university. There he was greeted with ridicule, and his preachings were hooted with derision. Following the Jesuit custom of endeavouring to obtain the favourable assistance of those in authority, not, as they asserted, because of their wealth and position, but merely because their power and influence could benefit, through Xavier and his followers, the souls of those in need, he endeavoured to obtain an interview with the Mikado.

Realising, however, that he had been wrong in going amongst strangers in his humble and ragged robe, he returned in two weeks to the Court of the King of Amanguchi with a retinue of servants carrying gifts, and with letters from the Indian Viceroy and the Bishop of Goa. Xavier himself wore handsome ecclesiastical robes.   The King gave him a friendly greeting and offered handsome presents, which the apostle refused, only craving permission to preach in his principality.   After only two months Xavier had baptised five hundred people.

In December 1552 he died and was interred in his robes. Three months and a half later his body was exhumed and found exactly as though he had just passed away—" the clothes entire, and the colour as that of a living man, and exhaling a pleasant odour."   Roman Catholics regard the exhumation of Xavier's body as one of the best attested miracles within the pale of their Church.   The people in Goa, on the other hand, disbelieving in the supernatural preservation, concluded that it had been disembowelled and embalmed, although the doctor's examination is said to have refuted this supposition.

CHAPTER IX

VISIONARIES—(*Continued*)

EVEN as a boy at school Tommasso (1568–1639) argued on theological subjects with his masters and school-fellows. He joined the mystical order of the Dominicans when he was only fourteen years old. His intellect was as acute as his nerves were sensitive. When at Naples he happened to speak disparagingly of ex-communication, for which he was put in prison. On his release he went to Padua, and on the journey was robbed of all his manuscripts. He was then again imprisoned for threatening the General of the Dominicans, and a third time on account of the new doctrines which he openly professed. He had studied necromancy in the monastery of Cosenza from Brother Abramo, who prophesied that Tommasso would one day wear a kingly crown. His mind, thus started on a wild, ambitious road, he let his thoughts and imagination run riot, until he claimed to be indeed a monarch, and even more—a demigod—in opposition to the power of Spain and of the Pope. That was the beginning—in the end, he died a zealous supporter of both, his whole life a contradiction.

When he was released from prison, where, in all, he spent three years, he became deeply interested in astrology. He talked much with astrologers and mathematicians, and was greatly impressed by their prophecy of the approaching end of the world. He then became entirely immersed in prophecy, devouring eagerly all of the prophecies the Bible and the ancient poets could teach him. In the white horses and the white-garbed elders of the New Zion he recognised the brothers of Saint Dominic.

In the political and social upheavals of that period, and in the happenings of famines, floods, comets, and earthquakes, Tommasso saw sure signs of the fulfilment of the predictions, and he spread these predictions far and wide, thinking thus to pave the way for the foundation of the 'Holy Republic' of his dreams. Unquestionably his words and exhortations came to the people as a call to rebellion, they fitted in so well with the crying need for change, which the miserable condition of Calabria rendered much longed for. To many who thirsted for revenge, the prophet's words came as a trumpet call. Marazio di Rinaldi and his bandit band were amongst the latter, and although neither religious reforms nor the seven seals of the Apocalypse were known to them, they grasped the fact that their help would be needed in the fight.

Tommasso's idea of the 'Holy Republic' comprised a universal monarchy reigned over by the Pope and himself —" Utopia, of the City of the Sun," he called it. Every human being was to be equally educated, and all the Solarians should call each other brother. Selfishness should be unknown, the one thought should be for the common good, and everyone should live together in happiness. The only strife would be the noble strife of intelligence. He visualised his Solarians using ships with neither rudder nor oars, cars that were driven by the wind, the art of flying in every-day practice, and an instrument invented for the discovery of new stars. The Solarians should practise never-ending adoration, offer up bloodless sacrifices, and pay homage (without worship) to the sun and the stars.

And this wonderful city Tommasso aimed at inaugurating in Calabria, with himself as head and ruler. Believing firmly in the practicability of his wild scheme, he felt sure that every other nation, seeing the happy lives of the citizens of the New Zion, would fall in with the new order of things, and that in due time he would rule as guide and king of the entire world, and thus reach the summit of his aspirations.

It does not seem to have occurred to him to doubt the possibility of reorganising the universe at one stroke, changing everything, governments, laws, ancient customs, ancient traditions, and human lives. Some of the reforms that he drew out were liberal and remarkable : " Law is the consent of all, written and promulgated for the common good." " Heavy taxes should be levied on articles that are not necessary, and are of luxury, and light ones on necessaries." " A national army should be established, education should be free, and medical aid should be gratuitous."

Thus, a simple monk, in a remote countryside, really imagined that, with his few followers, he could overturn all that was, and all that had ever been, and that he would become the reformer and monarch of the entire universe. When crushed by adversity, Tommasso once again sought comfort in Catholicism and returned to his angels and miracles. During the last few months of his life he fasted rigorously, in penitence, he said, for his revolutionary sins, but even then he despaired of pardon and believed himself to be damned. Richelieu writes of Tommasso : " I shall always hold him for a man wilder than a fly, and less sensible in worldly affairs than a child."

Bartolomeo Brandano (1584–1637), a tenant of the Olivetan monks who had their monastery near Monte Amiata, was suddenly seized with intense religious fervour, perhaps partly through grief at the sufferings which the occupation of the Spanish army was causing to his beloved country. He was convinced that he was John the Baptist, and wore a hair shirt which reached barely to his knees. In this garment—his feet bare, a crucifix in his hand, and under his arm a skull—Brandano journeyed through Siena, preaching and prophesying as he went, working miracles, and gathering proselytes ; thence he travelled to Rome, and preached in the square of St. Peter's inveighing against the Pope and the Cardinals. The Pope Clement VII, being more pitying than indignant with the self-styled prophet, did not command that he should be burnt at the stake, as was the custom with those ' possessed of demons,' but instead had him secluded in the Tordinova prison.

John Bunyan (1628–1688) was very wild as a boy and much addicted to " lying and swearing." He had " fearful dreams and visions." Pestilent spirits, orgies of devils, and even archangels, appeared to him and continued to do so until his seventeenth year ; then they disappeared for two years, during which period he gave himself over to every evil passion and led an utterly riotous life. He knew an old man who kept an ale-house, and he often tormented his son just to make him curse his father and wish the devil had him. " The devil did at last have the ale-house keeper, and rent and tore him till he died." Bunyan writes, " I was an ear and eye witness of what I here say—I saw the father himself possessed, his flesh being gathered up in a heap about the bigness of half an egg, to the unutterable torture and affliction of the old man."

When Bunyan's visions and dreams returned to him they took a benign and celestial form. He heard heavenly voices, and saw the face of Christ himself looking down upon him, which affected him so strongly that his life completely changed, he put all the vice and ungodliness from him and became a great and earnest preacher, and, in due course, wrote the *Pilgrim's Progress*, most of which was doubtless not only suggested but ' seen ' by him in his dreams and visions. O'Donoghue appears to have been the first to realise that Bunyan was insane—in the technical and medical sense of the word—for three or four years of his life, say between 1650 and 1653. His book *Grace Abounding* contains particulars sufficient to fill up the certificate and case-book of the mental specialist. " When I was but a child, about nine or ten years old (*c.* 1638), after I had spent this or the other day in sin, I have in my bed been greatly afflicted, while asleep, with the apprehension of devils and wicked spirits, who still, as I then thought, laboured to draw me away with them."

Bunyan relates that until his marriage (1649) he indulged in all manner of " vice and ungodliness " with youths of the village, " cursing, swearing, and playing the madman." His marriage brought better elements into his life, and it seemed to his neighbours just as if ' Tom of Bedlam ' had become a sober man. Premonitory symptoms, however, of the latent disease manifested themselves from time to time, and in 1651 the " great storm came stealing " upon him, and " floods of blasphemies "—unprovoked and un-expected—overwhelmed his mind. The " unpardonable sin " began to have a horrible fascination for him. He " desired to commit it," and soon came to believe that he had committed it. Sometimes he " felt the tempter pull his clothes," sometimes the devil seemed to " take the form of a bull, bush, or besom," inviting him to fall down and worship him. Then for a whole year one sentence iterated and reiterated itself on the anvil of his diseased brain—" sell Christ," " sell Christ," " sell Christ." [1]

" I could neither eat my food, stoop for a pin, chop a stick, or cast my eyes upon this or that, but still the temptation would come, ' sell Christ,' ' sell Christ.' " The agitation of his mind was reflected in his restlessness ; he could not sit still for a moment, nor occupy himself in any way. At last—in a paroxysm of exhaustion—he seemed to himself to let the fatal words of surrender escape from his lips, " Let Him go, if He will." For two whole years at least the " masterless hounds of hell ran over his soul, roaring and bellowing. He had, at last—committed the unpardonable sin : he was now racked day and night with the anticipation of descending into Hades before another day had passed. Like other victims of religious melancholia he added to his physical agitation and mental agony by ransacking the Scriptures to justify the appalling sentence of everlasting damnation pronounced against his soul ! "

Unfortunately another book in his starved library did him infinite mischief. Francesco Spira, a lawyer of Cittadella near Padua, became a Lutheran, but in an access of terror in 1548 was persuaded to make a public recantation before the Papal Legate at Venice. He felt that he was an apostate from the truth, and he soon believed himself to have, on that account, forfeited for ever the mercy of God. Religious melancholia followed with suicidal impulses, which baffled both the theologians and the physicians of Padua. The story of Spira was written in Italian to prove the judgment of God against

[1] O'Donoghue, *History of Bethlehem Hospital.*

Protestantism, and was translated into English by Nathaniel
Bacon, as a proof of the falsehood of popery ! Neither
the man who translated it, nor Bunyan who read into it
an irrefragable assurance of his own damnation, had the
least idea that the story of Francesco Spira illustrated a
case of religious mania.

Such was the fiery trial which made John Bunyan what
he came to be. Out of it came the iron, dug in darkness,
heated red hot in the furnace of his afflictions, tempered in
the bath of his own tears—which went to the building up
of his greatest work, the *Pilgrim's Progress.*

The armour of Christian is dinted with the marks of
his terrible conflict with Apollyon. But it was John
Bunyan himself who could find no firm ground under his
feet in the slough of religious despondency. It was he
who had been in the iron cage, when he thought that he
had " sold Christ," and " committed the sin against the
Holy Ghost." John Bunyan—and none but he—had been
through the valley of the shadow of death, before he wrote
about it : in it he had uttered the grievous blasphemies
which the fiend seemed to have put into his mouth : on
his pilgrimage through it " clouds of confusion " had sometimes settled on his head, sometimes " doleful voices "
moaned in his ear or he heard a " company of fiends rushing
and yelling " around him.

The wonderful inventive genius of Swedenborg (1688-
1772) was in a great measure the outcome of morbid
exaltation. Among his remarkable and shrewd observations, he upheld that the angels read the full story of a
man's life in his brain after he is dead. All his thoughts
and conclusions came to him suddenly as the result of
visions. In his boyhood he was able to suspend his
breathing completely, a sure sign, to his own mind and

to those of his disciples, that he was privileged to wander during his lifetime into the spirit-world.

He was an earnest student of astronomy, magnetism, and other sciences, until the strange thing happened which caused him to become a prophet. After a good dinner one night, a mist rose before him, and toads and beetles and other hideous crawling things seemed to surround him. He writes of that vision, " I was astonished, having all my wits about me, and being perfectly conscious. The darkness gradually passed away. I now saw a man sitting in a corner of the chamber. As I had thought myself alone, I was greatly frightened, when he said to me, ' Eat not so much.' My sight again became dim, and when I recovered, I found myself alone in the room." The same vision returned to him the next night and said, " I am God, the Lord, the Creator and Redeemer of the world, and I have chosen thee to unfold to men the spiritual sense of the Holy Scriptures. I will myself dictate to thee what thou shalt write."

After this, Swedenborg looked upon himself as the Messiah ; but in spite of his announced conviction, he always evaded every attempt to put his powers to the test. During an epileptic attack he stripped himself and fell rolling into the gutter. In earlier life, before the Great Vision which turned all his thoughts and labours to spiritual matters, he had constant visionary dreams, sometimes ecstatic, sometimes tragic—often full of sensuous passion, for there was little of the ascetic in his nature.

He asserted, and fully believed, that he could, and frequently did, hold communication with a world beyond. His friend Sprenger found him one day raising his hands to heaven and speaking and moving continuously. Then suddenly he dropped his hands, and said, " I had a long conversation with the angels and with my heavenly friends, and am now quite wet with perspiration." He himself also related that when in London an angel came to him and warned him not to give way to gluttony. A mist appeared to emanate from his body, this formed itself into worms, which were destroyed by flames, leaving only a brilliant light where they had been.

Swedenborg constantly had visions and dreams, and seemed unable to differentiate between the two. One of these dreams is described in his own words. " At ten o'clock I lay down in bed, and was somewhat better; half an hour later I heard a clamour under my head. I thought that then the temper went away. Immediately there came over me a rigour so strong, from the head and the whole body, with some din, and this several times I found that something holy was over me. I thereupon fell asleep, and at about twelve, one, or two o'clock in the night, there came over me so strong a shivering from head to foot, as if many winds rushed together, which shook me, was indescribable, and prostrated me upon my face. Then, while I was prostrated, I was in a moment quite awake, and saw that I was cast down, and wondered what it meant. And I spoke as if I was awake, but found that the word was put into my mouth, and I said, ' Omnipotent Jesus Christ, as of Thy great grace Thou condescendest to come to so great a sinner, make me worthy of this grace.' I held my hands together and prayed, and then came a hand which squeezed my hands hard—immediately thereon I continued my prayer."

He believed that he had conversed for days and months with the spirits of the different planets, that he had actually seen the inhabitants of Jupiter walking on their feet and hands at the same time, those of Mars talking through their eyes, and those of Saturn out of their stomachs.[1]

Julie de Krudener (1766–1824), after having been disappointed in love, turned her thoughts to the faith of the ancients, and believed herself to have been chosen to redeem humanity. She preached at Bale, and announced the speedy coming of the Messiah. The Senate of the city took alarm and banished her, and twenty thousand pilgrims wished to follow her. Julie then went to Baden and found twice that number of people awaiti g her, eager to kiss her hands or the hem of her robe. Exiled also from Baden, she returned to Switzerland. Crowds followed her everywhere. She was followed by acclamations and blessings as she passed from one town to another —the hostility of the police notwithstanding. Julie's preachings were delivered with a burning eloquence, which she explained by saying that the words and all her works were inspired to her by angels.

Margaretta Peter (1794–1823), the youngest of John Peter's five daughters—unlike all her sisters and one brother was extremely clever from childhood, constantly receiving praise for her school work, and winning the admiration of the village pastor for her religious devotion and eagerness to probe the depth of all questions relating to theological and spiritual knowledge. Already at six years of age Margaretta delivered sermons to her family and exhorted her father and sisters as to the manner of life God would wish them to live, and they attributed her great spiritual ardour to a special grace which had been accorded to her owing to the fact that she was a Christmas-born child. Her intellect and strength of character were

---

[1] *Swedenborg*, by M. de Baumont-Vassy, 1842.

so far beyond those possessed by the rest of farmer Peter's family that she unconsciously drew them under her influence, and her ascendancy grew with her years.

When Margaretta was eighteen she went to Illnan to keep house for an uncle, and so successful was his work and home life under her sway that he soon began to believe, as her own household did, that she carried with her the benign blessing of God. Whilst with her uncle, Margaretta attended the meetings of the Pietists at Shaffhausen, and at the end of twelve months she told her sisters that the Almighty was gradually flooding her with wondrous revelations which aroused her to a fuller sense of her own sins, and that she was also endowed with the spirit of prophecy. On leaving her uncle the ' holy maiden ' started on a preaching tour as a revivalist. Margaretta had grown into a tall, good-looking girl, with fair hair and large soulful eyes, which, however, glowed with intense spiritual fervour.

Jacob Gavoz, also a roving apostle, met her at Zurich, and his description of Margaretta to one of his disciples, Jacob Morf, made the latter hasten to make her acquaintance—an acquaintance which ripened so speedily into a close friendship that Jacob paid long and protracted visits to her. She told him on ' Ascension Day ' that it was the will of Heaven that they should ascend together into the mansions of the blessed and occupy one throne together for all eternity. Mysticism, resulting from spiritual exaltation, invariably, and apparently inevitably, glides into licentiousness, for the ardent mystic obeys only the laws which, in his extravagant fancy, he considers to be mapped out for him and him alone.

But a change soon came over the holy maiden; she stayed for whole days in her room, with drawn shutters, reading the Bible and, when Jacob was not with her, writing long letters addressed to " her dear child, Jacob." The evenings were spent with her family in the big living-room, where she preached and prophesied to them and to the ardent neighbours, who thronged to the house and hung upon her words. Often she bade them pray for strength, as a great trial of their strength was at hand. One day she exclaimed, " I see the host of Satan drawing nearer and nearer to encompass me. He strives to overcome me. Let me alone that I may fight him." She then began to strike the air, as she feared that she alone could not shield the whole world against the power of Satan. She even told her family that the devil had ensconced himself in the walls of their house, and that it would need terrific force and faith to send him forth. Not one of her family either doubted her word or hesitated to obey her commands, so absolute had become her authority. A sharp pop in the fire brought the maid Gaggli to her feet with a jump, crying out that the devil was knocking. Margaretta performed the spiritual movements of the Pietists for expelling evil spirits, and cried out, " Depart, thou murderer of souls, accursed one—to hell fire. Wilt thou try to rob me of my sheep, whom I have pledged myself to save ? "

On another occasion she said, " Lo, I see Satan and his first-born floating in the air. They are dispersing their emissaries to the corners of the earth to summon their armies together." Her sister Elizabeth echoed this by saying that the spirits were visible to her also. Margaretta immediately commenced to dash up and down the room, overthrowing the furniture and striking it with all the force of her bare hands, until she found a hammer with which she attacked the walls. " I see in spirit," she cried,

" the old Napoleon gathering a mighty host and marching against me. The contest will be terrible. Go—fetch me axes, clubs, whatever you can find. Bar the doors, curtain all the windows in the house, and close every shutter." " Strike, Strike," cried Margaretta as soon as they arrived with the weapons. " Cleave everywhere— on all sides—Smite on till I bid you stay. Smite and give your lives if need be ! " There were ten in that room, and each and all hacked away at furniture and walls for upwards of three hours, encouraged always and goaded on by the holy maid. " Strike him, cut him down, the arch-fiend ; whoso loseth his life shall find it. There he is in yonder corner ! He is a murderer, he is the young Napoleon, the coming anti-Christ, who entered into me and nearly destroyed me."

But before an hour had passed she commanded them to rise and continue the battle on their own bodies—to strike their heads and their bodies. Elizabeth, beyond herself with exaltation, cried out, " O Margaret, do then strike me, let me die for Christ." Margaretta did so without delay, and with so much force that her sister screamed with pain. " Bear it," said the saint; " it is the will of God." She kept watch that none should slacken in their self-inflicted blows. " Father," she said to old Peter, " you do not beat yourself sufficiently," and struck him with all her strength, saying, " I am only driving out the old Adam, father ; it does not hurt you."

The whole of the following day and night were spent in the Pietest spiritual exercises and in silent prayer, but on the ensuing morning the holy maid, standing on her bed, addressed her family : " I see the many souls seeking salvation through me ; they must be assisted. I have given a pledge for many souls, that Satan may not have them—among them is my brother Caspar. But I cannot conquer in the strife without the shedding of blood."

Again she exhorted all present to continue their efforts to drive the devil out. Seizing an iron wedge, she struck her brother Caspar many times with great violence, and he submitted without a murmur, as though deprived of all power of resistance or even self-assertion. When a crashing blow sent him half-stunned to the ground, old Peter and Gaggli the maid-servant carried him to the safety of his room, and although Peter must have known that still more terrible tragedies might be consummated, he tacitly approved, inasmuch as he did not return to the fated room, nor would he admit anyone to the house, making the excuse that a surgeon was busy upstairs.

Margaretta asked the others if they were prepared to offer up their lives, and all replied with vivid enthusiasm in the affirmative. She asserted, " I see you will not really die. But I—I must die ! " Elizabeth, who was still weak and half stupefied, cried out, " I will gladly die for the saving of the souls of my brother and father ; strike me dead." Without hesitation, she commenced to hammer at her own head. Margaretta said, " It has been revealed to me that Elizabeth will sacrifice herself." She picked up the heavy iron wedge with which she stunned her brother, and brought it down on her sister's head. That was the cue—and in wild spiritual fanaticism, the others took it up, and hammered at poor Elizabeth. Margaretta inflicted wounds on Ursula and John Moser, so haphazard were the blows she directed at her sister, and gripping Ursula's arm, she commanded her to deal the death blow to Elizabeth. Ursula, by nature full of love and tenderness, sobbed aloud. Even in the midst of the wild frenzy which possessed them all, she said that she could not obey, seeing how well she loved Elizabeth. " I am ready to die," said the latter, who was already more than half dead. Margaretta promised to raise her again in three days, and to rise herself again at the same time. Then all rained more blows on Elizabeth and battered her to death.

Margaretta's eyes blazed with the spiritual fire of ecstasy as she took her seat by the side of the murdered girl, and she said with amazing calmness, " More blood must flow, I must die now—you must crucify me. It is better that I should die than that thousands of souls should perish."

When, with bitter tears, the family said it was impossible, that they could not obey such a behest, she told them solemnly that they would be responsible for every soul that might be lost, and implored them once more to bring nails to form a cross. " Go on," she said, " God strengthen your arms." No sign of pain escaped her as the terrible work of crucifixion was enacted, even though her murderers grew dizzy and sick and sobbed with agony as they carried it through. It is noteworthy, as showing the extraordinary depth of Revivalist ecstasy at that period, that even after all those who had participated in the terrible murders had been tried and sentenced to long terms of imprisonment, and the house owned by John Peter ordered to be levelled to the ground, Pietists and other fanatical believers visited the place, gazing at the holy maiden's house, and not only feeling but openly expressing the deepest admiration for her life and for the manner of her death. " Oh, that it had been I who had died ! " " Oh, how many souls must she have delivered ! " were among the utterances overheard in the crowd of sight-seeing worshippers.

Mesmer (1734–1815), the Austrian physician, studied medicine at the Vienna University, and devoted much time and thought to the influence of the planets upon the body. Following in the footsteps of the old astrological physicians—and going a step further—he stated this influence affected the nervous system most keenly, and he then commenced to try experiments with magnetic plates. His rapid success surprised everybody—himself most of all, so he worked at his theories, experiments, and cures until his theory of animal magnetism evolved. A girl he was attending had a convulsive complaint, which he soon ameliorated by his planetary method of treatment. Mesmer could not for some time be sure whether there existed among the diverse bodies which form the world a like action to that of the heavenly bodies. As soon as he had assured himself on this point, he came to the conclusion that metallic plates were quite superfluous, and he thought he was able to effect his cures equally well without them, by merely passing his hands in the direction of the feet of the sufferer. He sent a detailed report of his amazing discovery to every university and school of learning in Europe, challenging them to investigate his claim. With the exception of the Berlin Academy of Sciences, one and all ignored both his letter and his discovery, and the reply from Berlin was discouraging to his theory and insulting to himself. But he upheld his views and beliefs with great firmness, and asserted that the whole world and every human body was filled with a magnetic matter, and that any person could pass on some of his own to another person merely by will power. Mesmer said there was scarcely any substance that he could not magnetise, *e.g.* glass, wood, paper, stones, etc., and that he was able to fill any receptacle with magnetic matter.

The old adage as to no man being a prophet in his own country could assuredly have been applied to Mesmer—all his statements, even his cures, being either ignored or treated with contempt. He left Vienna and travelled for a time. In Switzerland he came upon the well-known alchemic physician Father Gassner, who made quite a good business by casting out devils and—like Mesmer—by curing the suffering by laying hands on them. His house was daily overrun with patients—the blind, the deaf, the lame, and the hysteric.

Mesmer approved his cures, being, as they were, on his own lines; and he assured Gassner that unconsciously he was using his personal powers of magnetism. At Gassner's request Mesmer treated some of his patients with the same success. Following on this, he, to quote his very own words, succeeded in working some amazing cures, though we have only his assurance on this subject. He professed his ability to cure a lady who was inclined to convulsive fits and who was also blind, and protested that he had been successful, or if not, the lady herself was alone to blame. A well-known oculist who examined her eyes after the treatment declared that her sight had not been restored, nor had her convulsive tendencies been checked. Mesmer adhered to his first statement, adding that the lady merely pretended to be still blind in order to harm his fame, that in truth she was in a conspiracy to ruin him.

He found on his arrival in Paris that the Parisians were much more inclined to be amused than attracted by his pretensions. But with great perseverance and supreme self-confidence Mesmer leased a magnificent apartment and invited all who were in trouble or sickness to give his new power of nature a trial. He secured an unexpected ally in M. d'Eslon, a physician of great renown, and when the fact of d'Eslon's becoming a convert was mooted around, animal magnetism, or Mesmerism, as some people called it, became suddenly the rage of Paris. Rich and poor, old and young, came in crowds to Mesmer's salons in order to judge for themselves of the powers of this self-confident magician, the women especially being intensely enthusiastic. The richly stained glass, the pale tender lighting of the rooms, appealed to them, as did the mirrors which almost covered the walls. They were attracted also by the costly scents and incense which fun i from antique vases, and by the odour of orange blosso which pervaded the passages, the harp melodies, and the soft religious music whose sighings came to them from other rooms.

In the middle of the largest salon was placed a large oval vessel containing bottles filled with magnetised water. The vessel was then filled with water, and iron filings thrown in from time to time to increase the magnetic effect. The vessel was next covered with a lid of iron in which many holes had been punched. A long iron rod projected from every hole—for application to any part of the patient's body that might be affected, the sufferers being instructed to sit round the vessel holding each other's hands, with their knees pressed together to assist the passing of the magnetic fluid.

The assistant magnetisers then entered the room to pour the marvellous fluid from the tips of their fingers into the sufferers. These assistants were always chosen for their strength and good looks. They approached the patients, " embraced them between the knees, rubbed them gently down the spine and the course of the nerves, using gentle pressure on the breasts of the ladies, and staring them out of countenance to magnetise them by the eye. All this time the most rigorous silence was maintained, with the exception of a few wild notes on the harmonium or the pianoforte, or the melodious voice of a hidden opera singer swelling softly at long intervals. Gradually the cheeks of the ladies began to glow, their imaginations to become inflamed, and off they went, one after the other, into convulsive fits. Some of them sobbed and tore their hair, others laughed till the tears ran from their eyes, while yet others shrieked and yelled till they became insensible altogether." [1]

At this crisis the High Priest, in the person of Mesmer, made his effective entry, clad in a long and gold-embroidered robe of violet silk, and carrying a white magnetic rod. As soon as he fixed the more ecstatic and noisy patients with his eye, most of their violence disappeared, and the insensible he brought back to consciousness by tracing imaginary figures on their breasts and abdomens. These experiments of Mesmer had an extraordinary effect on the excitable people of Paris, the majority lauding him up to the skies, though some condemned him as a quack to whom evil powers had been given because he had sold himself to the devil. Marie Antoinette the Queen was amongst his earnest supporters, and to her Mesmer wrote, entreating her influence to secure for him the Government's protection and sheltering arm ; he even hinted that unless he were presented with a chateau, lands, and a large income, he might feel it necessary to take himself and his wondrous discovery to another country.

But this letter only brought him the offer of a small pension and a cross of the order of St. Michael, if and when he should make a discovery in medicine and send

[1] *Memoirs of Extraordinary Popular Delusions*, Charles Mackay, i. 279.

a report to physicians of the King's nomination. These conditions were not appreciated by Mesmer, and under pretence of taking the water cure, he left Paris for Spa, followed by many of his wealthy and titled patients. One of these promised to start a subscription for him of one hundred shares, each of one hundred louis, if he would reveal his secrets to them. Mesmer unhesitatingly agreed, and in an incredibly short time the subscription had grown far above the original figure. Mesmer pocketed the money and renewed his experiments in Paris, whilst his wealthy and admiring disciples inaugurated ' Societies of Harmony ' in many parts of France. The scenes enacted at these ' Reunions,' under the name of magnetism, were a scandal to morality.

A Royal Commission which had been ordered by the King to enquire into Mesmer's methods and beliefs and M. d'Eslon's share therein, issued a report which struck a death-blow to Mesmer's reputation in the gay capital, by giving as its verdict that imagination and not animal magnetism produced the phenomenal effects on his patients. He left Paris in much haste, and took his subscribed fortune with him.

Prospère Enfantin (born 1796), an able and level-headed engineer, railway director, and mathematician, believed himself to be the founder and head of a new religion. He himself had not the smallest doubt as to his infallibility on every subject, whether industrial or philosophical— musical or culinary. The new religion had for its object the equalisation of men and women, and the poetising of financial and industrial language. In his own person he stood for the Father, and hoped always to find the Mother, Eve the free woman—a woman, who whilst able to reason like a man, also knew the capabilities and needs of women and would declare them unrestrainedly, and so supply the material for a declaration of the duties and rights of women. It is perhaps not strange that the right woman was never discovered. George Sand and Madame de Stael were suggested, but they merely smiled when they heard.

Although Prospère and his followers were at last put into prison, he adhered to his illusion, saying that only a great man was capable of founding a new religion. He and his party called themselves ' Supreme Fathers,' wore a symbolical dress, consisting of white trousers, red waistcoat, and blue coat, the three colours standing for love, work, and faith. Each member had his name written on his shirt front, and wore a collar embroidered with triangles and a semi-circle, which was to become a circle whenever the Mother Eve should be found, and it was said amongst their doctrines, that " Man recalls the Past, Woman represents the Future, and the two united are the present." Prospère's kindness was remarkable, he was selfless to his followers—whom he called his sons. He was for many years director of the railway from Paris to Lyons, and he anticipated and even attempted to undertake the building of the Suez Canal.

David Lazzaretti, when a boy, wanted to become a monk, but when old enough he followed his father's trade of carter. He gave early signs of extraordinarily striking contradictions of character. Unlike his father, he possessed handsome and distinguished features, very marked intelligence, and strange piercing eyes, which to some people had a singular attraction. Like his father, however, David was an inveterate drunkard. Yet he studied assiduously and devoted much of his time to intellectual reading. But the rules of grammar he never could master. He was so extremely bad tempered, quarrelsome, and such an object of dread, that one day he and his brothers put all the inhabitants of Castle del Piano to flight. Yet whatever was fine and noble—a sermon, speech or poem—appealed to and attracted David, and he had a great reverence for Christ and Mahomet. Although he at one time asserted that he abhorred three things—women, churches, and dancing—yet at that same period he very much admired a Jewess of Pittigliano, probably moved by her eloquent defence of her faith. He joined Pialdini's army, and before marching to the war wrote a patriotic hymn, which, in spite of the crudity of its phrasing and its many grammatical mistakes, was both original and beautiful. It is supposed that Lazzaretti was impotent during his youth, but he married in his twenty-fifth year and seems to have felt a poetic tenderness for his wife, to whom he wrote love sonnets. After the war he returned to his life of debauchery and coarse language, but continued his writings, hoping thereby to win name and fame. His tragedies and some of his verses read like burlesques. When he was thirty-three years of age he was seized with violent religious fervour. The Madonna appeared to him in a vision and ordered him to proceed to Rome and remind the Pope of the divinity of his mission. It is recorded that when he reached Rome, the Pope at first refused to receive him, but afterwards did so, advising him, however, to try the remedy of a shower bath.

After his stay at the hermitage of Montorio Romano David's character underwent a complete change. He became gentle and abstemious, subsisting on bread, water, and herbs. Even his burlesque writings became more elegant in style, and they teemed with forceful images contributed by a faith as vivid as that of the early Christians.   His calm, grave manner and inspired eloquence of speech, as well as his changed habits, surprised the people who crowded to hear him.   They formed a procession, Lazzaretti leading and priests walking at his side.   He was welcomed with rejoicings wherever he went, even the parish priests kissed his face, his hands, his feet.   In 1870 he founded a Mutual Assistance Society, which he called ' the Society of the Holy League.'   When about to start for Monte Cristo, Lazzaretti invited his followers to a Last Supper.   Whilst at Monte Cristo he wrote sermons, epistles and prophecies, and when he returned to Monte-labro he wrote a description of the visions and prophetic inspirations which he had received.   For this he was arrested and imprisoned for sedition.   On being released, David founded another Society, to which he gave the name of ' Christian Families.'   On a false charge of this being a fraud, he was again sent to prison for seven months. When in Italy, he compiled the ' Rules and Discipline of the Order of Persistent Hermits,' and evolved a new system of cypher with a numerical alphabet.

" Mysteriously carried by the Divine Power " to France, he wrote a book entitled *My Wrestling with God*, a mingling of Genesis, Revelations, and rhapsodies.   In a manifesto which he addressed to all the princes in Christendom, he referred to himself as the Great Monarch, and advised them that, " at an unexpected time, the end of the world shall be manifested to the Latin nation in a way quite opposed to human pride," and in the same document he claims himself to be the " Leader, Master, Judge, and Prince over all the rulers of the earth."   He also boasted descent from the great Constantine.   " I am the King of Kings and Prince of all rulers.   I bear on my shoulders all the princes of the world.   All the carbineers and soldiers there are, are mine and dependent on me, and there are no ropes that can bind me."

He adopted a singular emblematic device—the double C, about which he was most concerned, and which stood for the first and second Christ—Christ, the son of Joseph of Nazareth, and Christ, the son of the late Joseph Lazzaretti of Arcidosso. With his habitual contradictoriness, David later on attacked the priesthood and even the Catholic Church, which, he asserted, had become a shop-keeping Church, whilst the priests merely profited by the faith of others without having any of their own. He entreated all true believers to disassociate themselves from the world by " abstaining from food, and from sexual intercourse, even in the case of married persons, who, however, if they indulged, were required to pray for at least two hours, naked, outside the bed," concluding his exhortation by declaring himself to be the " man of mystery, the New Christ, the Leader and Avenger." David then gave out that he would perform a great miracle, and had special banners and robes made, embroidered with all the grotesque animals which, at different times, had appeared to him in dreams.

The Prophet administered the oath of loyalty and sub servience at the foot of the Cross, his banner bearing the words, " The Republic is the Kingdom of God." One of his brothers warned him of the perilousness of this enter-prise, but he merely said that " he could ward off the bullets with his hands, and render harmless the weapons directed against himself and his faithful followers, and the government carbineers themselves would act as a guard of honour to them." He even went so far as to threaten all unbelievers with the Divine wrath if through want of faith they rebelled against his will. For this ceremonial,

David was attired in a royal cloak of purple embroidered in gold and crowned with a tiara bearing a crest with plumes ; he held a staff which was a rod of command. His principal associates wore robes of different colours, strangely fashioned, but less costly than his own.

David's brother had not erred when he foresaw the coming danger. The authorities made war upon the Prophet, imagining him to be a rebel, and he who had considered himself invulnerable fell struck by a shot. But even as he fell his imagination still held sway, for he cried out, " The victory is ours." Although Lazzaretti had first called upon the Church to free Italy, he wrote denouncing Papal idolatry, and though he desired to die as a member of the Catholic Apostolic Church, he wished to abolish auricular confession. When a surgeon hesitated about performing an operation on his son of whom he was intensely fond, David took the knife from him and himself performed the operation. His son died under it, but he only repeated in an unperturbed way, " The son of David cannot die."

CHAPTER X

THE PECULIARITIES OF MEN OF GENIUS

DANTE (born 1265) wrote his first sonnet to Beatrice at the age of nine. He possessed in such an unusual degree the vanity of most poets that he asserted his superiority to all his contemporaries, and declared himself to be the special favourite of God. He possessed a fierce hatred of his own country, as did Goethe, Heine, and Leopardi.

Villon (born 1431), so named after he had adopted the life of a thief, came of a good old family whose honour had never been sullied. Gaming and women compassed his downfall. At first he stole on quite a small scale, so that he might entertain his friends and mistresses, whose wine he took for the banquets. When a woman, who practically kept him, turned him out of doors, cold and hunger drove him to bigger thefts. Yet, in his will, he bequeathed her his heart. Eventually he became one of a band of road robbers, and narrowly escaped hanging.

Ariosto (1474–1533), the great Italian poet, was so beside himself with excitement when Charles V crowned him with a wreath of laurels that he rushed up and down the streets like a wild man.

The genius of the great sculptor and painter Michelangelo (1474–1564) triumphed over the great opposition of his parents, who endeavoured in every possible way to induce their son to adopt some other career. It may not be widely known that Michelangelo was also the author of some poems. His art and his work appear to have given more pleasure than did the man himself, for he was petty-minded, bad-tempered, and suspicious. He suffered from nerve trouble, which doubtless increased these characteristics. He slept badly, his sight was weak, and he suffered from attacks of giddiness. After receiving an injury through a fall, he not only forbade anyone to come near him, but remained shut up in his room, where he gave way to one of his terrific outbursts of temper. His speech was frequently incoherent, and his letters still more so. Indeed some of his missives are curious and meaningless.

Barthey (1544–1590) was so utterly grief-stricken when, on reading the printed copy of the *Génie*, he found the accent on the E was accidentally divided into two, that he spent sleepless nights of agony in consequence.

Tasso (1544–1595), like Socrates, imagined that a familiar spirit went with him, with whom he could converse on heavenly subjects. He constantly saw apparitions which were either gloriously beautiful, or evil and devilish. Sounds of laughter in the air and the ringing of bells were common auditory experiences of his. Once he beheld a wondrous cloud and, in its midst, the Virgin herself.

Giordano Bruno (1550–1600) openly expressed his settled conviction that he was a Titan who could destroy Jupiter ; and also a messenger from God, who knew the source of all created things. " What others see far ahead," said he, " I leave behind."   Bruno also believed himself illuminated by celestial light.

Malherbes (1555–1628) the poet, on being asked by Princess Conti to look over some verses " the most beautiful in the world," she said, " and which you have probably not seen," he replied pompously, " Pardon me, madam, I have seen them, for since they are the most beautiful in the world, I must have written them myself."

Richelieu (1585–1642) at times imagined himself to be a horse, and neighed, trotted, and jumped like one.

Milton, like Bacon, found that if he heard music before commencing work, he made far better progress. He always wrote with his head hanging over his armchair. He asserted that his muse was sterile in winter, and that he was able to write only between Spring and Autumn. " Cold," he used to say, " hinders the free development of the imagination."

Harington (1611–1677) conceived a strange notion that diseases adopted the shapes of " flies and bees," and because he believed this to be so, he armed himself with a long broom in order to brush them away.

Turenne (1611–1675), like Charles V, fought down bodily ailments and became a great general, proving again the oft-proven fact that the greatest military commanders have so frequently been sick men, many of them epileptics, almost implying that such men possess a greater spirit of reckless daring, a greater energy and quickness, combined with an equally greater disregard for destruction than healthy-bodied men. As a schoolboy Turenne showed no brilliancy, and he hated all restraint. He had an incurable stutter in his speech, and a slight nervous twitch in his shoulders. But he was also possessed of a dogged staying-power, and never abandoned any plan or enterprise on which he had set his mind.

Carlo Dolce (1618–1666), the celebrated Dutch painter, was so swayed by religious fervour that he made a vow never to paint any but religious pictures.   On the day of his wedding he did not present himself for the ceremony, and for many hours was searched for in vain.   At last his friends found him prostrated in front of the altar of the Annunciation.

Isabella Eugenia, Gouvernante of the Netherlands, brought into fashion a colour which became popular as ' Coleur d'Isabelle.'   It was a dull shade of brown, and this was how it was brought about.   When Ostend was besieged, and Isabella swore to capture the town, she made a vow that she would not change her chemise until the town surrendered, and as the siege went on for over three years, the ladies and gentlemen of the Court endeavoured to select their garments to match the colour scheme attained by those of Isabella.

Pascal (1623–1662) was, from boyhood upwards, a great nervous sufferer and had many odd fancies.   When quite a little child, the sight of water sent him into convulsive fits.   He was the victim of agonising headaches, which eventually developed into epileptic attacks.   Pascal could never endure to see his parents together, and always felt that he was walking by the side of a great abyss.

George Fox (1625–1690) believed himself to be possessed of a kind of second sight, which enabled him to discern the ' worthiness ' of others.   And in this way he asserted that he could ' discern witches.'   This founder of Quakerism was fully convinced as to the reality of the visions which continually appeared to him.   It was in one of these, he said, that he had received the consecration of the Spirit.   He frequently heard the voice of the Lord, and of one of these visions he writes that " the creation gave another smell to me than before and beyond what words can utter."

Lulli (1634–1687) composed much glorious music, but lived entirely for his art and was intensely unpractical. A friend of his frequently made excuses for his gaucheness, saying, " Pay no attention to him, he has no common sense, he is all genius."

Sir Isaac Newton (1642–1727) was so absent-minded that one day he rammed his niece's fingers into his pipe, and if he went to fetch anything, he usually came back without it. When he discovered the solution of a problem, his emotional joy was so intense that he was entirely incapable of going on with his work. He always asserted that his system had been suggested merely by the falling of an apple, and that many of his mathematical problems came to him in his sleep. His mind, even as a boy, was incessantly working at his great problems, and he frequently omitted to fulfil the instructions of his parents. He was usually the last in his class at school, but showed remarkable cleverness in the designing and making of mechanical toys. Newton's colossal mind is said to have conquered humanity—but he himself was strange and incoherent in his speech, and he suffered much through a dread of persecution. One of his letters addressed to Pepys contains these lines : " I neither ate nor slept this twelve month, nor have I my former consistency of mind."

He suffered in middle age from what he himself described as a distemper that seized his head, and kept him awake for five nights together. As a matter of fact, the burning of his laboratory and papers in 1684 caused him intense grief and doubtless preyed upon his mind. After his forty-ninth year, he turned his thoughts to theological subjects and prophecies. He was supposed to have been a woman-hater, and he never married.

Swift (1667–1745), Dean of St. Patrick's, poet and

essayist, was called ' the Mad Parson.' He even wrote extremely irreligious books, so much so that it was suggested that he ought to be baptised before being made a bishop. Swift was much addicted to ostentation and self-aggrandisement with great people, but his private life was most wild and dissipated. When his adored ' Stella ' died, he was completely grief-stricken, and yet almost simultaneously he wrote one of his most frivolous burlesques—*Directions to Servants*. He lost his memory for a time, and, during over a year, did not speak or even read, and took no notice of anyone.

Peter the Great of Russia (1672–1725) was extremely fond of taking the law in his own hands, and never hesitated, so writes De Villebois, to strike any person who gave him offence, whatever his rank might be, and he was extremely lavish with his blows. The same writer tells us that Peter liked to surround himself with men whom he secretly hated, and whom he invited to Court only so that he might note down what they said when they were in their cups ; or he would endeavour to lead them on to drink themselves to death, so that he might be rid of them. He held orgies of the most depraved and drunken kind, and sometimes pretended to solemnise a Papal election among those debauched surroundings. He finally contracted a terrible disease, probably caused by the atrocious life in which he indulged. He had a habit of making twitching movements of his face, which distorted it horribly.

Marie Casimire of Poland (1674), wife of King Sobieski, delighted in going out in the pouring rain in magnificent clothes, and sometimes she would ask one of her ministers to walk with her, especially if she knew that he did not like to get wet.

Handel (1674–1759), like Michelangelo, had to suffer blows from his parents in consequence of his determination to devote his life to music, as Angelo had done to art ; but his genius for music must have been remarkable, for, even prior to his receiving a lesson, he was a very capable musician, and at eight years of age a clever composer. When he was fifty he had a paralytic seizure, which left him very changed. Indeed for over one year after the attack he rarely went out at all. Even his handwriting became changed. He suffered severely from highly strung nerves, and his temper was stormy and irrational. Only he, of all the large family to which he belonged, showed any artistic faculty.

Concato (1679–1764) was one of the most brilliant of European physicians, yet there were times when he regarded himself as one of the lowest of men. Violent tempered himself, he believed that " to be in good health, one must be angry at least once a day." One night he dreamt that he was a murderer, and suffered acute terrors. When quite young he had a fear of sudden death ; and at twenty he had a longing to become a monk, although in his childhood he had been conspicuously undevout. After having had a quarrel with an Austrian officer, he became terrified of all soldiers and sentinels, and never permitted an officer to come into his house with his sword by his side. The sight of one of the city guards made him tremble with fear even in his old age.

Voltaire (1694–1778) expressed himself in one of his letters thus : " All the manifestations of genius are the effects of instinct. All the philosophers of the world put together would not be able to produce Quinault's *Armide* or the *Animaux malades de la peste* which La Fontaine wrote without knowing what he did. Corneille composed

Horace as a bird composes its nest." Regarding his own body, Voltaire said, " It is moribund. Diseases more cruel even than kings are persecuting me—doctors only are needed to finish me." (*N.B.*—Voltaire conceived part of his *Henriade* during sleep.)

Buffon (1707–1777), the French naturalist, was very absent-minded. He one day ascended to a tower, and instead of returning by the winding staircase, slid down by some ropes, absolutely without any consciousness of what he was doing, and as if he were walking in his sleep.

Dr. Johnson (1709–1784) continually distorted his face by violent grimaces. He had the habit, when walking in the street, of touching every post he went by, and if by chance he missed doing so he always returned. Likewise he invariably made a point of entering or leaving a door with either his left or right foot first (Boswell in his biography is not sure which), but Dr. Johnson was most assiduous as to which should first pass over the threshold, and if he made any error about it, he went back and solemnly went through what he considered to be an obligation, after which he seemed greatly relieved.

He suffered from bodily ailments as well as nerve trouble. Even as a boy he constantly had convulsive cramps, and irritation of the skin. Irritability of temper was also his constant companion, and often it would plunge him into the deepest despair. One of his eyes was useless, but his vision with the other remained unimpaired. If his vast powers of genius and understanding were an endowment to the world, to himself they brought no pleasure, his personal life being one prolonged fret and worry. Boswell writes thus to illustrate one of the learned Doctor's strange beliefs: " One day at Oxford, as he was turning the key of his chambers, he heard his mother distinctly call ' Sam,' although she was then at Lichfield."

Rousseau (1712–1798) always turned his head to the full glare of the sun when pondering over new thoughts for his work. He was always dominated by his senses, which he had no power to fight against. Of himself he writes : " I have very ardent passions, and while under their influence my impetuosity knows no bounds. I think only of the object which occupies me, the entire universe besides is nothing to me, but this lasts only a moment, and the moment that follows throws me into a state of prostration. A single sheet of fine paper tempts me more than the money to buy a ream of it. I see the thing and am tempted . . . the most insignificant pleasure, so long as it is present, fascinates me more than all the joys of Paradise." Actual sorrows and troubles affected him in a very minor degree, but imaginary ones tormented him.

In his *Confessions* he says : " My imagination has never been so cheerful as when I have been suffering. My mind cannot beautify the really pleasant things that happen to me, but only the imaginary ones. If I wish to describe Spring well, it must be in Winter." He also fancied himself to be an object of persecution. He wrote that every country, as well as the king and all men and women, had taken offence at some of his works, and that they were persecuting him with such ferocity that his health was being undermined ; indeed, he attributed the internal pains from which he was suffering solely to this cause. The cruelty of his enemies, he said, was so refined that part of their torture was to pour praise and benefits upon him, and they actually corrupted his tradespeople,

so that they sold him cheaper and better food.   And all
this, Rousseau asserted, was their subtle way of proving
their generosity and his vileness !

When he began to study medical books, he at once
believed himself to be suffering from every malady of which
he read, and was actually astonished to find himself alive,
and in fairly good health.   Rousseau was certainly a
' Jack-of-all-trades' during his career—being a litterateur,
scientist, botanist, secretary, embryo diplomat, engraver,
watchmaker,   charlatan,   music   teacher,   and   servant.
" There are times," he says in his *Confessions*, " in which
I am so little like myself that I might be taken for a man
of quite different character.   In repose I am indolence and
timidity itself, but if I become excited, I immediately
know what to say."

When Rousseau was in England, he was seized with the
idea that Choiseul intended to have him arrested, whereupon he hurried to the coast, leaving his luggage and even
his money at the hotel.   Violent gales were blowing
which prevented him from crossing—and even in these
winds he read another phase of the plot to torture and
torment him.   In his excitement he made a speech so
full of hysterical incoherency and vituperation that the
people listened stupefied, and Rousseau quite thought he
had impressed them.

On his return to France he imagined his enemies to
have increased in number, spying and misreading every
trivial movement and calling his every action a crime.   If
he read a paper, they regarded him as a conspirator,
if he inhaled the perfume of a flower, he was brewing
some poison.   They prevented his door from shutting,
they prejudiced every caller against him—the shoeblack
had just used all his blacking, if the unfortunate Rousseau

needed his shoes cleaned ; the boatman had let out all his boats, if he wished to go over the river. The ancient custom of burning a dummy figure at the *mi-carème* had fallen out of use, but now he believed it was re-established so that the people might burn his cardboard effigy, dressed in clothes similar to those he wore. Brooding over all these imaginary agonies, he became so desperate that he begged to be put in prison.

At last he wrote his *Defence* and gave a copy to all passers-by whose faces did not seem to him to have been embittered towards him by his enemies. Losing all faith in his fellow-creatures, he wrote a tender and friendly letter to God, and in order " to make sure of its arrival," he laid the letter on the altar side of Notre Dame, with a manuscript of his *Dialogues*. And, because the railing was closed, he believed that Heaven was in the plot against him. Dussaulx, who was much with him during his latter years, writes that he even became distrustful of his dog, which he loved devotedly, and suspected some mystery in the animal's caresses.

Amongst his many complex characteristics, Rousseau's vanity was at times very evident. In his *Confessions* he defied the entire human race to show a finer human being than himself. In his relations with women, he was decidedly unusual, since they gave him no pleasure unless the women beat him naked, or threatened to beat him as they would a child. He had evinced great sexual precocity and perversion from early boyhood.

He was weak and puny as a baby, joyless as a child, melancholy as a man. He never could free himself from the idea that he was being persecuted, and that his life was always in danger. He was once heard to let fall these words : " My cousins employ more ingenuity in persecuting me than would be required for governing Europe." He frequently fell into paroxysms of frantic excitement, and whilst in these his eyes looked so wild and terrible that it seemed almost as though he saw himself pursued by some fearful horror, and if addressed, his reply was wide of the mark and not very coherent. He would then be seized with violent shuddering, or be attacked by sudden faintness, but the day after he could remember nothing of it.

Haydn (1713–1809) said, "When my work does not advance, I retire into the oratory with my rosary, say an *ave*—immediately ideas come to me." He always declared that the conception of *The Creation* was due to divine grace from above.

Diderot (1713–1764) wrote: "If nature has ever made a sensitive soul, it is mine. Multiply sensitive souls, and you will augment good and evil actions." He was so absent-minded that he frequently engaged vehicles, then left them at the door and forgot all about them—perhaps for the whole day, which naturally cost him an unnecessary amount of money. He often could not recall the time, the day, the month, or even the name of the individual whom he was addressing, and he had a habit of making long monologues to himself in the same manner as a somnambulist. Diderot said, " Il me semble que j'ai l'esprit fou des grands vents."

Klopstock (1724–1803) asserted, and was himself fully convinced, that a great many of his poems were conceived and inspired in dreams. Once when asked about the meaning of some lines in a poem of his, Klopstock answered, " God and I both knew what it meant once, now God alone knows."

Casanova (1725–1803) blended his career as a mathematical genius with swindling and lax living, full particulars of which he gives in his *Memoirs*.

Zimmerman (1726–1795), the famous doctor, philosopher, and physiognomist, had a dread of arrest, or of dying of hunger ; this fixed idea eventually brought about his death by starvation, he being convinced that he possessed no money for the purchase of food.

Foscolo (1728–1827) writes, in his splendid *Epistolaria*, that " the power to write is dependent on an obliging fever of the mind, and cannot be called forth at any moment." " I write," he tells us, " not for my country, not for fame, but for the secret joy which arises from the exercise of our faculties ; they have need of movement, as our legs of walking." Foscolo could not bear anything approaching irony or lack of approval. Once he became so furious at some words spoken half-jestingly by one of his friends, that he exclaimed, " You wish to see me dead, I will break my skull at your feet." He thereupon flung himself with all his force against the marble mantelpiece, and had it not been for the presence of mind of one of the company, who saved his head by pushing him to the ground, he would probably have received a fatal injury. He was also heard to confess that though " very active in some directions, he was in others inferior to a man, to a woman, to a child."

Oliver Goldsmith (1728–1774) had neither the brains nor the concentration to derive much benefit from his college life, and when that was finished, he for a long time evinced no desire to do any kind of work, preferring to be a ' remittance man ' dependent on the charity of his relations. It would be giving too much grace to the life he chose to call it ' Bohemian,' it was absolutely squalid. Even when he commenced to write, and with such success that the money positively poured in, he did not in any way change his habits, and only wrote when he chose, and very spasmodically.   He was always in debt, but this fact seemed to worry him not at all.   Surely there never was such an idler with such a marvellous capacity for doing good and remunerative work.   Even as a boy, his disposition varied constantly from brightness to moroseness, and he was accounted dull and stupid.   Nevertheless he scribbled poems even in his school days.   In fact, Goldsmith was by no means prepossessing, he had a thick receding jaw, thick lips, and a heavy vacant expression. In later life he suffered much from " a violent pain extending all over the fore part of his head," which was responsible for his death.

Kuh's sublime thoughts came to him by inspiration, and were dictated at a time when he was quite incapable of any concentrated thought or even of the simplest reasoning.

Restif de la Bretonne, at the age of four, had read much ; at eleven he had seduced young girls, and at fourteen he had composed a poem to his first twelve mistresses.

Barnardin de Saint Pierre (1737–1814), the composer of *Harmonies de la Nature*, writes therein : " Wherever they are, fleas throw themselves against white colours.   This instinct has been given them in order that we may catch them more easily."   And in another ' harmony ' we find, " The melon has been divided into slices by nature in order that it may be eaten *en famille*—the pumpkin, being larger, may be eaten with neighbours."   Hofmann (1738–1793) always averred, " When I compose, I sit down at the piano, shut my eyes, and play what I hear."

Paisiello Giovanni (1741–1816), the Italian musician, was unable to compose unless he lay between six quilts in the summer and nine in the winter.

Goethe (1749–1832), the great German poet, writes thus of himself : " When I closed my eyes and depressed my head, I could cause the image of a flower to appear in the middle of the field of vision ; this flower did not for a moment retain its first form, but unfold itself, and develop from its interior new flowers, formed and coloured, or sometimes green leaves. These were not natural flowers, but of fantastic form, although symmetrical as the rosettes of sculpture. I was unable to fix any one form, but the development of new flowers continued as long as I desired it without any variation in the rapidity of the changes. The same thing occurred when I figured to myself a variegated disc. The coloured figures upon it underwent constant changes, which extended progressively from the centre towards the periphery, exactly like the changes in the kaleidoscope." Goethe once saw a spectral figure on horseback. He undoubtedly possessed at all times an extraordinary visualising and visionary power.

Victor Alfieri (1749–1823) was best able to compose his tragedies whilst music was being played, or even directly after, whilst the airs rang in his mind. It is recorded that when this great writer heard music for the first time, he felt an extraordinary dazzling in his ears and in his eyes, and spent several subsequent days in melancholy but pleasing solitude, during which time floods of wonderfully fantastic ideas shaped themselves into his work. Like Dante, he fell in love at nine.

Alfieri tells us, " I compare myself to a barometer. I have always experienced more or less facility in writing according to the weight of the air—absolute stupidity in the great solstitial and equinoctial winds, infinitely less perspicacity in the evening than in the morning, and a much greater aptness for creation in the middle of winter

or of summer than in the intermediate seasons.   This has
made me humble, as I am convinced that at times I had
no power to do otherwise."   He expressed the opinion that
" every increase of knowledge is an increase of sorrow."
He described Italy most completely without ever having
been there.   He wrote a study in seven languages before
he was ten years old.   He always asserted with absolute
conviction that, on one occasion, he saw his own image,
which came to meet him.

Richard Brinsley Sheridan (1751–1816) came of a family
noted for its unstable, mercurial character, and its wonderful capacity for writing poetry.   He, like Goldsmith, was
the dunce of his school, thriftless, careless as he grew to
manhood ;   but he led a far more riotous life—always
poor, always in debt, and very often drunk.   If he wrote,
it was because writing came so easily to him—had it been
any effort, his masterpieces would certainly have never
been penned.   He ran away with Miss Linley, to whom he
proved an extremely bad husband, for he worried her
into her grave by his " unreasonableness and unintelligible
folly."   Sheridan married again almost immediately after
her death, and made his second wife as miserable as his
first.   With advancing years, his vices only increased,
until he alienated even the few friends who had remained
loyal to him.   After the age of sixty, Sheridan suffered
much from epileptic fits, which eventually caused his
death.

Thomas Chatterton (1752–1770) was strangely silent
and morbid as a child, but often he gave way to violent
fits of temper, or at times to quite sudden and apparently
reasonless floods of tears.   It has been said that it was
his extreme poverty, amounting to destitution, when he
found himself alone in a London garret, which caused him

to commit suicide, when only eighteen years old. In spite of his extreme youth, however, he was known as one of the most immoral lads in Bristol, as well as one of the vainest. Chatterton is said to have had a tendency to a " growing restlessness " and " sudden fits of vacancy or silence that came upon him sometimes while he was talking rapidly." And he was given to " Look steadily in a person's face without speaking or seeming to see the person for a quarter of an hour or more, till it was quite frightful."

De Maistre (1754–1821), in *Soirées de St. Petersburg*, writes : " It is the business of bishops, nobles, and the great officers of the State to be the depositaries and the guardians of the conservative virtues, to teach nations what is good and what is evil, what is true and what is false in the moral and spiritual world. Others have no right to reason on these matters. They may amuse themselves with the natural sciences. What have they to complain of ? "

Mozart (1756–1791) was haunted by the idea that the Italians desired to poison him. He always acknowledged that his music was not the result of his personal will or striving, but that it came to him, like dreams. His *Don Giovanni* was suggested to him by the sight of an orange, which, he said, brought to his mind a popular Neapolitan tune which he remembered hearing several years before. His fingers seemed to be always on the piano, but he cut them so continually when carving meat that he was perforce compelled to depute others to carve in his place.

Robert Burns (1759–1796) writes in one of his letters : " My constitution and frame were aborigine blasted with a deep incurable taint of melancholia which poisons my

existence." From his youth upwards he suffered from
a dull pain in his head, which increased in the evenings.
As he grew older this pain was replaced by palpitation of
the heart, and by frequent feelings of faintness and suffocation as he lay in bed. To allay these troubles, he often
plunged into a tub of cold water, which he kept beside
the bed.

The great Scotch poet always said that " poets had a
stronger imagination, more delicate sensibility, and a more
ungovernable set of passions " than other men. Perhaps
this opinion may have prevented him from any effort to
give up the habit of drinking too much. Certain it is
that the habit developed in him, and led to his death
when he was only thirty-seven. He certainly possessed
an extraordinary sensibility, and was easily moved to
tears by sights or even pictures representative of misery
or suffering. He had wonderful eyes, which " literally
glowed " when he was thrilled or interested. His brother
Gilbert said of him that " In love, the agitations of his
mind and body exceeded anything of the kind I ever
knew."

Schiller (1759–1805) had a habit of putting his feet in
ice when working. The joys and sorrows of the people
moved him fully as much as did the personal happenings
of his life. He once gave a full and perfect description
of the Swiss land and people—yet he knew neither.

Luce de Laucival (1764–1810) was not able to bear
criticism of any kind, it infuriated and agonised him, yet
he smiled cheerfully when his legs were amputated.

Fodera (1764–1835), the famous Sicilian physician and
medical writer, was fond of asserting with much conviction that he could conquer any army, though it
numbered a million, with forty soldiers, and that with

one single and easily constructed oven, he could supply bread for 200,000 people. Opposite to his house there lived a young girl, with whom he fell in love when he was about fifty years of age. He was in the habit of gazing longingly up at her window, and one day the girl, becoming annoyed at his rapturous adoration, poured a jug of dirty water upon him. Even this did not cool his ardour. He went home rejoicing at the attention, and meeting a fowl, which he said resembled the girl he loved, he bought it, smothered it with caresses, allowed it to mess up his clothes, his books, and even his bed, where it eventually died.[1]

Gioia (1767–1829), the Italian writer, grew so excited when in the midst of composition that he once wrote a chapter on the table, quite unaware that he was not, as usual, committing the lines to paper.

Chateaubriand (1768–1848) grew irate if anyone received praise in his presence, even though it were only his own tradesmen. He himself relates that in his youthful days he charged an old musket, which had a way of going off by itself, with three balls, then inserted the barrel into his mouth, fixing the stock in the ground ; but a passer-by made an interruption, and his resolution was not carried out. In his great work *Memoirs d'Outre-Tombe*, he writes : " My great defect is ennui, a distaste for everything and a perpetual doubt." It is significant that the idea of suicide remained with him all through his life, although he did not make a second attempt.

Lord Wellington (1769–1852) suffered throughout the whole of his long career from fainting fits and epileptic attacks. He came of an artistic family, noted for musical and poetic ability. During his late years, increasing

[1] *Costanza Follia Anomale.* Palerme, 1870.

infirmities—manifested though energetically repressed—struggling utterance, and tottering step told their tale.

Mrs. Siddons (1769), the renowned actress, possessed an extremely sensitive nature, and suffered from fainting fits, sciatica, and ' nerves.' She was also inclined to suspiciousness, and viewed any small slight, or unfavourable criticism, as proof of violent and malignant enmity. Her bodily health was so frail that she was forced to leave the stage at fifty, and died of erysipelas at an advanced age. Her sister, Mrs. Curtis, was strange in her manner, grossly immoral, and lame, in addition to being a poetess of no mean ability. She once made an attempt to end her life when in Westminster Abbey by taking poison.

Humboldt's nurse acknowledged that when she looked at the soft flesh of his child, she was quite unable to refrain from biting it.

Kleist always felt great emotion over his work. On being found weeping copiously after completing one of his tragedies, " She is dead," he sobbed.

Beethoven (1770–1827), though not an invalid, was constantly ailing, and suffered from eye weakness. He was notoriously unpractical and absent-minded, and had a passion for frequently changing his lodgings, which even his poverty could not eradicate, though it sometimes compelled him to pay two or three rents at the same time. He gradually became deaf from the age of thirty, although he continued his composition work. He was very absent-minded, and in consequence often went hatless. On one occasion he left his coat in a field, and, hatless and coatless, was arrested as a vagabond. Fortunately, however, he was identified by the leader of his orchestra and released.

Wordsworth (1770–1850), with great conceit, was fully convinced that he himself was the only poet of true transcendental genius, indeed the only man of real eminence of his time. And yet, genius as he undoubtedly was, his poems refer to simple rural scenes and places— a great limitation, since they never bear on the thrilling happenings of life. Indeed the big things of life seem to have left him cold—or perhaps he was subconsciously afraid of their devastating force. Wordsworth worked slowly—poetry did not flow abundantly from him, and the veriest trifle would put him off his work.

Schopenhauer (1770–1838) wrote that: " In the face of death I confess that I despise the Germans for their unspeakable bestiality and am ashamed to belong to them." The idea of persecution seems to have been with him from his earliest youth, for when he was six years old he fancied that his parents desired to abandon him. In spite of the continual change of scene into which his many travels brought him, he was always a ' bundle of misery.' He says of himself, " When I was eighteen, I thought to myself that the world could not be the work of God, but rather of a devil." Later he wrote, " If there is nothing to cause me misery, I am tormented by the thought that there must be something hidden from me." He felt in himself something demoniacal that urged him on " to open a new and only way to lead men of heart and mind to the truth." But the thought of working for his living he could not bear.

Schopenhauer's vanity was colossal. When in Italy, he wrote, " If I could only satisfy my desire to look upon this race of toads and vipers as my equals, it would be a consolation to me." Capable of turning out fine work with much haughty presumption, he could also descend to ordinary, almost puerile platitudes. In his work and personal life he was a teeming mass of contradictions.

He preached sexual abstinence, but wallowed in prosaic love adventures. Indeed, his friends had trouble in saving him from consequences of his follies, even at the time that he was busy with his great work which was to be the wonder-book of the world. He lived on the first storey, so great was his dread of fire, and he was afraid to trust himself to his hairdresser. He hid away money in the inkpot, and notes under the bedcoverings. He frequently talked and gesticulated violently when alone, even in the streets. All his life he believed that he was impelled by some demon or spirit. The slightest sound caused his hand to fly to his sword, and, if he received a letter, he at once concluded that it brought news of a great misfortune, and feared to open it. He reasoned and argued about the least important matters, believed firmly in ' table-turning,' and was convinced that magnetism could cure his dog's paws, and give him back his own hearing. He thought that all contemporary philosophers were in league to impede his success by ignoring his name and works, and these ideas continued to obsess him even when fame came to him. Although convinced that all other professors were maliciously depriving him of glory, he yet dreaded lest they should criticise his works.

Schopenhauer had the utmost contempt for patriotism, which he described as " the passion of fools, and the most foolish of passions." He was eternally preoccupied with himself, even with his own photograph. He hated women, and summed them up tersely as " long of hair and short of sense." " People of genius," he wrote, " are not only unpleasant in practical life, but weak in moral sense and wicked."

On New Year's eve, 1831, he dreamt that his death would take place in the New Year. Soon afterwards he went to Frankfurt-on-Main, where, he says, "I had a very distinct vision of angels. They were, as I think, my ancestors, and they announced to me that I should survive my mother, at that time still living. My father, who was dead, carried a light in his hand." After this vision he sunk in deep melancholy, not even speaking to anyone; but after a year his condition improved. All his life he was subject to fits of temper, and one day, when irritated because he heard his landlady chattering in another room, he went to her and shook her with such force that he broke her arm, for which he had to pay damages. The idea of illness was always intensely repugnant to him; fear of small-pox sent him flying from Naples, and at Verona he fancied himself poisoned by snuff. He was driven from Berlin by dread of the cholera.

Hegel (1770–1831) was convinced of his personal divinity. He always commenced his lectures by saying, "I may say with Christ that not only do I teach truth, but that I am myself truth."

Sir Walter Scott (1771–1820) possessed a very active brain and a remarkable gift of visualisation. "Show me an old castle or a field of battle," he said, "and I am at home at once, filling it with its combatants in their proper costume, and overwhelming my hearers by the enthusiasm of my description. In crossing Magus Moor, near St. Andrews, the spirit moved me to give a picture of the assassination of the Archbishop of St. Andrews to some fellow-travellers with whom I was accidentally associated, and one of them, though well acquainted with the story, protested that my narrative had frightened away his night's sleep."

Scott's four brothers and one sister all died young. Although gifted in some respects, they were extremely violent in temper.   As an infant of eighteen months, Scott suddenly lost some of the power in his right leg, which was followed by lifelong lameness.   Later in life he suffered from actual paralysis and apoplexy.   In his journal, he writes of feeling " a tremor of the head, the pulsations of which became painfully sensible, a disposition to causeless alarm, much lassitude, and decay of both vigour and activity of intellect."   When he laid aside his spectacles, he fancied he saw the rim of them, and put up his hands imagining he was still wearing them ; and at Byron's death, he thought his dead friend had actually come to visit him. Weakened by recurring paralytic attacks, he succumbed to an apoplectic fit at sixty-one.

Coleridge's (1772–1834) *Kubla Khan* was written during a deep sleep, under the influence of an opiate.   Fifty-four lines was all he could remember when sufficiently recovered to write.   Through the lack of will power and over-fondness for alcohol, he was never able to carry out the great works which he had in his youth dreamed of and projected.   His son, Hartley, summed up that " he wrote like an angel and drank like a fish."

There was nothing suggestive of labouredness in Coleridge's poetry.   He strung off his beautiful verses in the same way as he talked—quickly, impulsively, full of glowing intensity.   His genius had no need of concentration ; any moment or wherever he found himself—if the thought came to him—he would turn out a poem or a sonnet with amazing ease and speech.   He was a very imaginative child, extremely sensitive, and of feeble constitution.   When he was only six he ran away, because of a quarrel with one of his brothers, and spent the night in the pouring rain.   In a like way he bolted from college and enlisted in the army without apprising anyone of his intention, leaving his wife and family in a state of great anxiety.

He was a poet from the early age of eleven, indeed he appears to have entirely missed the childhood period of life, since he never indulged or took any interest in the usual amusements of children. He himself sums up this fact by telling us that " at a very premature age, even before my fifteenth year, I had bewildered myself in metaphysics and in theological controversy, particularly with reference to ' fixed-fate,' ' free-will,' and fore-knowledge absolute." Although never strong, Coleridge experienced no definite ailments during his early life. A violent attack of gout, however, laid him almost prostrate at thirty years of age, and from that time he degenerated. All the more so because the pain he suffered led him to take opium. He was by no means a handsome man even during his best years, he carried himself badly, walked with a shuffling gait, held his head down and his knees bent. He had the makings of a strong man marred in the making.

To Hartley Coleridge, his son, he bequeathed his poetical genius, his extreme sensibility, and even more than his vivid imagination. Hartley Coleridge thought out abstruse metaphysical questions when he was five years old, and facts blended themselves with amazing fiction in his baby mind. He visualised a new kingdom on an island which had been formed by the bursting of a cataract. He gave this island a name, and not only peopled it, but even planned its government ; he spoke of it as seriously and conclusively as though it really existed.

Throughout his boyhood Hartley Coleridge weaved stories of romance or adventure, and gave them forth with vividness and conviction. They were real to him, and if he fancied he saw doubt on the face of one of his listeners, he would fly into a violent fit of passion. Sometimes, in these fits of rage, he would bite himself. He was also liable to attacks of melancholy, and in one of these he heard an audible and sensuous voice foreboding evil. Had he possessed more power of concentration, so that the threads of his work might have been woven together instead of being loose and straggling, his remarkable intellect and high poetic powers would have placed him in the front rank of English poets. His energy and productive power were enormous ; but his love of drink and dissipation hindered his work, nor had he the self-control to regulate the flood of ideas which teemed in his brain.

Irving (1774–1841) averred that divine inspiration had made him conversant with several unknown languages. He originated the sect of the Irvingites.

Charles Lamb (1775–1834) once wrote some significant lines in a letter to Coleridge : " I will amuse you by the strange turns my frenzy took. I look back upon it at times with a gloomy kind of envy, for while it lasted I had many, many hours of pure happiness. Dream not, Coleridge, of having tasted the grandeur and wildness of fancy till you have gone mad. All now seems vapid or comparatively so."

Ampère (1775–1836) was much given to abstraction, and one day, when out riding in the country, he became so absolutely absorbed in the meditation of a problem that he dismounted and walked slowly along, leading his horse. When he arrived at his destination he was without the horse, which he had lost and not even missed, until his attention was drawn to the fact by his friends. He once wrote on the back of a cab a formula of which his mind was full, and when he saw the cab driving away, he rushed wildly after it. He was unable to do sedentary work ; he always said that in order to express his thoughts his body must be in a condition of continual motion. He was sincere in his belief that he had found the way to square a circle.

CHAPTER XI

THE PECULIARITIES OF MEN OF GENIUS
(*Continued*)

HOFFMANN (1776–1822), the German novelist and musician, drank to excess. It is said of him that his drawings ended in caricature, his tales in wildness, and his music in just a medley of sound. He himself wrote, "Disorderly ideas seem to rise out of my mind like blood from opened veins." He was so frightfully affected by atmospheric changes that he constructed a meteorological scale from his subjective emotions. He evolved ideas of persecution through believing that the fantasies of his tales were being changed into actualities.

Foscolo (1777–1837) wrote: "I keep near the fire. My friends laugh at me, but I am seeking to give my members heat which my heart will concentrate, and sublime within." (*Opistolario*, p. 395.)

Humphrey Davy (1778–1829) was that rare anomaly—a scientific genius, with a strong leaning to poetry and romance. As a boy he was very spasmodic in his attention to lessons, but, owing to his wonderful memory, he imbibed a large amount of knowledge without any effort of concentration. He was possessed of an extraordinarily vivid imagination, and fancied himself "pursued at night by horrible images." His health declined as his fame grew, he suffered much from rheumatism, had several paralytic seizures, and died of apoplexy.

Robert Southey (1774–1843) was a genius and wrote poems before he was eight. He was of so supremely sensitive a disposition that Carlyle spoke of him as " the excitablest man " he had ever encountered. " The shallowest chin, small, care-lined brow, the most vehement pair of hazel eyes. A well read, honest, limited, kindly-hearted most irritable man. I said to myself, ' How has this man contrived, with such a nervous system, to keep alive for nearly sixty years ? How has he not been torn to pieces long since under such furious pulling this way and that ? ' " (Thomas Carlyle, *Reminiscences*.)

Very soon after Carlyle's criticism, Southey began to suffer from loss of memory, a dimming of his understanding, and a confusion of persons, time, and places. The remainder of his life was spent in a condition of coma. His literary work was colossal, and it almost appeared as though the tension of constant and strenuous writing held him together, for he broke down utterly directly he was unable to continue.

Southey had several extraordinary dreams. One of them he describes thus : " I thought a fiend and a good spirit were shooting arrows at each other, many of which fell near me, and I gathered them, and endeavoured to shoot at the fiend also, who was very little, but could never get them to fit the bow. The good spirit at last heaped coals upon the head of his enemy, so as to bury him completely till he, by the fierceness of his nature, kindled them, and they blazed and burned, burning him who could not be consumed." In another dream he saw a human head, just the head only, with no bodily attachment of any kind, then he found himself in a great castle peopled with these heads, which appeared to be having quite a good time. They could not swallow, but possessed the full power of smell and taste, and were able to turn in any direction.

William Blake (1757–1827) wrote poems from boyhood, he even scribbled them on the backs of the bills in his father's hosiery shop. He lived in a weird, dream-world of his own construction, and frequently heard celestial voices calling to him. At twelve years old, his father apprenticed him to the engraving trade, but he spent his time either composing verses or seeing visions. These latter took the forms of people in history, and so convinced was he of the reality of the apparitions that he asserted that neither his engraving designs nor his poems were created by himself, but produced through and according to revelations made to him by the visionary visitors and voices. His exquisite method of tinting, he ascribed to the spirit of his dead brother, which also gave him valuable advice about one of his poems. Probably these facts may account for the incoherence of some of Blake's writings.

The following passage occurs in one of the poet's letters : " I am more famed in Heaven for my works than I could well conceive. In my brain are studies and chambers filled with books and pictures of old, which I wrote and printed in ages of eternity—before my mortal life—and these works are the delight and study of archangels. Why, then, should I be anxious about the riches or fame of mortality ? " " For many years," he said, " I longed to see Satan. I could never believe he was the vulgar fiend our legends represent him to be. I imagined him a classic spirit, with some of his original splendour about him. At last I had my wish. I was going downstairs in the dark, when suddenly a light came streaming amongst my feet. I turned round, and there he was, looking fiercely at me through the iron grating of my staircase window. As he appeared, so I drew him."

According to the biographer's informant, Blake's sketch represented the most appallingly horrible phantom glaring through a grated window. It had eyes like burning coals, teeth of extraordinary length, and claws like talons. Blake said that he was often visited by Milton, Virgil, Dante, Moses, and Homer, and that " they were all majestic shadows, gray but luminous, and superior to the common height of man." He once described a "fairy's funeral" which he had seen. " I was walking alone in my garden. There was great stillness in the air. I heard a low and pleasant sound, and knew not whence it came. At last I saw the broad leaf of a flower move, and underneath I saw a procession of creatures of the size and colour of green and gray grasshoppers, bearing a body laid out on a rose leaf, which they buried with songs and then disappeared." When drawing a portrait and looking apparently at an invisible sitter, he said it was " Lot, sitting for his portrait." In spite of Blake's visionary tendencies, he most certainly was affected by his inspirations, and many of his poems and engravings are masterly as well as delightful.

Turner (1775–1844) was a remarkably dull boy, indeed his intellectual faculties were totally undeveloped. He was put to work in an architect's office, where his remarkable sense of colour enabled him to wash in plans with blue skies and green grass and gravel walks marvellously well. Other work he could make no headway with at all, nor did he ever acquire any learning, or even knowledge of grammar, whilst his general behaviour left much to be

desired. He entered the academy as a student, but his
colour sense was always far more perfect than his drawing.
It was in colour that his genius lay.

Turner had a constitution of a horse, and never knew
fatigue. In character he was mean and avaricious. His
poems and other writings are a strange mingling of
muddled incomprehensibleness, with a slight sub-current
of the true poetic sense. He was generally morose, even
sullen, and quite lacking in sociability, preferring his own
company to that of others. Turner's extraordinary colour
schemes have been unfavourably as well as favourably
regarded, some of them being, as in his scarlet shadows
and white lights, invisible to the ordinary eye and mind
in nature. He frequently was so parsimonious that he
begrudged the most necessary outlay, and he allowed his
house to become absolutely dilapidated.

When informed of Haydon's suicide, Turner continued
his painting, muttering, " He stabbed his mother," and
repeated the phrase again and again, but either could not
or would not explain his meaning (if he had any). It has
been said of some of Turner's works, that they are " fitful
dreams, nightmares of beauty rather than distinct images,"
but this is said to be the " vision of the poet which, although
perhaps less definite, yet often catches further glimpses
of truth and beauty than ordinary sight can obtain."

Bolzano (1781–1848), the great geometer, fought duels
with thirteen officials whom he had provoked, and played
the violin between each duel. He was so poor at the time
that his house was quite bare of furniture. After he had
been pensioned, Bolzano printed his own funeral cards, and
made his own coffin. And in his will he enjoined his heir
to plant an apple tree on his grave in memory of Adam
and Newton.

Nodier (1783–1844) wrote an entire theory of future destiny, as well as his *Lydia*, from successive dreams of such vividness that the ideas transformed themselves into convictions.

Mangoni (1784–1873) was of such an undecided turn of mind that he never could resolve on any definite step, even the most unimportant. He was also in a constant state of dread, afraid to go out alone, and even afraid of drowning in a small puddle. Often, for entire days, he could not bring himself to any kind of concentration, and seemed quite incapable of thinking.

Grimm (1785–1863), author of the famous fairy-tales, always wished to appear ill or miserable. When speaking of his travels and amusements, he said that all these did not take from him the feeling that he was dead or dying, and if anyone ventured to suggest that he was well and strong, he flew into violent fits of rage.

Lord Byron (1788–1824) was extremely vain of his aristocratic birth and his handsome features ; his unfortunate club foot was a constant *bête noir* to him. He courted publicity and was an absolute egoist, insomuch as he regarded most other poets and writers with more contempt than admiration. He had an amazingly retentive memory and a receptive mind, except for arithmetic, which he never could master. In character, Byron was at once mean in trifles, and wildly extravagant in bigger things. He used to say that the power of poetry had " burst upon his mind unexpectedly," to his great surprise. He was always very odd and wayward in his conduct, also supersensitive and inclined to extreme morbidness. He was also a great lover of women ; but his affections were mostly ephemeral. His wife, Lady Byron, left him a year after their marriage.

Byron's diary contains some strange entries, such as, " When I am tired, as I generally am, out comes this and down goes everything. But I can't read it over, and God knows what contradictions it may contain. If I am sincere with myself (but I fear one lies more to oneself than to anyone else), every page should confute, refute, and utterly abjure its predecessor." And again, " What have I seen ! The same men all over the world. Aye, and women too ... Hang up philosophy ! To be sure I have long despised myself and man, but I have never spat in the face of my species before. Oh fool ! " Byron was so emotional that when watching a performance of Kean's, he grew extremely excited and fell into convulsions, and once in a fit of temper he threw his watch into the fire and hammered it to pieces with the poker. He also discharged a pistol in his wife's bedroom.

Byron's life in Italy was one wild course of licentiousness. In Venice he acquired a harem. All his evil passions were let loose, and he was seldom sober. This depraved life increased his naturally violent temper and morbidness, whilst his bodily sufferings either kept him awake at night or he endured the torture of painful dreams when he did sleep. Even his once musical voice grew harsh and discordant, and his handwriting became illegible. He had several attacks of epilepsy shortly before he died. In his works can be read the working of his volcanic mind, wealthy with divine fire, swift as the lightning, but changing always from grave to gay, from storm to calm, from merriment to misanthropy and gloom.

Rossini (1791–1868) lost himself so completely in his work that when conducting the orchestra during a rehearsal of his *Barbiere*, which was a dire failure, he did not even observe until the close of the act that the audience and the performers had departed. He had such an intense dread of travelling by train that, once having let himself be persuaded to do so, he fell in a faint, and said on returning to consciousness, " If I was not like that, I should never have written *Barbiere*." As he grew older, he became parsimonious, and suffered keenly on buying a horse at a small loss. Gradually he became convinced that he was reduced to utter misery, and that he would be compelled to beg. He also got the idea that he had developed into an idiot, and that not only was he quite incapable of composing again, but he could not even endure to hear music spoken of.

T. Grossi (1791–1853), referring to the apparition of Prina, which he described in one of his works, asserted that it actually appeared before him, and he was only able to procure its departure by re-lighting his lamp.

Shelley (1792–1822) was very shy and also excitable in his boyhood, much addicted to waking visions, which left him in a condition of trembling ecstasy. These characteristics grew with his youth. He also had night terrors, and walked in his sleep. Shelley's personality was extremely vital and vivid, his conversation full of intellectuality and enthusiasm. His nerves occasionally ran away with him, and he took laudanum to " force them to calmness." Hogg says of him : " He always looked wild, unearthly, like a spirit that had just descended from the sky, or a demon risen at that moment out of the ground. . . . Shelley was unconscious and oblivious of time, place, persons, and seasons ; falling into some poetic vision or day dream, he quickly forgot all that he had repeatedly and solemnly promised. Or he would run away after some imaginary urgency and importance which

suddenly came into his head, setting off in vain pursuit
of it, he knew not whither."

During the whole of Shelley's short life he was troubled
with terrifying dreams. In one of his waking visions he
met a figure shrouded in a long cloak, and when the hood
was thrown back he saw that the form was his own
phantasm. Another time he heard a noise outside the
country cottage where he was staying, and went to open
the door. As he opened it he was struck a heavy blow
which rendered him unconscious. He also saw a nude
child rising out of the sea waves radiant with joyful smiles
clapping its little hands. These visions apparently came
to him whenever he was in a more than usually nervous
mood.

Donizetti (1792–1848) was inconceivably brutal in his
home life. One day, in a fit of savage rage, after beating
his wife with more than usual ferocity, he composed his
beautiful melody, *Tu che a Dio spiegaste l'ali*, whilst
sobbing under the after effects of his furious outbreak.

Lamartine (1792–1869) had a queer notion that in his
writing it was not himself who thought, but that his ideas
thought for him.

Scéchényi (1792–1860), who founded the Magyar
Academy, inaugurated Danubeian navigation, and pro-
moted the Revolution of 1848, imagined himself responsible
for the misfortunes into which he foresaw that his country
would be plunged, and became extremely morbid. He
refused to see anyone, and often recited a long list of the sins
of which he fancied himself guilty. Only in chess did his
melancholy moroseness find an outlet, and he would play
without a break for ten or twelve hours. An unfortunate
student who was hired to play with him went mad under
the strain ; but Scéchényi himself improved, and even

began once again to see his relations, though it was a long time before he could be persuaded to leave his room. When he resumed his writing he showed all his old power and took the keenest interest in all matters relating to his country and the university he had founded. The following lines from one of his works proves that they were not lacking in the forcefulness of his earlier efforts : "To remain at one's post in spite of the mud that fanatical or frivolous patriots throw in the faces of their brothers and companions in arms, to remain obstinately there even when insult strikes one in the face, that should be the *mot d'ordre* of the present day."

With satire, of a strange terribleness, Scéchényi wrote the history of Hungary's torments under Bach's brutal *régime*, and urged a policy of concord, on the same lines and equal to that prevailing in Austria—and afterwards he says of the work, " in truth, this book is miserable, but do you know how the Margaret Island was found ? According to an old legend, the Danube once occupied its site. Some carrion once, no one knows how, settled on to a sandbank and became attached there. Whatever the river swept down—froth, leaves, branches, trees—all were piled up there, and at last a magnificent island arose. My work is something like that carrion. Who knows what may arise out of it at last ? "

When Hübner ruled in Bach's stead, and terror gave place to liberalism, Scéchényi was delirious with gladness, and in his humble room wrote papers of the joyful renewal of the life of his country, and made plans of reform, all of which he sent to Hübner. But his joy-bells did not ring long, for Thierry soon took over the reins of government, and Hungary was in a worse plight than ever. The new minister even wished to imprison Scéchényi, who, stricken with remorse, imagined he had been neglectful of his country and too sparing in his efforts for her good. The unhappy man flew to his old comfort, chess, but as that could not give him ease, he shot himself.

Carlyle (1795–1881) found torture in even the most trivial worries or bothers inseparable from daily life. The thought of ordering clothes, buying gloves or handkerchiefs, ties, or any small need, rendered him positively ill, and when he had to pack his portmanteau, it was a most solemn and portentous matter, about which he worried for hours beforehand and was completely worn out after the ' feat.'

Carlyle's unhappy wife was once heard to express the opinion that a " man's genius is no sinecure." In spite of her charm and intelligence, the great man treated her with less regard than he showed to his servants. He only saw her at meals, forced her to ride for miles carrying his messages, and often never spoke to her for weeks. Even when travelling, he never allowed her to be in the same carriage with him, he continually neglected her for other women, and gave out that she had no love for him. After her death, which was certainly hastened by his cruelty, he wrote of her touchingly and penitently, but, in the words of his biographer, " had she lived he would have tormented her afresh."

Leopardi (1798–1837), the poet, judged by his poetical writings, would be considered romantic and benevolent. But from his letters he was evidently quite the reverse— harsh and unsympathetic in his home, unfriendly to his friends. He turned day into night, night into day. He wrote exquisite stanzas about life in the country, but he hated it so much that if ever he journeyed thither, he longed to return before he even arrived there, and never even remained for a whole day. In character also he was mean, and suspicious of everybody, and constantly thought he was being robbed. It is said that his miserableness was caused by supersensitiveness and by a boyish hopeless love. He wrote of himself, " Thought has long inflicted on me, and still inflicts, and it will kill me if I do not change my manner of existence."

Balzac (1799–1850) was so inordinately vain, that his great delight was to speak about his works. He frequently asked advice from even quite young children, but seldom waited for a reply, or else opposed their remarks with the supremest contempt. He actually wanted to go out one evening in an extremely handsome dressing gown and carrying a lamp, so that all might admire him.

Nicholas Lenau (1802–1850), the famous Hungarian poet, even in his childhood had a longing for sad music, and was inclined to mysticism. As he grew older he frequently lapsed into mournful reveries, and sometimes wandered all night in the garden playing his beloved violin. He returned from a futile visit to America to find himself famous. After a bad attack of heart trouble he could not sleep, and terrible visions came to him. He wrote, " One would say that the devil is hunting in my belly. I hear there a perpetual barking of dogs and a funereal echo of hell. Without joking, it is enough to make one despair."

When Germany was erecting triumphal arches in his honour, he ran away—he had suddenly become afraid of all men, felt himself incapable of work, and was constantly fretful and enraged. He went from one country to another, until at last the mysticism of his childhood came back to him. He studied the Gnostics, and eagerly again drank in all the tales of sorcerers which had fascinated him in his younger days. He wrote constantly, travelled much, planned great and wonderful works, and even contemplated marriage, but none of these materialised.

He had another serious attack of illness which left him much calmer. "I enjoy life," he says; "I am so glad that the terrible visions of old have been succeeded by pleasant and delightful visions." Lenau fancied himself at Walhalla with Goethe, also that he had been crowned King of Hungary, and that his wars had been victorious. He even began to make puns on his family name of Niembsch. Gradually he lost all sense of recognition, and also of smell, but a lyric of his, penned at that time, had much of the old beauty of his work and was full of wild mysticism. Shortly before his death Lenau happened to hear someone say " Here lives the great Lenau," and he replied sobbing, " Now Lenau has become very small." His last words, spoken like a child, were, " Lenau is unhappy."

According to Dumas, Victor Hugo " was dominated by one idea—to become the greatest poet and the greatest man of all countries and all ages." He could not endure a government or a religious faith in which he could not take first place and give full expression to his opinions. Thus, imagining himself a superman, it is not surprising that the people of his creation are never convincingly real. They always soar above human possibility because, for him, nature had forms which were not apparent to other men. He saw everything out of proportion, always in exceeding magnitude, a little mouse to him was a huge lion. Like most authors he now and again made some strange errors, as when he says in *Les Misérables* : " She did not know Latin, but understood it very well." He sank into a state of despondency when he was sixty years old, but a few years later recovered all his buoyancy of life, and at seventy a renewal of life came to him.

Grimaldi, feeling far from well, went one day to consult a physician, who advised him to seek distraction and amusement. " Go and see Grimaldi," he said ; " he will make you laugh, and that will be better for you than any drugs." " My God ! " exclaimed the patient, " but I am Grimaldi."

Alexandre Dumas at times so completely lost himself in frenzies of rage that during a quarrel with his wife he tore at her hair. She was in great despair and wanted to find peace in a convent. But Dumas soon recovered his composure and wrote an amusing scene to one of his plays, saying to one of his friends, " If tears were pearls, I would make myself a necklace of them."

Berlioz, when he heard music, felt, in his own words, " first, a sensation of voluptuous ecstasy, immediately followed by general agitation, with palpitation, oppression, sobbing, trembling—sometimes terminating with a fainting fit."

Bulwer Lytton was a delicate imaginative child, remarkably clever at school, and wrote poems at the age of nine. He was always filled with an amazing energy, but, as he grew older, his fits of depression were more frequent, and alternated with a temper so fiery that at times no one dared to go near him. Every small jar or fret appeared to him to be of colossal magnitude and exasperated him to the extent of actual bodily and mental agony and even incited him to violence. Once he struck his wife, then, springing upon her like a tiger, made his teeth meet in her left cheek.[1] He also kicked her savagely just before the birth of a child. He was an inveterate

---

[1] *Life of Lady Rosina Lytton : a Vindication.*

worker, and constantly wrote until two or three in the morning.

Baptiste Bernadotte, afterwards Charles XIV of Sweden, like Napoleon, had faith in his special destiny. He believed himself to be under the protection of a tutelar divinity—a certain fairy who was said to have wedded one of his ancestors, and it had been predicted that an illustrious king should descend from her race. We are told that when he wished to send his son Oscar to lead an army into Norway, he beheld an old woman weirdly clad. "What do you want?" asked the King; and the strange being replied, "If Oscar goes to the war, he will not give, but receive the first blow." The King thereupon changed his plans, made an honourable peace, and kept his son by his side.

Gérard de Nerval (born 1808) held conversations with Moses, Adam, and Joshua, who spoke to him through chairs and tables. He had long fits of exaltation and depression. Sometimes he danced Babylonian dances and performed cabalistic exorcisms. With honey drawn from flowers, he traced signs which encircled the form of a giantess who represented Diana, Saint Rosalie, and an actress named Jenny Colon with whom de Nerval fancied himself in love. He sent her huge bouquets and bought opera glasses of abnormal size so that he might see her more clearly. He bought a beautiful mediæval bed with a view to its being a resting place for him and his *inamorata*, hired a suitable apartment and bought superb furniture. Time passed, de Nerval fell on evil days and soon had to sell the furniture. The bed he kept as long as possible, even after it stood alone in the room; then he had it moved to a barn. But at last even the bed had to go, and he himself spent his nights in common lodging houses and

low taverns.   Often he wrote under trees or in doorways.
He declared that she was one of the incarnations of Saint
Teresa.   One day when walking along a balcony, he saw
a phantom figure and heard a voice which called him by
name.   He ran forward and fell over the balcony, but
escaped with his life.   Later on, ideas of personal grandeur
grew in his mind, he discoursed largely about his chateaux
at Ermenonville, and of his personal perfection of face
and form, of which he was convinced.   He bought all
the coins of Nerva, saying that he did not wish his
ancestral name to circulate as money, and yet Nerval
was not his own name at all, merely a *nom de plume*.
He quoted the Lapps, who, he said, enjoyed superb
health, as his excuse for adhering to his summer clothes
throughout a severe winter.   He ultimately hanged
himself.

Cavour, when a boy, gave way to paroxysms of rage.
Once, when told he must attend to his studies, he tried
to kill himself with a knife, and finally threw himself from
a window.   All his life he fancied himself alone, shorn of
family, love, and friends, and would have again attempted
suicide but was doubtful as to the morality of so doing.
" I will not kill myself," he said ; " no, but I will put up
an earnest prayer to Heaven to send me a rapid consump-
tion which may carry me off to the other world."

Charles Darwin wrote of himself : " I have no great
quickness of apprehension or wit . . . my power to follow
a long abstract train of thought is very limited . . . my
memory is extensive yet hazy."   Darwin had a kind of
impediment in his speech, he stammered slightly when he
commenced to talk, and had a difficulty in pronouncing
the letter W.   He was a sick man always, suffering from
giddiness and a " swimming in the head."   " His life was

one long struggle against the weariness and strain of sickness.''

Mendelssohn was very self-willed and fretful as a boy, wanting things which gave him no pleasure when obtained. When he heard music which did not please him, he threw himself into perfect furies of rage. All national melodies he hated as infamous, vulgar, out-of-time trash. He worked at such tension that at thirty-five his constitution was "hopelessly impaired." He looked haggard and worn, and his irritability was distressing. Mendelssohn fainted when he was told of the death of his sister, and afterwards had a premonition that he would not live much longer. He became afraid of publicity and any form of public life. Then fits of epilepsy developed, followed by terrific headaches and long periods of unconsciousness, which grew in force until the end came.

Chopin often wandered in a half ruined convent in Spain, which fascinated him even though it filled his imagination with fears and phantoms. When George Sand did not return from a walk with her son at the hour he expected her, he fancied all kinds of terrors, and even was convinced that they were both dead and that he himself was dead also. Chopin gave himself constant and needless worry over everything, however trivial. A fly, a little ink stain, a crumpled petal, made him utterly miserable and frequently moved him to tears. He deserted a woman to whom he was devotedly attached because she did not on one occasion offer him a chair before she offered one to others in the room. In his will, Chopin left instructions that he desired to be buried in a white tie, dress shoes, and short breeches.

Schumann, even in his early life, suffered from attacks of melancholia, and during these he felt impelled to take his own life. He " heard spirit voices, melodies, and harmonies, and had perturbations of smell and taste." [1] He was short and stout and had a square, intellectual head.

Gogol Nicolai, the great Russian novelist, was often compared by his admirers to Homer, and he was made much of even by the government. An unhappy love affair in Gogol's youth cast a cloud over his whole life, and though his splendid books might never have been written but for it, the bitterness of his mind caused him to look with strange criticism on his work. He got the idea firmly implanted in his mind that his books were so crudely true to the life of his country, so realistic, that they might tend towards a terrible revolution, of which he would feel himself the cause. This thought so preyed upon him that he gave up work, stayed indoors, prayed to the saints, and beseeched them to crave for him God's forgiveness for his revolutionary sins. Gogol then made a pilgrimage to Jerusalem, which brought him comfort until the Revolution broke out in 1848. Then his grief and remorse became tenfold. He was continually tortured by visions of the triumph of the Nihilists, and he was eventually found dead of exhaustion before the shrine at which he spent days and nights praying for pardon and grace.

Alfred de Musset alternated fits of passion with outbursts of remorse and great charm of manner. On one occasion his mistress said to him, " If there are two different men in you, could you not, when the bad one rises, be content to forgive the good one ? " [2] De Musset owns that in his conduct to her he behaved either with

---

[1] Wasilewski, *Life of Robert Schumann.*
[2] *Souvenirs*, p. 73. Paris, 1883.

brutal temper or else with extremest affection, " an exaltation carried to excess made me treat my mistress like an idol, like a divinity, a quarter of an hour after having insulted her." [1] Musset, like Carlyle and Flaubert, felt every vibration of sound so keenly that bells and street noises were to them unbearable; they were always moving from one place to another in the endeavour to get away from the din, and eventually sought the seclusion of the country.

John Humphrey Noyes, of the United States, professed and believed that he was endowed with the spirit of prophecy, and established at Oneida the sect called ' Perfectionists,' which recognised no human laws, looked upon property and marriage as robbery, and were assured every action, even the most trivial, to have been inspired by God.

Charles Kean, the famous tragedian, was most unreliable in his performances. Often he failed to appear at the theatre through drunkenness or mere carelessness. When being shown over an American asylum with a party of friends, they had the utmost difficulty in preventing him from throwing himself from the roof when he walked to the edge and said, " I'll make a leap, it is the best end I can put to my life." Kean had many sudden and unusual impulses; he once rose at three in the morning, ordered a coach, put into it a dog, a pair of pistols, some brandy and lighted candles, and quite seriously enjoined the driver to drive to hell. Kean was only thirty-seven when his health completely broke down. He was carried from the stage during a performance of *Othello*, having fallen down unconscious, and was never able to play again. He died at forty-six.

[1] *Souvenirs d'un Enfant du Siècle*, p. 218.

Wagner always said that he did not choose a musical career—it merely happened, and he explained it thus : " I only know that I heard one evening a symphony of Beethoven's, that I thereupon fell ill of a fever, and that when I recovered I was—a musician."

George Eliot was very susceptible to night terrors as a child, possessing a highly imaginative and sensitive temperament. To quote her own words, "All her soul became a quivering fear." Fits of depression were frequent with her, often she would fling herself on the ground and weep bitterly. After the age of thirty she suffered from almost maddening headaches, followed later by palpitations.

George IV was grossly intemperate, and if we are to believe Lord Holland, on the Prince's wedding day he was so drunk with brandy that he could scarcely keep upright between two dukes.

Baudelaire amused himself by throwing pots from his house and by breaking shop windows; the sound of the shattering glass delighted him, and, because he hated to stay in any place for long, he changed his lodgings at least every month. He stated that he felt the necessity of freeing himself " from an oasis of horror in a desert of ennui." Often when he sat down to write he would waste his time looking through references which in no way affected the subject at issue. He nearly strangled his mother's second husband after a violent quarrel. Baudelaire was sent to India with a view to taking up some business there, but he came back after losing everything. He did not come back alone, he brought with him a negress of whom he had become enamoured and to whom he wrote sonnets. His one idea seemed to be to make himself conspicuous, and to this end cultivated originality, even

aggressiveness.   He dyed his hair green, wore winter garments in summer, summer ones in winter, and deliberately
got drunk even in the presence of aristocratic and influential personages.   He had quaint and morbid ideas of
love.   He loved plain, even hideous women, negresses,
giantesses, and dwarfs.   He once told a beautiful woman
that he would like to see her hanging by her arms from
the ceiling in order that he might kiss her feet.   Kissing
the naked feet of a woman is said in one of his poems to
be equivalent to sexual intercourse.

Baudelaire was continually planning work, dreaming of
work, working out how soon it would enable him to pay
his debts, but very little work was accomplished.   He
writes in one of his books : " I desire to redeem myself,
to regard myself with a little pride in the silence and
solitude of the night.   Souls of those I have loved, souls
of those I love, sing, strengthen me, sustain me, remove
from me the ties and the corrupting vapours of the world.
And then, O Lord my God, grant me grace to produce
some fine lines which will prove to myself that I am not
the least of men, that I am not inferior to those whom
I contemn."   Baudelaire certainly had only abuse for
contemporary and earlier writers, calling them imbeciles,
stupid, idiots, etc.   Even George Sand he summed up as
" without delicacy."   And yet delicacy must have been
foreign to Baudelaire.   As he grew older his speech often
troubled him, he used words which had an opposite
meaning—cold when he meant warm, in when he meant
out, and so forth.   He had the sense of smell so finely
developed that he said he found it impossible to live in
Belgium, because the trees of that country possessed no
fragrance.

Amiel, the famous philosopher, wrote in his journal,

" As life flees, I mourn the loss of reality. Thought is sad without action, and action is sad without thought. The real is spoilt when the ideal has not added its perfume, but the ideal if not made one with the real becomes a poison. I have never learnt the art of writing, it would have been useful to me. . . . This journal will be useful to no one, and even for me it will serve rather to plan out life than to practise it—it is a pillow of idleness. And even in style I am unequal . . . I see before me several expressions, and do not know which I ought to choose. I discovered very early that it is easier to give up a wish than to gratify it. . . . The idea may be modified, but not the action, so I abhor it, for I fear useless remorse. I thrust aside the idea of a family because every lost joy is the stab of a knife, because every hope is an egg from which may proceed a serpent as well as a dove. Action is my cross because it would be my dream. It is my passion to injure my interests. When a thing attracts me, I flee from it." [1]

Flaubert wrote of himself : " The deplorable mania of doubt exhausts me. I doubt about everything, even my own doubts." He also said : " There never was a liberal idea which has not been unpopular, never an act of justice which has not caused scandal, never a great man who has not been pelted with potatoes or struck with knives. The history of human intellect is the history of human stupidity, as M. de Voltaire said." Guy de Maupassant relates of Flaubert : " From his early childhood, the distinctive features of his nature were a great naïveté and a horror of physical action. It exasperated him to see people walking or moving about him, and he declared in his mordant, sonorous, always theatrical

[1] Amiel, *Journal Intime.* 2nd ed. Geneva, 1889.

manner that it was not philosophic." [1] Flaubert wrote in one of his letters : " My good friend Von Bouilhet often said to me, ' There never was so moral a man who loved immorality as much as you.' There is truth in that. Is it the result of my pride or of a certain perversity ? "

Rénan described himself as " a tissue of contradictions." " One of my halves," he said, " is constantly occupied in demolishing the other, like the fabulous animal of Cterias, who ate his paws without knowing it." [2] Rénan, though a layman and a sceptic, writes of himself : " I took the vow of poverty and the paradoxical vow to preserve the classical virtues without the faith which serves as basis for them and in a world in which vows are not made. . . . My dream would have to be housed, fed, clothed, and warmed without having to think about it, by someone who would take charge of me and leave me free."

Rénan's gentle charm of manner did not even allow him to show authority to a dog. He longed to write, even from early childhood, but with his modesty and lack of worldliness it does not seem to have occurred to him that his work might bring in money. " What was my astonishment," says he, " when I saw a gentleman of agreeable and intelligent appearance enter my garret, compliment me on some articles I had published, and offer to collect them in a volume ! He brought a stamped paper, stipulating conditions which I thought amazingly generous, so that when he asked me to include all my future writings in the same contract, I consented. The idea came to me to make some observations, but I paused

[1] *Étude sur Gustave Flaubert.* Paris, 1885.
[2] *Souvenirs*, p. 73. Paris, 1883.

at sight of the document, the thought that that beautiful sheet of paper would be lost stopped me." Challemel-Lacour, a shrewd observer, summed up Rénan's character consummately in these few words : " He thinks like a man, feels like a woman, and acts like a child."

Of himself Rénan has also written : " Notwithstanding all my efforts to the contrary, I was predestined to be what I am, a romantic protesting against romanticism—an Utopian preaching materialistic politics—an idealist uselessly giving himself much trouble to appear bourgeois—a tissue of contradictions. I do not complain, since this moral constitution has procured me the most vivid intellectual joys that may be tasted."[1]

Alexandre Dumas almost ruined the fine reputation he had built up by the vastly inferior work which was all he could grind out during his latter years when he had to pay toll for the follies, excesses, and vain-glorious aggressiveness of his earlier life. He gradually became " quite helpless and almost unconscious of what was going on about him," and died without any return from this condition of oblivion.

Tolstoi's philosophic scepticism led him into dangerous labyrinths. " I imagined," he writes, " that there existed nothing outside me either living or dead—that objects were not objects, but vain appearances. This state reached such a point that sometimes I turned suddenly round, and looked behind me in the hope of seeing nothing where I was not."

Thomas Lloyd mixed miscellaneous objects with his food, saying that each ingredient would impart some virtue of its own—carbon had a purifying effect, stone gave mineral value, and so on—thus coal, paper, tobacco,

[1] *Souvenirs d'Enfance et de la Jeunesse.*

pebbles, sand, etc., were included in his meals. When dissatisfied with his verses, he placed them in a glass, saying that in that way they would be polished.

Junius Brutus Booth was as unreliable as Kean in theatrical work, failing to turn up at the theatre whenever he did not feel in an acting mood. And during his performances he sometimes indulged in any freak that came into his head, quite regardless of the play. One evening, during a performance of *Richelieu*, he suddenly halted, tripped over to one of the characters, the priest Father Joseph, and seizing him in his arms, waltzed with him round the stage, to the amazement of the house and the horror of the manager, who had the curtain dropped on this mad prank. Booth then disappeared and was not seen for some days.[1] He once jumped overboard when at sea, crying out that he had a message for an actor he had known and who had drowned himself there, and he was rescued only just in time.

Sarah Bernhardt, the famous actress, had through most of her life such a dislike to business that she kept most of her money in an open drawer, and when bills had to be met she would say, " Allez au tiroir "—and if sometimes her secretary or her maid came back with the information that there was nothing in the drawer, she merely smiled her wonderful smile and said, " Attendez alors, jusqu'il-y-en-a ! " She possessed an extremely retentive memory, and whilst on foreign tours would remember even the hobbies of her friends' children, and bring home minerals for one small boy, stamps for another, and so forth. For a long time she travelled always with her coffin, of which the inside was exquisitely upholstered. Amongst her ' retinue ' she had also two young bears, and a baby

[1] J. F. Nisbet, *The Insanity of Genius*.

lion which used to walk on the table at meals. Even long after middle age, the great actress delighted in swinging and all childish amusements. It can truly be said of her that, with all her genius, her worldliness, and her eccentricities, she herself had the heart of a child.

CHAPTER XII

THE REMEDY

By now the reader will doubtless have arrived at several conclusions, *viz.* : that the mental, moral, and practical characteristics as recorded in the history of humanity ' within and without ' have much in common. Mental, moral, and practical conventionalities are shared alike. For those whose names are recorded in the pages of this volume have contributed by their art to the aesthetic health of the art galleries of Europe, by their music to devotional practices in cathedrals and churches, by their architecture to the construction of edifices for the economic activities of mankind, and by their writings to the evolution of mentality ; the only difference being that those ' within ' have been protected from those ' without ' and have been free to pursue the trends of their inspirations.

The outside world is ever intolerant of inspiration, in spite of the fact that we rise in mentality according to the nature and quality of our inspirations. It seems strange that it should be necessary to point out that inspirations are prerogatives of mankind, and that they cannot always be explained as having had their origin entirely in, although apparently emanating from, the regions of the subliminal or subconscious. To be inspired is to grasp meanings or truths. The most brilliant of inspirations have come to those who are neither on, or over, the borderland, and it must be conceded, by even the intolerant of degeneration-mongering, that genius is indeed akin to madness. With regard to the imitators, the ' Toms o' Bedlam,' who trade upon such inspirations, quite another view may be held.

It is but natural for human beings to form conjectures as to possibilities of self-realisation in the hereafter. The egoist, or megalomaniac, is sufficient unto himself, and, declining to subscribe himself to a secondary *rôle* of sub-servience, meanders along bye-paths which lead to no-where; whilst a greater mentality posits self-realisation on the higher platform of relativity, and forms conjectures as to his being but an integral part of the totality of energy, life, mind, and spirit, pervading both time and space. Thus it is that the trend of thought should, in order that it may be free, be allowed to grow ever upwards, and not be strangled or even impeded by the weeds of subversive tradition or ignorance.

One lesson to be learned from history is,[1] that " if you can impress any man with an absorbing conviction of the supreme importance of some moral or religious doctrine ; if you can make him believe that those who reject that doctrine are doomed to eternal perdition ; if you then give that man power, and by means of his own ignorance blind him to the ulterior consequences of his own act— he will infallibly persecute those who deny his doctrine ; and the extent of his persecution will be regulated to the extent of his sincerity. Diminish the sincerity and you will diminish the persecution." That history furnishes us with many examples of this law cannot be denied. The persecutions of the early Christians by the Roman

[1] Buckle, *Civilization in England*, vol. i. p. 141.

Emperors (*e.g.* those of Commodus and Elagabulus) have their aftermath nowadays. The earnestness of Marcus Aurelius has been but replaced by the setting up of medico-legal restrictions as to the limits of freedom of thought and conduct.

That faddism, fostered by ignorance, has begotten many activities no one can deny, and we now witness many organised persecutions in the realms of thought, feeling, and conduct, which have their ramifications throughout religion, law, medicine, art, and industry, and in connection with which the main characteristic is intolerance. The great war of the future will be that of self-realisation, with its consequent freedom from the artificial bonds of slavery in which each individual has become so enmeshed that he is no longer free to think, feel, or act for himself. Real freedom is not to be gained by restriction in belief, prohibition by law, or constraint as to industry. The self-imposed restrictions and pro-hibitions of so-called civilisation have but resulted in hypocrisy and conventionality adopted as a means to cloak inner convictions and impulses ; and this has been necessitated by a knowledge of the fact that any unveiling of the real inner convictions would but be met by in-tolerance, and by further impositions of restraint.

That repression of normal sexual functions has much to do with variations in mental states both ' within and without ' asylums cannot be gainsaid. With regard to asylum administration this question has always been of importance, and its solution is attended by almost in-superable difficulties. Briefly stated, segregation and deprivation of marital rites may be beneficial to some, whilst harmful to others. This, however, is only one part of the question, and does not take into account the effects of repression upon those who are not segregated. That biologic and eugenic principles become involved no one will deny, and it is to those principles the physician applies his attention. There are, however, many sociological and religious principles which must be taken into consideration, and, needless to say, mere gratification of human instincts, even though such gratification be natural and hygienic, should not inflict mental pain and intensify the sufferings of those who are by reason of mental disease already suffering from the effects of an enforced repression. That further legislation with regard to divorce and re-marriage is indicated is manifest to all who have experience in connection with such problems, but it must be confessed that further legislation should take the form of rescinding state-enforced regulations rather than by making further restrictions. In fact, civilisation will have to consider, sooner or later, the biological as well as the sociological aspects of the question. The science of eugenics concerns itself with biologic principles of evolution of humanity, and where it comes into conflict with sociological or religious observances these observances must give way ultimately to what is beneficial to mankind. How long it will be before reason derived from knowledge takes the place of precedent derived from tradition seems difficult to gauge ; but there are indeed signs of an awakening from the cloud of unreason and of an emergence to the light of reality. In other words, theologians and physicians must ultimately work in harmony in maintaining such eugenic principles as may prove themselves to be true and incontrovertible. That any divergence from, or intoleration of, such principles should become manifest is one of the dangers of the future, and the evolution of mankind would but be hindered were legis-

lation devised to enforce any tendencies which are either
obstructive or subversive.

With advance of education and acquirement of knowledge, despotism, arrogance, and prejudice have tended
to give way to reason, but there is still much to be desired
in this respect.   With regard to almost every platform of
human endeavour we still witness party conflicts which
tend but to constrict and narrow the outlets of escape.
Indeed it is manifest to every medico-psychologist that
warring of motives, desires, feelings, and acts, when carried
to extremes, are productive of vitiation of energy and
nerve exhaustion.   Many of the ' exhaustion-psychoses '
are but the products of undue strain and friction on the
various scales of endeavour ; and, needless to say, the
meshes woven by tradition, religion, and law have oftentimes tended but further to impede freedom of thought
and action.

To attempt to give credence to what is apparently unreasonable involves an output of effort in controlling
expressions of revolt, and this effort, if long continued,
is in itself productive of fatigue.   When authority gives
way to unaided reason the individual then becomes independent and free, *i.e.* he is unhampered by the dogmata
of any school, the formulae of any observance, and the
controls of any man-made law.   That each one of us
should so expand his mental horizon becomes possible
only when a mental flight is made above church, court, or
palace.

The main difference between the sane and many of the
insane is that in the latter there is loss of control over the
hypocritical and artificial bonds of convention, which loss
places them out of harmony with their advisedly more
secretive brethren.   Thus we have the curious fact that

when an individual believes the word of his pastor, and frankly states he believes his soul to be lost, or that he is in danger of eternal damnation, he is certified as insane and relegated to an asylum. If he soars into the region of philosophy, science, aesthetics, or conjecture, he is regarded as a crank ; and if he be eccentric, unconventional, or abnormal in his behaviour, he is treated with ridicule by the community, irrespective of the fact that he may be a God-fearing, law-abiding, self-supporting, and responsible human being. These are but some of the shackles of so-called civilisation, and, needless to say, this trend is in itself not only subversive but also explanatory of the fact that many of the world's geniuses have had to seek asylum or protection against the intolerance displayed by their fellow-beings. That such havens of refuge exist for those who receive inspirations denied to the majority is, without doubt, beneficial so long as the public continues to treat them with ridicule. It would, however, be better advised were it to take more cognisance of the Toms o' Bedlam who subvert those inspirations, and gull the public with their own spurious imitations. Were religion, science, art, industry, to become more tolerant of the inspirations and aspirations of others there would result a considerable reduction in the numbers of those who have to seek protection from their interferences, restrictions, and prohibitions.

For those who, by reason of their lack of control over frank expressions of convictions, feelings, and activities, have found 'asylum' and protection, much can be done, both physically, mentally, socially, and industrially, and, until the community recognises its own personal responsibilities in the matter of toleration and individual protection, no effort will be spared by those who have the

welfare of suffering humanity at heart. The barred
windows, the locked doors, the padded rooms of asylums
are not for such as these, but for the irresponsibles who
require them. Unfortunately the custom of receiving the
harmless, as well as the harmful, into asylums has resulted
in a loss of freedom for both classes, irrespective of their
individual claims. Thus we witness the sad sight of
harmless, and even benevolent, human beings, gazing
wistfully at the busy world without, sighing in despair at
the thoughts of home, and craving for the sympathy of
their friends and relatives. Sad indeed are the reflections
of those who have to minister to the mind diseased.

When Tennyson penned the lines :

" My life has crept long on a broken wing
    Thro' cells of madness, haunts of horror and fear,
    That I come to be grateful at last for a little thing,"

he little knew how he echoed the thoughts of those who
have to do with the insane. That the stress and strain
of modern times necessitate care and control of some of
those who are mentally afflicted is true ; but that it
necessitates so serious a loss of freedom for all who are
now confined in asylums is open to question.

The Royal Commission on Lunacy and Mental Disorder
will doubtless fully consider the following questions :
(1) Scope and method of certification ; (2) Classification
and treatment ; (3) ' Responsibles ' ; (4) ' Irresponsibles ' ;
(5) Methods of administration ; (6) Right of appeal. That
many curious and vexatious anomalies do exist is beyond
question ; but a solution for the main difficulties is to be
anticipated, and doubtless the community will extend a
hand of sympathy to all who are now either suffering or
rejoicing in their segregation.

It may well be asked of what use is education if our

intellectual acquisitions do not serve to counteract and control the intolerance of outer barbarians. For those who wave the red flag as a danger signal there can be little or no claim to mental cultivation. That combative instincts are by their nature incompatible with reasoning is exemplified by their gradual separation in the course of human evolution. Solon, Themistocles, Socrates, Plato, Antisthenes, Archytas, Melissus, Pericles, Alcibiades, Demosthenes, Sophocles, and many others combined military and mental distinction. Descartes, Raleigh, Napier, Cromwell, Washington, and Napoleon also attained to eminence in both, whereas Gustavus Adolphus, Frederick the Great, Marlborough, and Wellington were comparatively deficient in regard to questions of social administration. That combativeness will ultimately give place to reason there is but little doubt when viewed as from above downwards; but among the irresponsibles want of reason tends but to bring about active measures of subversion which tend to express themselves in violence.

Perchance some of the sufferings of those who are now segregated, repressed, and deprived of their home influences, familiar relationships, and personal freedom may yet be relieved; but, before a 'charter of liberty' may with security be granted, it behoves the public to ponder deeply upon its responsibilities as well as its dangers, and to distinguish more fully between those who are harmless and responsible and those who are dangerous and subversive. If the contents of these pages have in any degree helped to throw light upon a most painful problem, the effort will not have been made in vain. In any case, however, there is always some consolation in the assurance that truth and justice will out at last.

Before any great changes can be effected in administration with regard to the insane, insight must be attained through knowledge, knowledge must be gained through incontrovertible data, and each individual, throughout all classes of society, must give his own verdict. Then, and only then, will civilisation be relieved from one of its present intolerable restraints, and be better able to enforce another charter of liberty. After all, legislation is devised merely to meet current requirements, and the emissaries of law have but to uphold its enactments. With regard to the ebb and flow of history, the affairs of the world have undergone a perpetual flux. Some ideas, some activities, and some inspirations have lived through all the ages, and of these, liberty of thought, feeling, and belief has prevailed in spite of human intervention. That this liberty has at times been perverted or subverted seems to have made no difference, and this alone affords cumulative evidence as to the upward trend of humanity towards freedom and a greater subservience.

That civilisation is not yet ripe for exhaustive generalisations on many important problems is obvious; but that it is ripe for its decision as to what is good or bad for its individual units, who, by reason of defect or perversion, are unable to think or act for themselves, is evidenced by the Royal Commission of Enquiry. Whether the Commission will get down to bed-rock and lay bare the vital and pressing needs of the moment is yet to be seen. That it can deal exhaustively with the individual right of freedom and self-realisation is not to be expected, for such a right can only be determined by each separate unit which possesses a mind to think, a heart to feel, and a body to direct; but that it can, and doubtless will, do much to relieve the sufferings of some, and awaken a deeper sense of personal responsibility in others, we have every confidence.

When at last each individual unit awakens from his adoration of idols and its mummeries, and revolts against being enchained by legends and subversive contracts, then, and then only, will he become independent and free. That civilisation has in great part rejected truths and hoarded shams is no reason why it should continue to do so, and it may not be too much to hope that Great Britain may yet through its humane activities deserve the great title of *Lux Mundi*.

The credulity which people of the twentieth century manifest towards obvious absurdities is evident to all. Those who now dare to doubt the claims of astrology, necromancy, witchcraft, thought-reading, telepathy, and the occult are in an advisedly passive majority. They display a spirit of complacency so long as it suits them to do so. Directly, however, medico-legal cognisance is taken of the vagaries, not only do they acquiesce in but further the segregation of those who have the courage of their beliefs. The three fundamental errors of olden times, *viz.*: intolerance in religion, credulity in science, and confidence in politics, have their aftermath in present-day restrictions and prohibitions. Present-day civilisation, instead of burning such heretics at the stake, invokes the aid of law and medicine for the purpose of imposing segregation, little dreaming that the administrators of the same medico-legal restrictions may themselves be, by their interference, the real sources of danger to the community. That this is so we have evidence derived from the sometimes ill-advised activities of those who have to carry out the various medico-legal enactments with regard to the insane. That laws are made to be carried out is

manifest ; but that they should be so zealously administered as to be regardless of due consideration of individual
circumstances is apt to be productive of harm. That the
regulations and bye-laws pertaining to lunatics are far-
reaching and explicit no one can deny ; but laws, like
structures, are more efficacious and more lasting if they
possess a certain degree of pliability or elasticity. With
regard to lunacy administration it must be confessed that
their degree of plasticity has of late years become so
lessened that those whose activities bring them within its
provisions have had cause to ' fight shy ' of it altogether
as being fraught with considerable danger. Needless to
say, the faculty of medicine would be well advised were
it to avoid constituting itself as the criterion as to what
religious, scientific, or philosophical hypotheses may be
valid in the eyes of the law ; for although the law takes
but little notice of hypotheses pertaining to the mind, it
is nevertheless apt to penalise any medical restraints
upon them, even though they may be the outcome of
medical research or experience. In other words, the
medical practitioner should avoid certifying as insane
those whose only indications of unsoundness of mind are
manifested by individual expressions of opinion with
regard to religious, scientific, or philosophical matters.
By observing this restriction there would result a considerable reduction in the numbers of those who are now
relegated to asylums. Not until the last gasps of religio-
medico-legal bigotry have ended in personal freedom from
the red-tape of officialdom should any person subscribe
himself as being a perpetrator of inhuman impositions.

The refusal to certify incipient forms of insanity may
result in harm through delay in treatment, but the harm
occasioned by the delay would be in great part mitigated

by the fact that the sufferer is not being relegated to an insititution where the benefits he might receive might also be counteracted by locked doors, barred windows, and the companionship of irresponsibles, all of which are but ill-compensatory for the loss of home, liberty, and conjugal relationships. As there is no definite criterion of religious, scientific, or philosophic truth, it is obvious that no super-human tribunal can be constituted to deal with such questions. The only real tribunal is that which is presided over by common-sense and a spirit of tolerance.

With regard to the future, it is to be hoped that the mentally perverted who are still amenable to social observances may have their own special ' retreats,' where they can pursue their intellectual, æsthetical, or industrial bents in safety ; that the morally perverted, who are a danger to themselves or to the community, may be relegated to ' Homes of Detention,' where special provision can be made for their care and safety ; and lastly, that Great Britain should deny itself the thankless task of offering itself as an ' asylum ' for alien perverts and subversivists. Certain it is that England has been in danger of becoming the dumping ground, or ' Asylum of the World,' owing to the misguided hospitality it has extended hitherto to alien degenerates, irresponsibles, and undesirables. When these changes are effected, and not till then, will justice be done to the various types of our afflicted fellow-beings.

It will be readily seen that, in order to meet the needs of the times, a complete revision of our methods of certification, classification, and administration is of urgent necessity.

Our mental cupboards have become so replete with stores of prohibitions enacted and constitutionalised in

consequence of the misguided enthusiasm of cranks and
faddists that each individual now finds himself enmeshed
both mentally and physically by numberless irritating
bonds which are comparable to those by which Gulliver
was held captive in Lilliput.   To multiply prohibitions is
psychologically unsound.   Undue statutory interference
with freedom of thought and action not only restricts the
potentialities of self-expression, but it also goes far towards suggesting possibilities of divergence from the
fenced path of the law.   The absurdity of making trifles
illegal also tends to make most of us potential criminals.
Just as the true gentleman in every sphere of life is in no
great need of guidance by rules of etiquette, so common-
sense requires no artificial bonds for self-control.   It is a
curious prerogative of the human mind to be combative
in reaction to ideas, *i.e.* to adopt the opposite point of
view in argument.   This natural tendency to opposition
has rendered it possible to treat others by contra-suggestion, *i.e.* by suggesting the opposite of the conclusions
which are desirable.   Hence it is that prohibition suggests
freedom, and the contra-suggestion of freedom merges
into auto-suggestion of the committal of acts which otherwise might never have attained to prominence in the
mind.   In other words, the ' daring ' to act is provocative
of action.   Hence it is that prohibitions have, by contra-
suggestion, led to impulses which in their turn have led
to the undoing of many an otherwise fairly healthy power
of control.

INDEX